GIVEN AT THE GENERAL REGISTER O
SOMERSET HOU

Application Number......564

helsea in the _County of Middlesex_

7	8	9	10*
Signature, description and residence of informant	When registered	Signature of registrar	Name entered after registration
M. F. Taylor Mother 2 Cooks Ground	Fifth of March 1843	Thos Long Registrar	/

District above mentioned.
d Office, the 29th day of _January_ 1971.

Act 1953.   Section 34 provides that any certified copy of an entry purporting to be
ed as evidence of the birth or death to which it relates without any further or other
e said Office shall be of any force or effect unless it is sealed or stamped as aforesaid.

cate, or (2) uses a falsified certificate as true, knowing it to be false, is liable to prosecution.

Laura Keene

LAURA KEENE

A Biography

BY

Ben Graf Henneke

Council Oak Books
Tulsa, Oklahoma

Council Oak Books
Tulsa, Oklahoma 74120

Printed in the United States of America
97 96 95 94 93 92 91 90   5 4 3 2 1

Library of Congress Catalog Card Number 90-81816
ISBN 0-933031-31-9

Designed by Carol Haralson

FRONTISPIECE:
Laura Keene, photographed by Matthew Brady National Portrait
Gallery, Smithsonian Institution

*Illustrations which bear no source credit
are from the collection of the author.*

Contents

ILLUSTRATIONS

Foreword

T he green-uniformed guide of the National Park Service tells of the presidential party changing its plans for the evening. General and Mrs. Grant will not attend the theatre; Mrs. Lincoln wishes to go to Ford's Theatre, not Grover's. The guide talks of Laura Keene, the actress whose benefit it was, of John Wilkes Booth, of Major Rathbone and his fiancee; talks of the moment in the play, *Our American Cousin,* chosen by Booth for his murderous attack upon the President of the United States. . .

The guide tries to give a sense of the enormity of the deed; of the confusion of the moment . . . Tells of the efforts of Dr. Leale to save the president's life with mouth-to-mouth resuscitation . . . Attempts to give an impression of Mrs. Lincoln's desperation, Major Rathbone's confusion, Laura Keene's control. . .

The Park Service guide directs the attention of the group to the house across the street where President Lincoln breathed his last; tells of the tribunal organized there which took evidence from those who had seen what happened; tells of the closing of Ford's Theatre, its confiscation by the War Department. . . .

But what of this woman, Laura Keene, whom Mrs. Lincoln wanted to honor on her benefit night? What of this woman who had pillowed in her lap the head of the dying president?

What of her?

Hers is not a straightforward story.

Tracing the path which led to Washington, D.C., that particular Holy Week in 1865, following where she went after the assassination, has been my obsession for many years.

When my curiosity was first aroused I turned to the *Dictionary of American Biography*, where Constance Rourke had written,

> She was beautiful, with chestnut hair and eyes, and exquisite pallor, and a fine carriage. Slight and graceful, she had "the water-color touch," and did not so much draw details of character and action as suggest them. . .
> Little is known of her personal life. The few faint glimpses reveal a distinguished and complex character.

What did *The Oxford Companion to the Theatre*, Third Edition, have to add?

> Keene, Laura (/? — 1873), actress and theatre manager, born in England. The date of her birth has been variously given as 1820, 1826, 1830, and 1836, and her real name may have been Moss, Foss, or Lee. She is said to have been trained for the stage by an aunt, Mrs. Yates, and to have made her first appearance. . .

Since, I have read what has been written; walked the ways she took. There has been a fatality rough-hewing the outcome of the search. Fire destroyed the Joseph Jefferson collection of theatre memorabilia, fire destroyed Laura's house in Massachusetts and virtually every theatre in which she acted. Records of her activities in San Francisco were lost in the earthquake and fire of 1907; parish registers in London were victims of the blitz.

But little by little, as a letter was found here, a legal document there, a person began to emerge; a person of infinite variety. One who deserves better than the sleazy notoriety of an unwitting part in assassination.

LAURA KEENE.

Chapter 1

The Changeling Daughter

There's a divinity that shapes our ends,
Rough-hew them how we will . . .
SHAKESPEARE, *HAMLET,* ACT V, SCENE 2

S he — who later was to be Laura Keene — was the fourth child of Thomas King and Jane Moss, born in 1826, and christened Mary Frances. There is reason to believe the Moss family lived in Prince's Street in the Parish of St. James, Westminster, but since Thomas Moss was a gentleman, it was not necessary that he be listed in the city directories of the time.

The family appears to have been a close one. Jane dedicated her life to easing the path of her changeling daughter. Edward, the eldest child, accompanied his mother and Mary's children when they came to the United States. Hannah, the next eldest, with her husband, William Stewart, stood surety for Mary Frances in later legal troubles. Thomas,

Laura Keene's career spanned the decades in which illustration was evolving from sketch to photograph, and in which theatrical personalities became public property. The image at left is not Laura's earliest likeness. O.A. Roorbach, theatre book publisher, speaking of her London debut, said, "the Lady's picture was exhibited in the West End print-shops, along with the pictures of other public performers." THOMAS BAKER SHEET MUSIC, LIBRARY OF CONGRESS.

the child closest to Mary in age, was lost at sea the year before she married.

Mary Frances was eighteen when, on April 8, 1844, she appeared at the registrar's office in the district of Saint Martin in the Fields. The groom, Henry Wellington Taylor, age 27, was said to be a godson of the Duke of Wellington. The story told later by her friends was that she met Taylor while serving as a retoucher of "old masters" in the St. James Gallery, managed by Taylor in his father's senescence.

Before that time she had acquired a remarkable education. She played the piano, she sang (her mother's pet name for her was "Birdie"), she danced; her knowledge of literature and history was extraordinary in a female of her time. The obituary dictated by her daughters claimed she had full run of an aunt's fine library.

The magazine, *Fine Arts,* which she published and edited in her last year of life, bore witness to her educational attainments, as well as giving credence to the story of her activities in an art gallery.

The Taylors are next heard of after the death of the elder Taylor and the closing of the gallery. They are domiciled at The Plough, 305 Oxford Street, in the Parish of St. George, Hanover Square, where Henry Wellington was publican and owner. There is little doubt that Mary Frances assisted here. One of the most frequent jibes at Laura Keene's acting was that she played the barmaid scenes in Goldsmith's comedy *She Stoops to Conquer* so well because of her early experience in a tavern.

Mary Frances Taylor, née Moss, is last heard of when she responds to the census taker on the night of the 30th of March, 1851. She then attested that the persons abiding at The Plough, after Henry and herself, were their two children, Emma Eliza, age six, born January

23, 1845, and Clara Stella, age 2, born October 3, 1848; a maiden aunt of Henry's, age 76; and three house servants.

Laura Keene is first known through the *Times* (London) of Wednesday, October 8, that same year, 1851. An advertisement of the Theatre Royal, Richmond, reads, "First appearance of the talented young actress Miss Laura Keene — this evening Romeo & Juliet . . ."

From the moment she became Laura Keene, Mary Frances Moss might never have been. T. Allston Brown, her manager, the man closest to her in later years, reported in 1870 that "her maiden name we have heard was Lee."

He, no more than anyone else, told where she found her stage name, Laura Keene. It may have been some echo of names in her mother's family. Her mother, who came to the United States to be with her and care for the Taylor children, forsook the Moss name for her daughter's sake. She lived, died, and was buried as Jane Keene.

The Taylor children were taught to call their mother, "Aunt." Throughout her life in America, the girls remembered to speak of her so, except once, so far as records show.

What happened to the Taylor family of The Plough Public House was another secret close guarded by Mary Frances. Between spring and fall the disruption of the family was complete. Henry's name does not appear again in the directories of London, nor does it appear among those malefactors transported to the colonies, although he later appears in Australia.

What separated the Taylors must have been shattering. In Queen Victoria's day, cosily established young matrons did not strike out on their own without provocation. There was so little women could do to support themselves and their families, they suffered almost any indignity. But not Mary Frances.

Since she was personable, intelligent, pretty, and vital, she chose the theatre as a way to support herself and her children. She assumed a persona, "Laura Keene," who had her way to make.

The proper way to learn to act, professionals believed, was to work one's way up through a stock company. Begin as a child, a ballet girl, a walking lady, saying two or three words in the course of an evening, but learning such important skills as standing, walking, curtsying and dancing. The young aspirant would learn from exposure to the senior members of the company, would learn by precept as well as from shop talk at rehearsals and performances. Such an apprenticeship was impossible to Henry Wellington Taylor's wife. For her, at age twenty-five, there was only private tuition.

She chose to study with Emma Brougham. Ladies and gentlemen wishing to make the stage their profession had the opportunity of training and practicing with a company of recognized ability, according to the advertisements for Mrs. Brougham's theatre in Richmond, England. From Mrs. Brougham she learned how to recite; how to send a word, a phrase, a sentence bouncing off the back wall of the theatre. Take care of the consonants and the vowels will take care of themselves. "Spit it out, duckie, drive a nail with d or t, burst a sack with b or p." All the clichés of diction became the new minted phrases of her education.

Her voice and manner had been deemed too slight for heavy roles, so she was prepared for Juliet and Rosalind in the Shakespearean canon, Pauline in *The Lady of Lyons,* Julia in *The Hunchback* and Juliana in *The Honeymoon.*

Following her debut, the *Era* newspaper reported that her reading was "musical, emphatic, and correct."

Two weeks later, after witnessing four of her five roles, the *Era* concluded, "She has been tutored in a high and legitimate school. We congratulate the stage in having made so promising an acquisition as this lady proves to be. . . . When we consider how little effective *youth* we have upon the boards, and what the coming ten years must inevitably bring about, we are the more pleased with the advent of this young actress."

The reviewer was able to announce that she had been offered employment in London by William Farren at the Olympic. It was only for a few nights; only for a few plays. However, before she could panic over her future, it was assured. Charles Mathews came backstage to offer her the young woman's role in *The Chain of Events*. It was to be a spectacular he and Madame Vestris were preparing for the Lyceum, their very fashionable theatre.

ii

Seldom do two people so alike in temperament, talent and ambition as Laura Keene and Madame Vestris have the opportunity to work together. There was no thought of competition; Madame was 55 years old, suffering from a terminal illness and the tired possessor of every honor the public could offer.

She was still sufficiently the woman to give glimpses of her former madcap behavior. She could dance and sing, and prance and preen. She no longer attempted "breeches parts" but recommended them to young women of good figure. She knew why men came to the theatre. The settings of her plays represented drawing rooms which promised much,

Programme of the Scenery by Mr W. BEVERLY

ACT I.
A STREET IN PARIS

ACT II.
A STORM AT SEA

ACT III.
THÉRÈSE'S SHOP.

ACT IV.
BONNEAU'S HOUSE

ACT V.
APARTMENT
At the MARQUIS DE MELCY'S.

ACT VI.
ROOM at THÉRÈSE'S

ACT VII.
MARKET OF THE INNOCENTS.

WITH THE FOUNTAIN BY MOONLIGHT.
HOLIDAY FÊTE.

Procession of Market Girls, Masqueraders, Miniature Millers and Poissardes,

BALLET.
LA FRICASSEE,

By Mesdames Mars, Wadham, Hodson, Wa'son, Wiltshire, Barnett, Edwards, Ford, C. Ford, Maile, Hunt, Webber, Cutmore, Graham, Smith and Barnes and 16 Children.

PAS DE POISSARDE,
By Miss ROSINA WRIGHT.

ACT VIII.
THE FLEUR DE LYS,
ILLUMINATED SALOON,
LOOKING INTO THE COURT of the PALAIS ROYAL.

TAKING BY STORM
AND
A CHAIN OF EVENTS
EVERY EVENING.

Stage Manager, - - Mr. ROBERT ROXBY

Dress Circle, 5s. Upper Boxes, 4s. Pit, 2s. Gallery, 1s.

The Purchase of Tickets for the DRESS CIRCLE, at the Box-Office, will ensure the Places for the whole Evening.
NO HALF PRICE TO ANY PART OF THE HOUSE.

Doors open at half-past Six. Performance to commence at Seven o'clock.

Mr ALLCROFT, 1, New Bond Street, is appointed Sole Agent for the Private Boxes, to whom all applications must be made.

PRIVATE BOXES, - - Two Guineas and a Half and Two Guineas.
The BOX-OFFICE, adjoining the Theatre, in WELLINGTON STREET open daily from 10 till 6 o'Clock, under the superintendance of MrT. P. HENNEKY

Applicants remembering the bills to be addressed (post paid) to Mr H. BARNES, at 1, Exeter Street, Strand

S. G. Fairbrother, Printer, 31, Bow Street Covent Garden

and the women in her companies were as evocative as selection and dress could make them.

To be part of Madame Vestris's company was a cachet of beauty and fashionableness, and to be of her company was a cause for presumption of easy virtue. Madame Vestris had given the drawing rooms of London much to gossip over.

Three ladies of her theatrical company gossiping about her marriage with Charles Mathews were reported.

"They say that before accepting him, Vestris made a full confession to him of all her lovers! What touching confidence!"

"What needless trouble!!"

"What a wonderful memory!!!"

Madame Vestris not only controlled every detail of a production while it was in rehearsal, she checked every detail of the run of the show while seated out front. She expected the acting and the decor and the stage effects to be as fresh after a long run as they had been the night the production opened.

Laura saw Madame Vestris apply her theories of production. The climax of *The Chain of Events* was a shipwreck scene. For it the stage mechanics contrived a solidly built vessel which was rocked in a sea of waving gauze. Calcium flares flashed through transparent openings in the back cloths. Sheets of silver-green paper, illuminated from behind, cast the lurid glow of an impending hurricane upon the mimic scene. The effect was breathtaking. Unfortunately it could not save the play. Laura had been a disappointment. She gave a tame performance on the opening which deteriorated to a listless one during the run. Her problem was that she did not yet know how to act.

She relished the Lyceum experience. In that greenroom was the headiest theatre talk in the English-speaking world, and she was permitted to listen, even to chime in. The theatre greenroom in Laura's time was the most civilized of conventions. It was the actor's club; and, for a beginner like Laura, a schoolroom. Here there was a perfect democracy. Here everyone met as fellow workers in a common cause. The star could have a separate dressing room for her clothes, her wigs, her powders, and her beaux, but she met on an equal footing with the supernumerary in the greenroom. There the entire company gossiped and chatted the waits away — their lives away. Old stagers' memories were always full of the good talk in the greenrooms of their time. Furniture not needed on the stage, but only on loan from the property room, was distributed about the greenroom, and always, right at the door was a full-length mirror in which each actor could give a final glance at himself as he left the room in response to the pipings of the callboy. Somewhere nearby was the cast-case, a glass-fronted box in which the working information of the company was displayed: notices of rehearsals and of the distribution of parts for the succeeding day. An actress's concern for the future taught her to look there first, as her vanity prompted her to look last at the mirror.

Laura learned about "lines of business" in the greenroom. It seemed the foolishness of a by-gone age. The company had lived its past and would fight the future in the professional framework of leading lady, second lady, juvenile, old woman, singing chambermaid, walking lady, and general utility. Laura learned that Juliet's nurse would be played by the "old woman," Juliet's mother by the "second lady," and Lady Montague would be taken by a "walking lady." She, Laura, as Juliet, had been the leading lady. Now, in *The Chain of Events,* she was a juvenile. The categories for men were more splintered than those for women.

Madame Vestris had many unconventional ideas about the theatre. She had been the first to rid the stage of borders and wings and to drop a ceiling down upon the three walls of a stage setting. Borders were pieces of cut-out canvas, fluttering in the drafts of the burning gas lights, a tired convention for a cornice. They were a means of hiding stage machinery from the spectators. Wings were similar. They ran parallel to the front curtain and tried to represent the side wall of a room in painted perspective. Madame Vestris's innovation, eventually called the box set, created a new illusion of reality. Her first box set was especially painted for a specific play, *London Assurance*.

Madame Vestris had demanded a specific drawing room from her scenic staff, not a generalized salon; the playwright, Dion Boucicault, had wanted carpet and window draperies. He got them because Madame Vestris thought of the theatre as a reflection of the great world of fashion. Laura absorbed the thinking: later, she modified it to her own beliefs. Laura saw the theatre as the model for society, the arbiter of fashion, not its reflection.

Madame Vestris, an exponent of the quieter school of acting, thought of her acting company as representatives of British society. Plays at her theatre were not about the lowly born, but about the concerns of the gentry. When a model for a character in one of her plays was needed, the actor went into the club world of London. Again Laura absorbed and again later she adapted. In the United States, Laura conceived of her actors as models for manners, not imitators thereof.

Whether you thought the theatre the reflection, or the model, of fashion, both Madame Vestris and her pupil Laura Keene believed that the theatre should be fashionable. They shared the belief that the women should be beautiful and the men attractive, the settings handsome and the furnishings rich, and the playhouse itself a place for laughter and gaiety.

Laura's theatre would hold up models of deportment on the stage and models of elegant living in the playhouse. She would have her ideal theatre designed by an architect with ideas of beauty and elegance; there would be symmetry and proportion and elevation of the senses. The lobbies would be galleries for the fine arts. The decorations of the auditorium would be such that the ladies of the audience — society needed the uplifting influence of womankind — would have models for the decoration of their own homes. The actors and actresses would be models of behavior as well as of fashion. Laura's ideal theatre would instruct the women of America in the paths that they should go.

Laura was one of that vast army of Victorian ladies determined to change the world. She was as single-mindedly sure of her definition of salvation — ladylike behavior in elegant surroundings — as Florence Nightingale was certain that physical well-being came in a room with the window open wide all night. Laura differed from Mrs. Trollope, Amelia Bloomer, Lucy Stone, Dorothea Dix, Susan B. Anthony, Carrie Nation, and others, in her goals, not in her sense of mission or in her assumption that she knew best for others.

"The influence of an elegant theatre, presided over by an accomplished woman, is superior to all other influences — procivibus servantis."

iii

As determined to be successful as she was, she realized there was little opportunity for her in London. She wouldn't be permitted to manage for years, maybe never. As for acting, so far she had appeared only some fifty times. She had played seven roles; she had been acceptable in two? three? Perhaps she could find a place with a company in the provinces. Emma Brougham spoke of America. During the run of *The Chain of Events,* Laura was sought out by J. Hall Wilton, the agent who had successfully negotiated the Jenny Lind contracts for P. T. Barnum. He too suggested America.

The states were not like England, with one theatrical center, he told her. There were centers all over the sprawling continent: San Francisco, New Orleans, St. Louis, Cincinnati, Philadelphia, Boston, New York. Each of those cities had at least one theatre company running a 40-week season. An actress could travel back and forth among them. For an actress of Miss Keene's limited experience, touring would be ideal because she could move on to another town as soon as she had run through her small repertoire of roles.

Leaving her children with Jane, she sailed with Wilton, on the *Arctic* of the Collins Line, arriving in New York City on September 6, 1852.

That evening, the New York theatres were jointly staging a special production of *The Merchant of Venice* in celebration of the centenary of the first professional theatre performance in the United States. It could be an omen. The Hallams had been the stars opening the first hundred years. She, Laura Keene, would begin the second.

She was lucky. James Wallack, one of the best actors in Britain and America, was again attempting management. He had no leading lady worthy of the name with his company. He gave Laura an audition; he offered a contract; he stipulated she needed more, much more, instruction before she could head the bill. She must begin again. Wilton assured her it was an offer she could not refuse.

In the days that followed, Laura began to know the lovely drudgery of the acting profession. At Mrs. Brougham's theatre in Richmond she had been a paying student whose whims would be catered to; at Madame Vestris's she had been cosseted. Now she was learning her trade.

James Wallack was remarkable among his contemporaries for his gentleness in handling a beginner. He also had a wary eye for detail and was strict about accuracy in a way then almost unknown. Laura later paid him the compliment of comparing him to Charles Kean and James Hackett, both far more noted than he. His trademark as a manager was his insistence on each actor's knowing "the why" of what he did. "We were like a set of school-boys under discipline," a later pupil wrote, "we had to give a reason for everything, and therefore study hard."

Since she was to take the place of the leading lady, she would be playing opposite Lester, Wallack's son, who was a matinee idol before there were matinees. His forte was standard and gentlemanly comedy. The Wallack stratagem was to prepare Laura in Lester's repertoire. She was to act in nothing she had performed in London.

Laura was held out of production while James Wallack gave her as much private instruction as his limited finances could permit. Not as much as she needed, but all he could afford. He finally announced she would make her debut on Monday, September 20, 1852, in the role of Albina Mandeville in *The Will*.

Why this of all plays? It was a public declaration that Wallack wanted his debutante to succeed. *The Will* was a play with a role for a saucy young woman that would captivate the men in the audience. Should the actress falter, she would be forgiven if she carried herself with an air. Laura's role was a breeches part; the convolutions of the

MADAME VESTRIS AS APOLLO.

Price Halfpenny   Pub.d by M & B. SKELT, 11. Swan St. Minories. London.   N.o 84

Stars of the British Theatre at the time of Laura's debut had collectible images for their younger fans. They were more like today's paper doll books than baseball cards. Drawings were sold Plain or Twopence Coloured. Madame Vestris, the second of Laura's acting teachers, is here shown in a half-penny plain drawing.

Robert Louis Stevenson in a familiar essay recommended to children that they buy plain and colour their own portraits of their favorite players. "With crimson lake and Prussion blue a certain purple is to be compounded, which for cloaks especially, Titian could not equal." J.W. Wallack was Laura's third teacher. UNIVERSITY OF TULSA THEATRE COLLECTION.

plot demanded she dress as a midshipmite of the British Navy. In England the part had been played in uniforms so tight the actress could not bend her knees to climb the stairs to the dressing room but had to be carried up and down.

The press, after ogling, foresaw a future for her in New York. The press unanimously complimented her on her figure, her classical features, her auburn hair, and her clear, ringing voice. Henry James, the novelist, writing of his memories as a small boy at the time of Laura's debut, spoke of the flutter in his family over her advent and the "relish expressed for that 'English' sweetness of her speech. . . . The Uncles, within my hearing, even imitated, for commendation, some of her choicer sounds." That her voice was particularly remarkable was attested by virtually every writer. Even the self-consciously quaint Jeems Pipes wrote, "the musikal voice of Lorer Keene still rings in my ear, and I find it diffikult to write about anything else."

After a successful debut, her life took on a pattern: learn a new role, perform it, and then learn another.

She was granted a first benefit on Thursday, November 11, 1852, a week-day night, not too good for a benefit, but she was going to be supported by Lester in the comedietta, *The Morning Call.* Lester's antics as Sir Edward Ardent in the play were well known to New York audiences. The James family attended, and Henry remembered for years the delightful game Laura made of Lester as she caused him to crawl about on all fours, covered with her shawl as if it were a horse blanket. The success of this brief afterpiece foretold better things to come.

Finally, the Wallack management found a formula for success. Lester Wallack in a romantic role, Laura the object of his affections.

That old, over-done, melodramatic improbable, *The Lady of Lyons*, established the pattern. It was immediately so popular that it continued for two weeks without interruption, a great run for those days. It and *Pauline*, another romantic pastiche, appeared in the bills at Wallack's for over three months.

Lester's performance in *The Lady of Lyons* filled the town with sighs. In his uniform as an officer of the French revolutionary armies, Lester was declared "too handsome to live." Young ladies wore the tricolor in their bonnets, his picture in their jewel caskets, and envied Laura. Young men were certain they would behave as devotedly as he, had they a woman like Laura to sacrifice for.

> We'd have no friends
> That were not lovers, no ambition, save
> To excel them all in love; we'd read no books
> That were not tales of love — that we might smile
> To think how poorly eloquence of words
> Translates the poetry of hearts like ours!
> And when night came, amidst the breathless Heavens
> We'd guess what star should be our home when love
> Becomes immortal; while the perfumed light
> Stole through the mists of alabaster lamps,
> And every air was heavy with the sighs
> Of orange-groves and music from sweet lutes,
> And murmurs of low fountains that gush forth
> I' the midst of roses! — Dost thou like the picture?

> *Pauline* (The Lady of Lyons)
> Oh, as the bee upon the flower, I hang

Upon the honey of thy eloquent tongue!
Am I not blest? And if I love too wildly,
Who would not love thee like Pauline?

Critics knew they were seeing superior acting. "I remember nothing more gallant, more perfect than this piece of acting," wrote one theatre historian. Critics were also aware that here was something more than theatre. Seldom before anywhere, and never before in America, had the theatre exploited the physical attractiveness of a young man and young woman. As one writer pointed out, "lovers go to Wallacks and study up."

Dion Boucicault's play, *Pauline,* gave Lester another he-man role and allowed Laura to be loved, betrayed, and rise unsullied, worthy of a good man's protection. It was full of incident. The *Times* reviewer enumerated: a murder, a duel, a thunderstorm, a robbery, a secret door, a subterranean cavern, an opportune arrival, and several shrieks, all interspersed with soft music and good scenery. The play was a fit subject for ridicule and lampoon. It also was good business.

John Brougham, the company's comedy Irishman and playwright, who was supplementing his activities with a fugitive magazine, *The Lantern,* had a metrical summary of *Pauline* which gave the flavor of the play, the character of Lester, and the appeal of Laura.

If you haven't yet been
To visit Pauline,
It's a presentation at Wallack's I mean
While Memory's green,
Let me tell you the terrors of sweet Laura Keene —
Fresh now in my mind — brought about by the hein-
ous offences of Lester, whose role is between

A dove and a hawk, if you know what I mean;
The most elegant scoundrel that ever was seen,
A Chesterfield cut-throat so aristocratical,
Graciously rude, and indeed problematical,
      Pale and piratical, —
Just such a "creature" as causes lymphatical
Boarding-school misses to feel quite ecstatical.

Brougham told the entire play, act by act, in verse. It was the kind of fun Laura most enjoyed: *Punch*-like satire, catchy rhythms, barbarous puns. After seeing her in her first week at Wallack's, Brougham had punningly touted her to the town, "Go to the Lyceum and pay Keene attention."

The Wallack season ended on Monday, June 13, with a performance of *As You Like It*. After it, the entire strength of the company made a final bow, and Mr. Wallack stepped forth to thank the public for its liberal patronage. In the year just past, Mr. Wallack reminded the public, exclusive of the standard repertoire, he had produced eighteen leading pieces, in a season of 239 nights.

What he did not say, but Laura could: Wallack's Theatre had successfully instructed a leading lady in the business of the stage, setting her forth in 34 different roles and in more than 250 appearances.

CITY STATIONS.

MESSAGES RECEIVED FOR ALL THE PRINCIPAL CITIES AND TOWNS
THE UNITED STATES. A REGULAR CITY COMMUNICATION IS NOW ESTAB-
LISHED, BY WHICH MESSAGES CAN BE TRANSMITTED FROM POINT TO
POINT IN THE CITY.

Stations other than those indicated upon the Map, will be opened as business requires

86 th. St.
YORKVILLE

CENTRAL PARK

79 th. St.

Blackwells Island

11 th. Ave.
10th. Ave.
9 th. Ave.
8 th. Ave.
7 th. Ave.
6 th. Ave.
5 th. Ave.
4 th. Ave.
3 rd. Ave.
2 nd. Ave.
1 st. Ave.

ALLERTONS HOTEL
44 th. St.

ALLERTONS WEST
44 St.

34 th. St.

M. R. R.R.
Depot

N. HAVEN R. R. DEPOT 27 th. St.
HARLEM R. R. DEPOT 26 th. St.
FIFTH AVE. HOTEL
24 th. St.

MADISON SQ. N.O.
EVERETT HOUSE
14 th. St.

NEW YORK
HOTEL
Amity St.

LAFARGE HOTEL

METROPOLITAN HOTEL
Houston St.

Bowery

Canal St.
West St.
Hudson St.
Broadway
Centre St.

Grand St.

Canal St.
Canal St.

East Broadway
South St.

First St.

So. 7th. St.

WILLIAMSBURG

Chamber St.

ASTOR HOUSE
Fulton St.

NAVY YARD

CITY STATIONS
AMERICAN
TELEGRAPH CO
Liberty St.
Wall St.

Sands St.

Flushing Ave.

GENERAL TELEGRAPH
OFFICE 145 Broadway

Fulton St.

Beaver St.

Myrtle Ave.

Remsen St.
BROOKLYN
Fulton Ave.

Chapter 2

A Woman Manager

A warrior woman, who in strife embarks,
The first of all dramatic Joan-of-Arcs!
Cheer on the enterprize thus dared by me,
The first that ever led a company.
OPENING ADDRESS BY MADAME VESTRIS,
OLYMPIC THEATRE, LONDON, JANUARY 3, 1831.

Laura was given a contract for the next season at $45 a week plus two benefits, from which she would receive the usual one-half of the gross proceeds. That was munificence! According to the New York *Times*, a family of four could live comfortably on an annual income of $600. If Laura were as popular the season of 1853-4 as she had been the season just past, her income from the proceeds of her benefits would equal that

Since theatres cluster near travellers' lodgings, this map showing hotels of the 1860s and 1870s bounds Laura's Rialto. Her theatrical life was lived in lower Manhattan between Grand and 14th Streets. Wallack's Lyceum Theatre was by the Metropolitan Hotel. The Varieties was adjacent to LaFarge's Hotel. Laura Keene's Theatre was at 624 Broadway, just south of Houston Street.

of the *Times* family of four, and she would have $1,800 in salary, as well!

Once the contract was set, she wrote her mother to come with the children. Her mother was asked to disembark in Philadelphia so that Laura could continue her masquerade of an unwed leading-lady. Laura would meet her there unseen by any of the stage-door Romeos.

Young New York — as it was called in the penny press — had acknowledged Laura's attractions by paying her their suit. Some had to be treated with more care than others. Pat Hearne dropped in almost every night. He was prodigal in his gifts to actors, and he could assure the success of a benefit. He was New York's most celebrated gambler, whose house at 587 Broadway, opposite the Metropolitan Hotel, was the resort of the wealthiest and heaviest gamblers of the city.

His brother, Edmund L. Hearne, specialized in the legal affairs of the theatre. The Hearneses were friends of John S. Lutz, another gambler, who became Laura's particular protector.

It was natural they should be drawn together. He was as solitary in New York City as she. His leisure hours were the same as hers. He was the American equivalent of gentry: his grandfather had been captain of General Washington's bodyguard during the Revolutionary War. His people were important in Georgetown.

He had been disinherited by his father in favor of his younger brother, Francis. John wanted no part of the family trunk-and-harness business in Washington and Georgetown; no part of the strict Methodism of his forebears. He had provided for his wife's support, settled his Georgetown property on his daughter Adelaide, then drifted north into the society of the Hearnes.

Laura had discovered in England that a woman living apart from her husband was without a champion. In the United States the situation

The leading man of Wallack's Company, his son, Lester, looked to William Winter, much like this etching. He described "the symmetrical, compact head; the close-curling . . . hair; the heavy, almost 'military' moustache; the clear-cut, aquiline, aristrocratic features; the handsome, piercing, dark eyes, . . . the kindling smile; the ringing laugh."
UNIVERSITY OF TULSA
THEATRE COLLECTION

was exaggerated. Public opinion about separation of husband and wife was as violent as the feeling against divorce. Catherine Beecher wrote Susan B. Anthony, "The Law of marriage demanding that in *no* case a man shall seek another wife while his first one lives is always imperative." Divorce for any cause was social ostracism.

Neither Laura Keene or John Lutz could find acceptance outside the ranks of their professions. They comforted each other.

When Laura's second season at Wallack's was filled with bitter struggle with Lester, when her performances gave evidence of her lack of experience, when a critic chided that she had "relapsed into a melodramatic style that chilled the whole audience," when she had nowhere to turn because the elder Wallack was away from his theatre touring the hinterland theatres, she unburdened herself to Lutz. He knew of her desire to manage; he'd listened to her dreams of the stage as a force for social uplift.

He knew of a theatre that could be rented in Baltimore.

Laura asked Lester Wallack for a day off so that she could visit Baltimore. He refused. She went anyway. He told the audience and the press, "Miss Keene is absent from her professional duties without notice to or permission from the manager." She bought an advertisement to respond to Wallack's charges. Lutz signed the Baltimore lease as her representative.

She was beginning again. What if management in Baltimore failed? Where could she go for an acting career? She was forever finished at Wallack's. Against all advice and reason she was risking herself. Why? She was spoiled, of course. When she couldn't have her way she pouted and looked adorable and did something outrageous, like a child. But she was a cool-headed adult, also. If she proposed management, she could see some advantage in it to herself. Obviously, if she were successful, the manager's net income would be hers; she, not Wallack, would get the $9,000 profit he had reported at the end of last season.

She was beginning to realize what she had undertaken. She was the sole wage-earner for her mother, two young girls, the governess and servants such a family required. They deserved better than the life she could provide at $45 a week — a precarious $45, dependent on her health, her looks, her ability to please. Unsympathetic managers could jeopardize her family's future, just as they thwarted her career.

Laura didn't yet know that every actress occasionally has trouble with a role, that every actress, sometimes, attempts a part that is not hers. Starting at age 25 she had no way to judge just how good she really was. She was working so hard to catch up she had no idea of how far she had come. The theatre columnist of the *National Intelligencer* said she is "always a far better actress than *she supposes herself to be.*" Having won acclaim displaying her figure and her fine voice and her waving golden hair, she didn't know that she was worth watching in roles where she flaunted none of those God-given assets.

ii

The Baltimore management gives Laura Keene a permanent place in American history. With her production of *Hearts Are Trumps* at the Charles Street Theatre on December 24, 1853, she became the first woman to manage a theatre in the United States.

She brought together a remarkable company considering that the season was well advanced and most actors had contracts with other managements. To play opposite her and lend elegance to romantic plays, she secured Charles Wheatleigh, but shortly come from England. For the bright young man necessary to set the comic tone, Laura employed another British newcomer, E. A. Sothern, acting under the *nom de theatre,* Douglas B. Stewart. His flair for outrageous comedy developed under Laura's tutelage, until he became the most popular comic performer in the English-speaking world. But that's later. Wheatleigh and Sothern with Laura formed the nucleus of a superior company.

A correspondent for the *Alta* of San Francisco reported that she was "adopting the course of Madame Vestris, in presenting her plays upon the stage, not only to have each character properly sustained, but to have all the accessories of costume, scenery, etc., correspond with the places, country and age, which the scenes are intended to represent."

What she wanted to achieve was unusual for her times. She wanted a company that worked together like the Comedie Française. She wanted that company to play long runs so that there could be time for the manager to oversee the acting company at rehearsals and performance, as Wallack and Vestris had done.

Her ideal had little to do with the audience. It was an ideal of production, which assumed that the spectator would like what the manager provided, the way the manager provided it. The theatre-goer in Laura's time was not necessarily a drama lover. He — and the audience was ninety percent male — went to the theatre as he might go to his club. He went to pass time, to meet friends, to pick up a girl, to get in off the street, to be seen.

Sometimes he went to see a play or a performer. The theatres in New York were clustered in a small area, close to the hotels and passenger terminals, close to all the other attractions of the night. Theatre performances ran from seven-thirty to eleven-thirty with two or three plays given in that span of time, so that the casual spectator could drop in for a while to see the part of the program he liked. If he liked Laura romping with Lester, he arrived at the theatre in time to see only that part — if his timing was off he could drink in the theatre bar.

The box-office managers encouraged the casual spectator. Tickets could be purchased at any time during the performance. Since there were few, if any, reserved seats, a person once inside the theatre could go virtually where he liked. If he found congenial company, he could stay or leave at will. When he left the theatre with the idea of returning he was given a pass-out check. This he could give to someone else, use later that same evening or another evening.

What Laura wanted was a playhouse in which serious theatre-lovers came on time to spend the evening. It never occurred to her that such a theatre-goer had nowhere else to go once a long run was achieved. It also never occurred to her that it would take a vast reservoir of play-goers to keep a long-run theatre in business. Two thousand people a night for a one-hundred-night run means at least 200,000 people who want to see Laura perform, a number infinitely harder to secure than two thousand people who are content to see a different, less well-done play every night.

Baltimore did not have a body of play-goers large enough to support her ideal.

What Laura did in her first try at management was what all other theatres in the United States were then doing. What she did no one in the theatre today attempts. She acted in from one to three different plays each night. During performance, she would prepare for the greenroom board a notice of the plays for the next night. She would confer with the stage artist about what scenery must be painted anew and what scenery would do just being retouched. At completion of the evening's bill, during the company call, she would curtsy on the hand of the leading man while the stage manager announced to the audience that tomorrow night the company would present such-and-such a favorite play followed by thus-and-so brilliant afterpiece, the whole to conclude with a tried-and-true, never-failing farce. Then she would pack the night's costumes, and since she was manager, she would pay a quick visit to the dressing rooms to say good-night to the members of her company.

The next morning, she would prepare bills of the play for the printer and newspapers, handle correspondence; consult with the stage manager and prompter over what plays they would present when that evening's play needed to be replaced, then attend the daily rehearsal at ten. Here she and the others went through the ritual checking of scripts: was there agreement on movement and positioning? Always there was someone in an unfamiliar part who needed extra attention, and always there was the problem of dress. The sleaziness of a scratch company was most apparent to an audience in matters of costume. The white trousers of Napoleon's soldiers were tucked into stockings to become the knee breeches of the courtiers of Louis XIV.

Rehearsal would last until three, after which time the actors would dine and lay out their costumes for the night's performance. So would Laura if there was no crisis needing her attention. All the actors were back in the theatre by six; curtain was at seven, another greenroom notice was up by nine-thirty, and good-nights were voiced around midnight.

In a season of sixty nights her company acted thirty-four different principal plays. Five of them she had learned in London, fourteen with Wallack, and the remainder she taught herself in Baltimore. While concentrating on management her acting became secure.

"Never having seen her before," wrote a Baltimorean, "I confess, I have been disappointed. . . . Of all the prominent actresses I have had the fortune to see, I have found that after a few weeks there was left on my mind a vivid impression of the woman and the character she represented, with a less distinct idea of the play or the other characters:

But with Miss Keene it has been the reverse. The vivid impression is of the play."

That unwitting accolade was followed by the news, "An agent is now here from California. His object is to induce Miss Laura Keene to trust herself among the golden population for six months. . . Since her advent in this city, she has won the good wishes and support of the citizens of Baltimore; of course all her true friends must rejoice at the advancement of her fortune, for the terms are almost fabulous."

Laura completed her contract with the owner of the Charles Street Theatre with a performance of *As You Like It* on Friday night, March 3, 1854, and the following Tuesday sailed from New York, with her mother and two daughters on the side-wheel steamer, *Ohio*.

iii

Although she thrilled at managing, she went to San Francisco to act.

The stories of gold-miners' wealth showered on actresses nowhere near so able as she, stirred her. It was common knowledge that the Chapmans had created a shortage of specie when too many miners had thrown too many buckskin purses onto the stage, that Mrs. Baker in October was presented with a valuable diamond bracelet, in March, a splendid diamond ring, in August, an expensive silver tea service, in January, a superfine diamond magic watch. The invitation to star lured her. The improbability of a role in the New York Theatre or a manager's job anywhere, convinced her.

Bella Union playhouse as it appeared in an 1850 photograph. Telegraph Hill is in the background; Portsmouth Plaza in the foreground. University of Tulsa Theatre Collection.

She could have served as a model for the imperturbable female English traveler, complete with mitts and parasol. She traveled to the gold diggings with her mother, her two children, a mountain of luggage, and all the play manuscripts so painfully acquired in Baltimore. She bought cabin accommodations, New York to Aspinwall, and Colon to San Francisco. She bought as much train travel from Aspinwall to Colon across the Isthmus of Panama as could be purchased in New York City. Since the rail line was unfinished, the half-day mule ride for the four women in the Keene party was a hardship to be borne just as one bore those other hardships aboard ship, vermin in the cabin, scoundrels in the lounge.

John Lutz had gone on ahead to negotiate the contracts for her starring tour; accommodations for her mother and the children. He made it to California only by the grace of God. The gold fever had pressed every ocean-going vessel into service. The one he had booked on was so derelict its seams opened in a moderate sea. Luckily, it foundered so close to shore the passengers could be saved. They unanimously signed a condemnation of the ship owners and booked passage on the next available boat.

John Lutz found places for the four women in the booming city of San Francisco and congenial work for himself. He — no more than she — realized she was not a star actress; that her success depended on an ensemble. She failed in her California debut.

"Miss Keene has not performed in San Francisco as well as she is capable of performing," wrote the editor of *The Pioneer*." In New York, she was surrounded and assisted at Wallack's by artists, several of whom were equally good with herself. They understood each other thoroughly, and this combination presented a marked attraction for the public.

"She being the lady of the troupe, gained a reputation which she is unable to sustain when acting alone.

"Her pieces came onto the stage without sufficient preparation. Some of the important actors around her were not perfect in their parts. We regret to say that this remark applies with too much truth to Mr. Edwin Booth."

Edwin Booth was not yet the dominant tragic actor of the nineteenth-century American stage, but rather the wild youngster who listed his profession in the city directory as "Comedian and Ranchero."

Laura denounced him after her debut performance. He confided to his cronies that "he felt it Keenely."

She was equally unsuccessful in the other towns of the gold-mine circuit.

Although the failure was hers, the fault was with the companies. No actor had his mind on the theatre; he would leave the stage for the diggings at the first news of another strike. While Laura was out of San Francisco she revised her repertoire, and announced herself in plays which depended less on others and more on her unaided appeal. She won the kind of reception as Lady Gay Spanker in *London Assurance*, in Sacramento, that she had coveted for her opening in San Francisco.

But those performances!

The acting style was that of the previous generation, all bluster and rant. And for the same reason. Stage lighting in Stockton was more primitive than the lighting of Shakespeare's Globe Theatre. Candle light was augmented by wicks floating in footlight troughs of whale oil. An actor to be seen to register disgust could not let a nostril flare, but had to twist his lips in such a contorted sneer that the white teeth showed to the back of the hall. The noisiness of the actor was indirectly due to the poor illumination, also. The spectators at the back could seldom see anything. They were kept abreast of the story by the stentorian voices on stage.

The audience was flannel-shirted and tobacco-chewing. It was all male, eager for entertainment, avid for the sight of woman.

She knew the reviewers were right. She was not a star. The saloon-hall theatre was not for her. She was a company performer. She and Lutz began to look for a vacant building in Frisco where she could assemble a company of her own and where she could display her skills as a manager. She was forced to agree with John Brougham's quip, "To star is human; to succeed, divine."

She found a playhouse, The Union, a former French Theatre. She recruited a company, sending back to Baltimore for Charles Wheatleigh, who had given her such support there. She announced a season of plays which had been successful in her previous experience.

But again it was a beginning over.

She who dreamed of a theatre like that of Madame Vestris's had to console herself that the theatre she did have was remarkable to the critics because "there was no halting and stopping and hemming; no gagging but each one gave the text of the play and all went off smoothly."

She learned again what she had first realized in Baltimore. Production comes before philosophy. The public wants a play, the actors want roles, the community wants an attraction. *Camp at the Union, A Review of California Dramatic Force,* filled that bill. However much she might want to produce elegant comedy, the public was happy with this extravaganza written by Dr. Yankee Robinson. It had songs and sketches that were reworked nightly to keep abreast of the changing San Francisco scene. The economic ups and downs, the discovery of new diggings, the arrival of celebrities, the completion of the trans-Panama railroad, all were skits for Dr. Robinson's revue. At some point there must have been reference to the "Laura Keene Diggings," placer mines discovered in the foothills near Douglas and Reany's Ranch in the San Joaquin valley, named in her honor. Also, surely, there must have been a bitter jest that the mines did not pan out.

The outside world reached into the private one of The Union. Lutz heard of the terminal illness of his wife. His place, now, must be with her. He returned to Georgetown. Laura had word of Henry Wellington Taylor. She packed her mother and the girls off to New York, while seeking passage to Australia. The first boat to leave was taking young Booth to try his theatrical luck among the Australian gold diggings. Laura booked passage on the same vessel.

Her visit to Australia was viewed as another example of aberrant behavior. "Where can Laura Keene run to from Australia? She bolted from Wallack's where she was favorite, and from Baltimore, where she was not; and now I see she has vanished from San Francisco," wrote a theatre paragrapher.

Taylor's existence was a secret kept from family and associates. Clara said all she knew of her father was that he was a loafer. John Lutz testified under oath he knew nothing of Laura's husband, Mr. Taylor. But of course, Edwin Booth knew.

He sent frequent letters to his friends in California and his family in Maryland. Jeems Pipes, his particular California friend, who corresponded for several newspapers, reported that Laura and Booth had acted together in Sydney and Melbourne; that Booth had sent him clippings from Australian newspapers reporting their doings. Pipes reported in a letter dated December 16, 1854, "Laura Keene (I heard yesterday) left Sydney . . . the day she arrived there. The cause of this was the unexpected meeting . . . with a near relation who had become immensely rich in the diggings and offered her any amount of money she wanted to return to the 'good old home.'"

Laura was interested only in a legal separation, which Taylor refused. He continued in Australia and there is no further record of him in Laura's life until Booth's brother-in-law, John Sleeper Clarke, in 1859, challenged Laura's right to own property because she had a husband in Australia, a fact he was prepared to prove.

That was in the future.

For now she would ignore Taylor's existence. Laura Keene still had her way to make. Times were hard; Australia was suffering an economic recession. She and Booth appeared in only twelve productions, then scurried for California.

Edwin Booth was much younger than he appears here when he acted with Laura Keene in California and Australia. This photograph is probably of the time of his debut in New York City in 1857 or of his marriage to Mary Devlin in 1859.
University of Tulsa Theatre Collection

iv

Her management of the American Theatre after her return from Australia was an artistic success story. San Francisco had changed. The city was reeling in financial panic. Actors were glad for jobs and careful to do as the manager suggested.

Midsummer Night's Dream was played every night for a week to crowded houses. The machinery which carried Titania and Oberon into the heavens at the conclusion of the play was so applauded that the entire effect had to be repeated as an encore. "Laura Keene, with her handsome legs and beautiful person, most exquisitely costumed as King Oberon . . . was a subject for a poet's dream."

Productions of *The Tempest, Comedy of Errors, Much Ado About Nothing,* and *Henry VIII* followed. She had experience of the success of a stock company. She had won the recognition of her peers. Her future in California seemed assured.

Then John Lutz wrote of his wife's death in late June, 1855. He was free! Long before, she had decided to behave as if she were. She would be returning to New York, as fast as she could honor all her local contracts. She booked passage on the *John L. Stephens,* a vessel sailing October 5.

"Miss Keene proceeds to the Atlantic States and will bear with her, if not the wealth of dollars, at least the golden opinion and good wishes of the community that has been enlivened by her art," said one reporter. The writer for the *Chronicle* said,

"Last appearance of Miss Keene. — Miss Laura Keene last night . . . bid our play-goers farewell. . . .

"It is now about a year and a half since Miss Keene first visited this country. Six or eight months of that time were occupied by her in a professional visit to Australia. During the remainder of the period Miss Keene has been almost constantly attached to one or other of the theatres in this city. The peculiarities of her acting must be familiar to most of our readers. She was the most graceful woman who has ever appeared on our stage. Her manners were elegant and refined, her taste in dress was unexceptionable, her elocution was clear, correct, and remarkably musical, she was generally well versed in her parts, and she was always 'at home' in the by-play and details of the scene. In truth it was a pleasure to see Miss Keene merely walk across the stage. All her movements were those of an intelligent, thorough-bred lady.

"She had a 'style' and merits of her own. She excelled in dashing and brilliant parts — in elegant comedy. We think Miss Keene was unrivaled by any actress who has yet appeared in San Francisco. During her recent management, the American Theatre was distinguished for the elegance and completeness of the various pieces produced there, and in which she always took the leading female parts. That period will long be remembered here with pleasure by lovers of the Shakespearean drama; and it may be some satisfaction for Miss Keene hereafter to think that her management at the American was truly the palmy time of theatricals in this city."

Chapter 3

Varieties Theatre

So far as my coin would stretch;
and where it would not,
I have used my credit.
SHAKESPEARE, *HENRY IV* PART I, ACT I, SCENE 2

Quince: Is all your company here?
Bottom: You were best to call them generally,
man by man, according to the script.
SHAKESPEARE, *A MIDSUMMER NIGHTS' DREAM*, ACT II,
SCENE 2.

S he was back where she wanted to be; back with her mother, her children, John Lutz. The New York newspapers told her that if she wanted to act, William Burton did not have a suitable leading lady; they told her, if she wanted to manage, John LaFarge was seeking a lessee for the Metropolitan Theatre. Would he be interested in the kind of theatre she envisioned? Would he be interested in her successes as a manager in California?

The ALBION *said of Laura Keene in a farewell comment before her departure for America, "She is passably pretty, with a face capable of a great variety of expression, and is blessed moreover with a neat figure and a pleasant voice."* THOMAS BAKER SHEET MUSIC COVER, AFTER AN AMBROTYPE BY BRADY. LIBRARY OF CONGRESS.

LaFarge asked nothing about her experience. He asked only if she had any money.

All parties were filled with trepidation. Lutz, of course, was concerned about cost. LaFarge was dubious about a lease where there was no security. The Hearneses, Laura's lawyer and Lutz's friends, were afraid of the contract that LaFarge was demanding and of the thinness of the Lutz-Keene finances. Laura was troubled over the availability of suitable actors and frightened by the immensity of the auditorium. Her ideal of elegant comedy required intimacy. In the Metropolitan the actors would need to exaggerate, to bawl out speeches. Such a theatre had been described as one where a speaking trumpet is required for the actor and a telescope for the spectator. LaFarge continued to advertise the building for lease or sale while negotiations were going on. Laura learned that a company could be assembled; many of Burton's actors were disaffected and would leave him to join her, including that most necessary of all creatures, a leading man of physical charm, George Jordan.

The crux now was money. They needed salary money for department heads and scenery builders and costume makers one week after they were employed. They needed money immediately for cleaning people to scrub down the auditorium. They needed money to make alterations.

At this point there must have been a series of emotionally charged exchanges, Laura wanting the theatre of her dreams now, Lutz counseling caution. He probably maneuvered her to a moderate expenditure on the auditorium by reminding her how much she would want to spend on her own department, the stage. But however less the actuality from her dream, it would take money — money before the business ever sold a ticket. The theory was that actors, dancers, musicians would not expect to be paid until after the first week of performances, when income could cover outgo. But Laura knew and Lutz was to learn that actors are impecunious and most would ask for, expect, and need advances just to have a wardrobe out of the pawnshops and in their dressing rooms on opening night.

They wouldn't have to pay playwrights, thank heaven.

Bill posters, printers, ticket printers, lithograph men, the gas company, the coal company would want money immediately.

What would LaFarge want?

He wanted $400 per week payable in advance promptly each Monday, and a long-term lease from December to December. Miss Keene could have the option to renew for four more years by giving notice in writing on or before May 1, 1856. He also agreed to certain alterations to the theatre building which Laura insisted upon.

Then must have followed long and heated discussions between Laura and Jane Keene, between Laura and John Lutz, between them and the Hearneses, the sort of talks that all beginning entrepreneurs have:

"Gas will cost us at least $55 a week."

"How do you know that?"

"Wallack's pays that much."

"I'm certain we could do it for less."

"What will the orchestra cost?"

Eventually much writing of numbers on a pad on someone's knee adds up to a bottom line of proposed salaries of $1,200 per week, with nothing in it for Laura or Lutz, and that's absurd because she's going to need money to buy dresses for herself as leading lady. Nothing she wore in California will do; styles have changed, hoops are now the fashion.

At least $1,200 for stage salaries. Then utilities, printing, advertising, cleaning people, ushers — make that another $400. Add LaFarge's $400 and it takes $2,000 a week just to stay open. Add $400 for Laura, Lutz, and emergencies. Say $2,400 all told.

What do you think your creation will sell for? Who can answer? If you believe in yourself and the value of what you have made, you of course believe buyers will beat a path to your door, but how can you make a budget on confidence alone? To calculate what might be possible, Laura and John Lutz took the proposed prices of admission, multiplied them by the number of seats in each price range. The parquet, for which they planned to charge fifty cents admission, had twelve hundred seats. The second and third tiers, for which they would charge a quarter, had fifteen hundred seats. Exclusive of the boxes, the theatre could crowd twenty-seven hundred people into its enormous maw. With the box customers, a full house at those prices could produce $1,000 a night. Business would be good during the holiday season and again in April when out-of-town buyers would be in New York. Business would be bad during the snow and sleighing season of February and March.

They would need an average nightly income of $400 to break even.

"This theatre having been leased by Miss Laura Keene for five years, parties of acknowledged talent desirous of engaging, will please apply —" read the advertisement in the newspapers of November 24. Laura announced to open the Metropolitan on Christmas Eve. Her lease with LaFarge began on December 17, on which day he was to receive his first $400.

ii

Laura had known of Thomas Baker, the musician, from her days in London. He was the first employee of the theatre, shortly to be called Laura Keene's Varieties. Baker became in time a fixture of her theatres and as popular as she with their audiences. He developed a skill "for doing the right thing at the right time, and making the music a noticeable feature of the evening." Baker announced a call for musicians for the theatre the last days of November.

Ladies and gentlemen desirous of engaging in the ballet were asked to apply at the box office the first days of December. As choreographer and principal dancer, Laura secured M. Montplaisir, whom she had seen and known in San Francisco.

But who were the actors to be? The newspapers outdid themselves in guessing. The members engaged were asked to convene in the greenroom at noon on Saturday, December 15, and the press finally had an inkling of the caliber of the company. Harry Hall, a respected member of "the old school of actors," had been secured from Burton's Theatre to be stage manager and second old man. Burton's had been levied on heavily. Kate Reignolds, a juvenile; Rosalie Durand, a vocal soloist; T. B. Johnston and John Dyott, character actors; Lotty Hough, an eye-poppingly beautiful soubrette; and George Jordan, leading man, were the principal defectors. Reignolds said they were unhappy at Burton's because of his high-handed treatment and were seeking a place to go; Laura, in other words, had not solicited them. However it happened, Laura earned Burton's enmity.

William E. Burton was an actor, writer, entertainer, manager, and publisher. Burton was never able to distinguish between competition and opposition. During his years of management in Philadelphia he

Rules and Regulations

OF

LAURA KEENE'S VARIETIES,

UNDER THE MANAGEMENT OF LAURA KEENE.

1.—Gentlemen, at the time of rehearsal or performance, are not to wear their hats in the Green Room or talk vociferously. The Green Room is a place appropriated for the quiet and regular meeting of the company, and to be called thence, *and thence only,* by the call boy, to attend on the Stage. The Manageress is not to be applied to in that place, on any matter of business, or with any personal complaint. For a breach of any part of this article, fifty cents will be forfeited.

2.—The call for all rehearsals will be put up by the Prompter between the play and farce, or earlier, on evenings of performance. No plea will be received, that the call was not seen, in order to avoid the penalties of Article Fifth.

3.—Any member of the Company unable from the effects of stimulants to perform, or to appear at rehearsal, shall forfeit a week's salary, and be liable to be discharged.

4.—For making the Stage wait, fifty cents.

5.—After due notice, all rehearsals must be attended. The Green Room clock or the Prompter's watch is to regulate time; ten minutes will be allowed, (*the first call only,*) for difference of clocks; forfeit, twenty-five cents for every scene—the whole rehearsal at the same rate, or four dollars at the option of the Manageress.

6.—A Performer rehearsing from a book or part at the last rehearsal of a new piece, and after proper time given for study, forfeits one dollar.

7.—A Performer introducing his own language or improper jests not in the author, or swearing in his part, shall forfeit one dollar.

8.—Any person talking aloud behind the scenes to the interruption of the performance, to forfeit fifty cents.

9.—Every Performer concerned in the first act of a play to be in the Green Room dressed for performance, at the time of beginning as expressed in the bills, or to forfeit five dollars. The Performers in the second act to be ready when the first finishes. In like manner with every other act. Those Performers who are not in the two last acts of the play, to be ready to begin the farce, or to forfeit one dollar. When a change of dress is necessary, ten minutes will be allowed.

10.—Every performer's costume to be decided on by the Manageress, and a Performer who makes any alteration in dresses without the consent of the Manageress, or refuses to wear them, shall forfeit one dollar.

11.—If the Prompter shall be guilty of any neglect in his office, or omit to forfeit where penalties are incurred, by non-observance of the Rules and Regulations of the Theatre, he shall forfeit for each offence or omission, one dollar.

12.—For refusing, on a sudden change of a play or farce, to represent a character performed by the same person during the season, a week's salary shall be forfeited.

13.—A Performer refusing a part allotted him by the Manageress, forfeits a week's salary or may be discharged.

14.—No *Prompter, Performer,* or *Musician,* will be permitted to copy any manuscript or music belonging to the Theatre, without permission from the Manageress, under the penalty of fifty dollars.

15.—Any Performer singing songs not advertised in the bills of the day, omitting any, or introducing them, not in the part allotted, without first having consent of the Manageress, forfeits a night's salary.

16.—A performer restoring what is cut out by the Manageress, will forfeit one dollar.

17.—A Performer absenting himself from the Theatre of an evening when concerned in the business of the Stage, will forfeit a week's salary, or be held liable to be discharged at the option of the Manageress.

18.—In all cases of sickness, the Manageress reserves to herself the right of payment or stoppage of salary during the absence of the sick person.

19.—No person permitted, on *any account,* to address *the audience,* but with the consent of the Manageress. Any violation of this article will subject the party to forfeiture of a week's salary, or a discharge, at the option of the Manageress.

20.—Any new rule which may be found necessary shall be considered as part of these Rules and Regulations, after it is publicly made known in the Green Room.

Ladies and Gentlemen bringing servants, must on no account permit them behind the scenes.

Ladies and Gentlemen are requested not to bring children behind the scenes, unless actually required in the business.

☞ It is particularly requested that every Lady and Gentleman will report to the Prompter their respective places of residence.

Ladies and Gentlemen prevented attending the rehearsal by indisposition, will please give notice to the Prompter BEFORE the hour of beginning.

☞ No stranger, or person not connected with the Theatre, will be admitted behind the scenes, without the written permission of the Manageress.

had tried to drive the other theatres into bankruptcy. Some said he attempted the same trick in New York.

He was a most complicated person. He owned one of the finest collections of books, mostly Shakespearean, in the United States. He had a three-story, fireproof library built next to his home at 174 Hudson Street to house the sixteen thousand volumes he had brought from Philadelphia. He lovingly produced Shakespeare's plays and grossly grimaced and wriggled in too-tight trousers as the low comedian in lesser shows. He was cruel to those out of his favor.

Laura had unwittingly and perhaps cavalierly offended Burton, but she hadn't time to bother. Baker had twenty in his orchestra, M. Montplaisir had thirty-six in the ballet, and Laura had attracted at least three times as many actors as she needed. "Every improvement that taste and judgment could dictate, and lavish expenditure procure has been adopted," the advertising said about Varieties. Laura had decreed that boxes be thrown together in the front of the house, that chairs be placed behind the benches in the parquet, that paint be spread and upholstery replaced.

In her department she ordered new sets of scenery prepared, and carpenters and machinists had managed to make the apparent size of the stage less. The acting area in LaFarge's building was large enough for equestrian demonstrations. Laura pulled the opening in to twenty-five feet. Backstage was immense. Painters and carpenters working in galleries along the building walls were hardly noticed; it was a hundred feet from wall to wall, or from the sidewalks of Broadway to those of Mercer Street. The audience sat parallel to Broadway with its back to Bleecker Street. Laura's office, the greenroom, and the actors' dressing rooms were under the stage; the stage door was off Mercer.

For her opening on Christmas Eve, Laura chose a gala from her days in London, *Prince Charming*. Although Laura's advertisements said that this "Grand, Romantic, Spectacular, Fairy Extravaganza" had been written expressly for the Varieties theatre, the fact that it had been written by Planche for Madame Vestris for the Christmas season of 1850 became obvious to everyone when Burton's Theatre announced the same play for the same evening.

iii

Spectators who tried to gain admission to Laura Keene's Varieties opening night were turned away from the darkened box office without an explanation. If they asked when the theatre would open, they were told to watch the newspapers.

Rumor was rife. Those who knew Laura and her tightly strung temperament assumed a nervous breakdown or physical exhaustion. Others, of course, guessed that a bout with liquor had washed out opening night. Some whispered that the show wasn't ready. What happened is more incredible than any of the guesses. A vandal had so slashed the principal scene of *Prince Charming* that it could not be shown to the public or repaired in time. Laura offered a reward for evidence to apprehend the culprit. Who was to blame was never revealed, but the destruction is like an act of Burton's in Philadelphia and in keeping with his confusion over the limits of legitimate competition.

What a Christmas Eve! The discovery of wrecked scenery some time that day, a decision to cancel for that night, and the second week's rent due to LaFarge. Lutz paid it and Laura didn't ask how. She was choosing another opening bill.

Salaries for the ballet, orchestra, and actors would be due on Saturday. Laura probably pawned the last of her jewelry to meet that expense. Everything else she and Lutz had, plus everything else they could cadge or extract from friends, had gone toward opening. Her mother, Jane, who later helped her through other financial crises, must have been called on for all she had. The situation was desperate.

Laura opened the Varieties on Thursday, December 27, with a ballet and a standard piece, *Old Heads and Young Hearts*. She was to have recited an opening address in verse but broke down and could not get past the first few lines. Two of the couplets she would have spoken were:

> I'll try the railroad-pace of this, our age,
> And "hurry up" by steam their slow coach stage —
> Variety is life's best spice, folks say,
> That be my aim, my motto "ever gay."

The "hurry up" of her age forced a change of bill on Saturday, when there was a snowstorm. There was a different bill on Monday, another on Tuesday, a change of bill and snow again on Saturday. Saturday was normally the best night for business. The next week was worse for the treasury: zero temperatures as well as snow, and the citizenry who could afford the theatre had gone sleighing mad. "This is a stern winter. The streets are like Jordan, 'hard roads to travel.' One has to walk warily over the slippery sidewalks and to plunge madly over crossings ankledeep in snow." But walking was better than attempting the sleigh caravans with which the city had replaced the omnibuses. The passengers stood in wet straw with their feet freezing, their ears and noses tingling in the wind, their hats always about to be blown off. "When the chariot stops, they tumble forward, and when it starts again, they tumble backward, and when they arrive at the end of their ride, they commonly land up to their knees in a snowdrift."

Luckily for Laura, she lived within some thousand feet of the stage door, and her only other journey outdoors, to LaFarge's each Monday with the rent, was equally short, since he lived on the property between his theatre and hotel.

The condition of the Varieties, although critical, was not mortal. Performances continued, but her grandiose plans trailed in the dust. Reviewers commented: "Everything is malignant, coarse and cheap. The courtiers look like flunkies, . . . with wigs that are evidently of raw cotton," "Miss Keene's acting was good enough to excuse the obtuseness of some of the company," "Miss Keene's energetic impersonation . . . is sufficient to redeem any amount of stupidity, clumsiness and bad taste."

Without audiences, there was no money; without money, there were inadequate costumes and scenery. When Laura arrived at the theatre the last Monday night in January after paying LaFarge, she discovered that the costumes for *Much Ado About Nothing* were not ready. All the ladies in the acting and ballet companies were pressed into service, and the unfinished dresses were sewn together on the performers. Then, calling the men together, Laura finished the borders of the jackets and trunks with great stripes of black scenery paint. She went off to dress herself for Beatrice with a final injunction, "Now, keep apart! Don't sit down! Don't come near the ladies!"

If the shows were as bad as that, why didn't the theatre fail? The theatre reviewers were asking themselves the same question, and their answers were surprisingly similar. It was Laura. She was not only admired for her ability as an actress and her industry as a manager, but was personally liked. "There is a widespread feeling of sympathy with and for her which renders her audience her friends," a columnist noted. "They seem to deem it a duty and labor of love to uphold her in all her efforts and to identify themself with her enterprises and her fortunes." This feeling was palpable. It survived the years and was commented on by succeeding generations of reviewers. Laura responded to it with intensified activity. Surely the weather would moderate? Some play catch the public fancy? She took a benefit on a Saturday late in February to stimulate the box office, but the stimulant had been found the night before, a one-act dramatization of her dilemma called *Novelty*.

Laura portrayed herself, a harried theatre manager, wanting to please an audience. The thin plot then introduced a tableau and actor imitations, which her company performed admirably. The imitations were "interspersed with song and dance, and some beautiful scenic effects." One newspaper writer, pondering its success, stated that it was originally a French play and added, "We wonder that it has never been stolen before." It had been, by Laura in California. The format permitted topicality; the lines and scenes could be changed with the times. It was just enough of a success that Laura and Lutz need no longer strain, but they couldn't relax. *Novelty* was the afterpiece, with a constantly changing main bill, until St. Patrick's day and then . . . the Varieties had a hit!

Camille, with Laura as the courtesan and Jordan as Armand.

There was shock value in that play. It was box office, when it could be adapted to the squeamishness of the audience. Laura presented the entire story of the courtesan's life and death as a dream, from which

Camille awoke in the last scene. The same bill ran for three weeks; even late snows did not dampen the public ardor.

With a play running, there was time to catch one's breath, to look about, to think, to plan. With spring coming on, the buyers from the country would be coming into town; they would add to the box office and plays of the winter could be repeated for them. Spring meant the season of players' benefits, and the thought of contract renewal. Jordan had been adequate, but for a theatre professing to be ever gay, "He carries a dead weight about him that drags him down, down," Laura wrote. "What a pity with his appearance and gifts." He would be continued, however. Where could she find a better leading man? The company needed a scenic designer. Laura wrote to agents in London and in May learned she could get a very proficient one, Charles J. Hawthorne, if she would advance the passage money.

During the time of thinking and reappraisal she tried to determine what had brought business. It was — not to put too fine a point on it — a play in which the audience could hear the worst about a woman but need not admit it to be true. The public found vicarious pleasure in admiring the wicked. They wanted to hear about the same scarlet sins they dreamed, but since, when awake, they praised virtue and chastity, they didn't want those other sinners — characters in a play — to get away unpunished. She looked through her collection of prompt books and conferred with the stage manager, Harry Hall. *The Marble Heart*, in which she had acted in California, fitted the formula. So did *Agnes St. Aubin* and *The King's Rival*. They couldn't find a script for *Agnes,* but the others were copied and readied for the time when Camille should cough her last.

Such activity was typical of Laura's days. She and Hall were forced to keep five and six weeks ahead on possible plays.

In a theatre such as Laura wanted to manage, play selection was the formula for success. It was not as important in 1856 as it was to become later, but obviously a theatre survived on the spectator's desire to see its wares. The public preferred to see a show that had a prior audience's seal of approval. If a play were called for repetition, that was an attraction for a second-night audience. If a play in Baltimore had had a success in New York, it was assured of less critical listening. A play in New York had its chances enhanced by a successful career in London, and the London stage aped the Parisian. France, with a copyright law that protected a share of the income in a play to the playwright, had the creative, innovative theatre of the period. As Laura had already demonstrated, *Camille* and *Novelty*, both French successes, were the material keeping her theatre open.

The principal theatres of London and New York kept a constant watch on the Parisian stage. A success in Paris could be in rehearsal in London within the week, or announced in the bills in America as fast as a vessel could cross the Atlantic. Three weeks from foreign stage to New York production was not unusual. Out of France, the French product belonged to anyone. Every theatre manager in London could present *Camille* if he wanted; every female star could add it to her repertoire.

When Laura began choosing dramatic fare for the theatres she managed, she operated under an American statute which, as nearly as she and the courts understood it, permitted her to produce any play in print without permission from, or fee to, the author so long as she named him.

All that was changing. Eighteen fifty-six was the year in which Congress was going to do something to protect and encourage native dramatic writers with a new copyright law.

iv

Laura was ahead of the government. She had been seeking new scripts through theatrical agents. She let it be known she preferred American playwrights who dealt with American subjects. She also let it be known that the Varieties would pay respectable royalties for such material. She received one such manuscript, *My Wife's Mirror*, which she and Hall began to prepare for the time when *Camille* would have faded in audience interest.

The play might serve another purpose. The author, E. G. P. Wilkins, drama critic for the *Herald*, was also part of New York's nascent Bohemia. Laura had been stung by the Bohemians' criticism. Would royalties pull their stings? "The drama is especially afflicted in the number and character of so-called Critics for the newspapers," a magazine article about Bohemianism reported. It called the men "long-haired and dirty-nailed" and the women "unhooped and uncombed." It said they gave criticism in New York "its low, egotistic, unfair, malicious character, its blind particularities and undying hates; its brazen ignorance and insulting familiarity." They were obviously feared by theatre managers, and particularly by Laura. They tried to outdo each other in outrageous comments. Laura's scenic department was their particular target at the moment. On the proscenium flats at the Varieties, one of the group said, "are depicted two hideous Jewesses playing on tambours in a state of cheerful intoxication. Taste cannot exist where such flats are tolerated." Laura's version of *Camille* drew this comment: "The scenery is beneath criticism, and it is too bad even for condemnation." So far, the writers had not aimed at Laura, and the same reviewer just quoted had been delighted with her performance: "It was spirited, arch, and lifelike with those cloudlets of thoughtfulness

which Miss Keene knew so well how to hang over her best imper-
sonations."

Laura's fear of critics was almost pathological. She went to great
lengths to propitiate them, and she exhibited an abnormal sensitivity
to their comments. Toward the end of her career she wrote a young
actress, "I understand the press have not taken you up tenderly. . . .
If there are two who can sympathize with each other it is you and I, as
we have had bitter experience from unjust criticism. I have lived
through mine, and so will you." To arrive at such an evaluation of her
treatment by the press, Laura must have allowed every slightly
uncomplimentary comment to hurt her like a scathing rebuke. Her
overreaction to the press was commented on by the *New York Picayune,*
"Laura Keene has been the pet of the newspapers from the first hour
she opened at Wallack's to the present time, and she shows a great
want of gratitude when she assails her best friends." Since the critics
were Bohemians, and since they wanted to be creative artists, Laura
set about neutralizing their power to harm her by employing them.
Producing Wilkins's play was an example of her strategy.

She became so busy in preparing *My Wife's Mirror* for
presentation at the Varieties that she forgot all else. To give it the best
hearing she could provide, Laura premiered it on the night of her
benefit. The play had special distinction as the first play copyrighted
under the new federal law.

Novelty had run over fifty performances, *Camille* was in and out
of the repertoire and still profitable, *My Wife's Mirror* was a *succès
d'estime.* Creditors were paid off. Given time and a little money, even
the scenery looked better, as Laura had always known it would. To her
delight the play of the second week of May was greeted in the press
with this paragraph: "The play is mounted and placed upon the stage

in irreproachable style. Wonderful improvements have lately been made here in this department."

With another triumph behind her, Laura and Lutz agreed to give notice to John LaFarge that they would exercise their options and keep the theatre for the next four years. Laura took the arrears of rent with her when she called on the landlord. He was complimentary of her management and congratulatory that she would continue her use of the house. He in fact forgave her one week's rent. She paid him $2,875 on May 19. The $75 was penalty on five weeks' back rent, and Laura paid one week in advance. The gift of a week's rent carried the lease up through June 9. LaFarge didn't say that he had received feelers from William Burton about buying the Metropolitan Theatre. Burton wanted to move his company uptown where the theatre-goers now congregated. Burton offered $80,000 to purchase the theatre and $10,000 a year for twenty-one years as ground rent. The deal was consummated on Saturday, June 7. Laura first heard of it on rent day, when she read the *Times* of Monday, June 9: "Mr. Burton has purchased in fee from Mr. LaFarge the theatre . . . and will enter in possession on the 1st of September next."

"The present lessee who holds a lease for five years," Laura fired back in the next day's papers, "has not relinquished any of her rights and privileges . . . It is impossible that any party can have obtained powers to interfere or interrupt the . . . season commencing September next." Harry Hall, Laura's stage manager, took out an advertisement to reassure the actors employed for the coming theatrical season 1856-7: "Take no notice of unfounded reports circulated by malicious parties."

Laura wrote an open letter for the next day's papers: "I have invested many thousand dollars, and all I possess in the world, in his building; and all the profits of my arduous exertions through the past season are visible in the improvements, scenery, and decorations. Were I to surrender my rights, therefore, I should leave the house with nothing but my will and energy."

But Burton now owned the theatre. Where would Laura go when she left LaFarge's? Back to acting? The *Times* suggested Burton employ her, since his company lacked a leading lady. Where could she act? Would she be happy acting now that she had known the headiness

This sheet music attention to Laura was her first such in the United States. In England, Wellington Guernsey had composed 'The Laura Keene Galop for Pianoforte," about which the ERA *said, "This though not a strikingly original composition, is a very spirited and pleasing one."* THOMAS BAKER SHEET MUSIC, LIBRARY OF CONGRESS.

of successful management? Would she continue to manage? If so, where? Where was there a theatre in New York? She would not trade theatres with Burton. Where else was there an unleased hall? She knew of none.

New York was ready for another theatre building. John M. Trimble, architect of some twenty-five theatres in the United States, thought so and sought out men who could finance such a new venture. While Laura was fulminating and threatening suits against Burton and LaFarge, while the daily work of the Varieties was somehow getting done, Trimble was exploring possibilities. The acting company, under the leadership of George Jordan and Harry Hall and Thomas Baker, announced a complimentary benefit for Miss Keene on the last night of the season, June 21. As a souvenir every lady who attended would be given a handsomely embellished copy of Thomas Baker's latest composition, "Laura Keene Schottische." The embellishment was a portrait of Laura.

On the last performance of the season, it was customary for the theatre manager to make a report on the season just ending. This gave Laura an opportunity to talk directly to her supporters. She omitted the usual statistical report: 153 nights of forty-five different plays. Instead she thanked the ladies in the audience for their powerful support and added, "Gentlemen, I am also indebted to you for the chivalrous appreciation of my efforts which ever distinguished the American character towards our sex, when engaged in advancing the interest of literature or art." She praised her acting company, pointing out that although the press had claimed she was paying only twenty-five cents on the dollar in salaries, the actors had all signed contracts with her for another year. She praised the musicians and Baker, and the stage mechanics, and Harry Hall, who had been "a friend and a father."

She repeated that she and the company would be performing at the same place in September. "On this spot we have placed our flag."

She was cheered to the echo. Whether it was her performance or her indomitable courage or the euphoria of the occasion, the press reported that the box office take amounted to $1,500, and that among the floral tributes tossed to Miss Keene from the boxes and carried forward by the ushers were some containing more substantial tokens of admiration; one bouquet held a check for $3,000.

Baker and the musicians serenaded Laura home while the stage was being cleared; then she returned to be hostess at a *petit souper* on stage for all the people who had made the season a success. The ladies of the company gave Laura a silver pitcher with drinking cups, and Jordan, speaking for the men of the company, presented a bracelet and a complimentary letter.

The sour note in the concord of sentiment was Burton's notice through the press that he would move in immediately.

W E Burton

Chapter 4

Laura's Own Theatre

*If this were played upon the stage now, I would
Condemn it as an impossible fiction.*
SHAKESPEARE, *TWELFTH NIGHT,* ACT III, SCENE 4

"In that hour of doubt, and almost despair, . . . one of
America's first architects . . . stretched forth his hand to
me, saying, 'Take courage, I will build you a theatre.'" Thus
Laura emotionally reported what had happened after her
eviction from the Varieties.

John M. Trimble, at 43, probably was just as emotional. He had
made himself the principal theatre architect in the United States by
skill, courage, and energy. Before his death in 1867 he had built
thirty-four theatres across the land. Laura's was his twenty-seventh. In
many ways Trimble was as naive and romantic as Laura. In building
her theatre to their combined requirements he fell into the hands of
sharpers. It is gratifying to report that the malefactors overreached
themselves and that Laura's theatre, which they wrested from Trimble,

*William Keese, Burton's biographer said of him, "He was at times
arbitrary, and could ill brook opposition. His vexation sometimes
magnified slight offenses . . . But if he made a few enemies he also made
many friends."*

reverted to his family as a dowry for his four daughters years after he and Laura were dead.

During the summer of Laura's discontent, Trimble approached Whitney and Earle, owners of the Lovejoy Hotel, proposing a playhouse on some lots on the east side of Broadway halfway between Bleecker and Houston Streets. The first proposal was that the theatre would cost $35,000, the hotel keepers to put up $15,000, Trimble to persuade Laura to put up $10,000, and then put up $10,000, himself. If it cost more than that, Trimble must supply the difference. Word of the negotiations began to reach the press in mid-July. The reporters thought the proposed location an excellent one for a theatre, half a block north of Niblo's Garden and just a block below the Metropolitan Theatre. They also thought it wise: "She has taken the easiest way of settling a dispute which had made a great deal of talk . . . and promised a rich harvest for the lawyers," one of them wrote.

Lutz represented Laura at a meeting of all parties on July 26 and the word-of-mouth agreement was talked about in the office of the lawyer for the owner of the land. Even the lawsuits later held to straighten the crooked paths could not make clear all the details. William H. Roberts owned the land and leased it at $6,000 per year. Working with Laura, Trimble was to complete a theatre for her by October 1, and would pay penalties — to whom was never specified — of $500 per week for each week's delay. Whitney and Earle would put up their $15,000 and keep a man on the spot to watch their interest in the building. Lutz agreed that Laura pay Whitney and Earle $10,000, which could then be deducted from her rent in installments. She would also take a five-year lease at $12,000 a year. Somewhere in all this it was agreed that Trimble would or would not share in the profits, or would or would not share in the property. Since he was hard-of-hearing, he was never clear on the matter.

The theatre cost $74,000 and was not finished until mid-November. Whitney and Earle had managed to freeze Trimble out by then, and when they had their names put on the lease with Laura Keene and he quite naturally asked, "Where am I?" Whitney told him, "You're nowhere."

Laura was to have the theatre she had dreamed of. From the ground up it was built the way she thought a theatre ought to be. She advised on backstage organization and needs and, being Laura, dictated decor and arrangements in front of the curtain. When the building was finished, the only part that was skimped and crowded was the box office area, Lutz's domain.

It would have been pleasant to watch the building going up. It was only a few feet from the Keene's lodgings. Laura, in crinoline, hanging over the barriers watching the workmen excavate the boiler and men's dressing rooms would have been an appealing picture to the Broadway stroller. But Laura had an acting company employed to begin a season in September. She also had enemies who would like to see her fail.

Her first action after she decided to build the new theatre was to gut her former theatre of all she had added: lights, draperies, and movables. She arranged storage for the costumes, scenery, properties, and other paraphernalia of production; even the "cerulean board" which had carried the legend "Laura Keene's Varieties" was taken with her.

Her next action was typically Laura. She feared further trouble from Burton. What if he lured some of her company from her while they lazed along the Rialto waiting for Trimble's theatre to be completed? How might she protect them from him? Why not take them out of town? . . . Could Lutz find bookings for an entire company complete with scenery and costumes?

So simply she pioneered the road show.

In September, the public was informed that the theatre would be ready on October 16 and that "Miss Laura Keene and her unequaled company will visit Washington and Baltimore until the completion of the building." They played to a $1,200 house in Washington on opening night, September 8. *Camille* and *Novelty* were the plays. A week later Laura took her benefit in *My Wife's Mirror* and the company moved on to Baltimore. There they played for a month. A sign at the construction site in New York said the season would begin there on November 1. It was later changed to read November 10. The company returned to Washington for a three-day stand when the newly elected President of the United States, James Buchanan, was inaugurated. From there, they went to Philadelphia for two weeks, and then, finally, back to New York, where the company was called together on the stage at eleven in the morning, Monday, November 3. Laura was giving them and herself two weeks to ready the opening show and allow for completion of decoration of the auditorium.

Touring the Laura Keene company had been a successful move. It had been profitable at the box office, and, more importantly, it had built an acting company. There was a holiday spirit to the journey. People were separated from their familiar pursuits and thrown together in travel and in performance. They lived around the theatres where they played. They polished their skills while being lauded by the local patrons. They acted twelve major plays and an equal number of afterpieces in the eight weeks they were on the road. Off and on, they performed *As You Like It,* to ready it for the opening of Laura Keene's theatre. In such fashion, she may have introduced the out-of-town tryout for Broadway shows.

Laura was enjoying herself. New people, new conquests. Her appearance in John Ford's Baltimore theatre was dubbed a "Keene encounter of wits." Her playbills were written in such a flowery fashion that she was called a "Poet Laura-ate." The bill for *She Stoops to Conquer* on Wednesday, September 24 caroled, "THE GLORIOUS PORTRAITURES of Miss Keene and her Professional Associates, presenting for the admiration and the study of the intelligent, and of those susceptible to the soft-toned poetry of art! Genius-created, passion-breathing pictures of life, which, like the world-honored works of Salvator, Raphael, or Corregio, startle not, but subdue the sense and charm each instinct of taste by their delicacy of contrasts, wonderful fidelity of resemblance and exquisite harmony!"

In Philadelphia, it was reported that "Capt. McLean presented a set of jewelry from the Columbia Rifle Corps to Miss Laura Keene. There is no repressing the promptings of gratitude or the tasteful dictation of true generosity, while the Drama holds her sway in the hearts of the people." When she checked out of Barnum's Hotel in Baltimore, she found herself charged for candles, because it was still the custom to put them in rooms. The clerk, upon discovering Laura had not used them removed the charge from her bill while handing her his autograph album. Over her signature, she wrote "As a little candle throws its beams, so shines a good deed in a naughty world."

Trimble's good deeds shone like limelight. Laura couldn't wait to see what had been done. She and Trimble must have met on Sunday morning to walk through the theatre. She could see the Corinthian columns framing the entrance as she rounded the corner from Bleecker. Over the door there would eventually be a sign in gaslight letters,

"Laura Keene's." Did she stop to exclaim over the black and white marble paving of the vestibule or the ornamental dome with colored glass that gave the foyer elegance? Or did she promenade the stairs like any leading lady, posing at the newel post for imaginary applause? The stairs could lead them up to the dress circle or down to the parquet. Both Trimble and Laura were aware that the entrance to the theatre was cramped. They hadn't had much room there to play with when planning the layout. The building was seventy-five feet wide and two hundred feet deep; much smaller than the Varieties, and the entrance off Broadway was correspondingly smaller, only twenty-five feet wide. But who wants to stand in the foyer? There was an elegant antechamber once the spectator had passed the pay box, and there was a promenade area behind the family circle.

The plaster decorations were not complete on the day Laura saw the building after her return from Philadelphia, but she could visualize them. Most of the decorations were to be in white with gold embellishment, and the ceiling was to be painted so chastely it could "serve for a shield to Minerva." The proscenium achieved its effect by form rather than color. Laura had wanted the whole auditorium to glow with warmth; this would be achieved with damask curtains at the boxes and on the parquet seats, but principally with light. There was no concentration of gas jets, but single brackets ran along the balcony facing, each reflected in pink satin. Opening night spectators were delighted to discover that there was a "general illumination produced, and shade in any part avoided." Since these lamps were controlled by the gas wheel backstage, the amount of light in the audience could be increased or diminished. Over the proscenium was a medallion containing the bust of Shakespeare flanked on either side by representations of fame.

Laura probably climbed over, around, and atop everything in the building at that first viewing. The building was more than fifty feet tall at the ventilator cupola; the stage housing was equally high. The stage was fifty-two feet deep. The wonder was the space. The orchestra had an instrument room as well as a gathering room. The greenroom, of a generous size, was between Laura's suite and the prompter. Laura had a suite — an office as well as a dressing room! The former had a fireplace, and in time it would also have carpeting and an easy chair. The ladies' dressing rooms and the costume department were on the second level above the greenroom. A separate building just outside the theatre provided for storage of scenery and properties.

They had tried to think of everything.

The building would be snobbish in its appeal: there would be no third gallery for prostitutes, there would be no gallery of any sort. Instead there would be an orchestra seating section for 200, a lower floor section, called the parquet to give it tone, seating 540, a dress circle (first balcony) seating 280, a family circle (second balcony) seating 480, and room for only 38 persons in the boxes. The house had a comfortable capacity of 1,538, but Lutz and his staff successfully crowded in 2,200 on many occasions, the first of which was opening night. In the dress circle tier there was a commodious drawing room for ladies, and across the house a similar accommodation for men. As the notices said, "Every required convenience is attached to these rooms." That was novelty indeed.

Laura and Trimble did not need to wait until opening night to know how New York would respond. "No such gorgeous a hall can be found in our city, or one better adapted for the light French drawing room comedy, in which Miss Keene and her company so excel," one reporter wrote. Until it was torn down for business buildings in 1880, it was referred to as a "bijou" establishment.

First night was a social event. "Long before the doors were opened a dense crowd beset the entrances," the *Herald* reported, "So great was the crowd that several hundred tickets were sold by speculators at double price to timid individuals who were afraid of the crush around the paying places. Before the curtain rose the sale of tickets was stopped. Receipts amounted to nine hundred and forty dollars."

Before the play, there were opening ceremonies with Baker conducting "The Star Spangled Banner" as the national anthem. Laura made an opening address, in which she reviewed the events connected with the loss of the Varieties, then told of the wonders of Trimble and her company, ending with, "No effort will be spared that industry can arouse — no results neglected that energy can achieve." Then Baker conducted his enlarged and improved orchestra in a new Shakespearean overture, and the swells who had paid one dollar and those in the family circle who had paid a quarter were treated to a show which all could see and hear.

She's done it!

She's built and opened the theatre of her dreams. She's made a social and artistic success. She's done it in less than five years since first landing in New York.

ii

From November 18, 1856, Trimble's building stood as the tangible expression of Laura Keene's dream. She had achieved the physical setting for her ideal. Now all that was left to do was to keep her theatre a place of social attractiveness, pay the bills, and improve the productions. For the next two years, the theatre seasons of 1856-57 and 1857-58, Laura either struggled and failed or struggled and succeeded. Sometimes the bill-paying was excruciatingly hard; sometimes improving the productions appeared impossible because as one part of the complex theatre microcosm grew better another part became worse. They were building years.

The mood of the new theatre was different from that of the Varieties. Laura somehow felt secure. She had survived Burton's malefic spite; she had skirted the financial pitfalls. There was a slower, stronger tempo now. Plays had runs of a decent number of days; not yet the long runs she hoped for but long enough for each new play to be prepared, long enough for her to develop herself as a manager.

To understand Laura's world, an examination of her first two seasons, not in detail but in selected activities, may be helpful.

The public said and the press repeated the primary truth, which could never be forgotten: Laura Keene, the actress, was the drawing power. On those rare occasions when she was ill or away for personal reasons, business at the box office fell off. She must therefore always keep in the forefront of her mind her responsibilities to herself. She must protect her voice, her health, her appearance. Young New York had been attracted by her figure; she must keep it. Her regimen and genes kept her flanks flat; her corsetier kept her bust high; her dancing and good movement kept her legs firm. "Until the Elves were introduced to us we may have *believed* but we did not know; how gracefully Miss Keene could dance and how well she was modeled," said a bemused reporter.

"It is no flattery to designate her as the best actress of the American theatre," Roorbach, who printed plays and visited all the theatres, said of her in 1856. When she debuted with Wallack, "She was pretty and interesting; she is now beautiful, and, in many parts we have seen her assume, great." Joseph Jefferson, who first acted with her in 1857, agreed: "She had the rare power of varying her manner." He it was who suggested they produce *The Sea of Ice*. In his

Our incomparable Jefferson! Long may the old-time sweetness of his speech
Dwell in our ears when he shall cease to teach;
Long will the memory hold his witching art,
As imagined in each finely-ordered part,
Where laughing wit lay close to throbbing heart — Verses by W.S. Keese. Thomas Baker Sheet Music, Library of Congress.

Autobiography, Jefferson described her versatile quality in that play: "In the prologue she played the mother, in which her quiet and refined bearing told of a sad life; in the next act, the daughter, a girl who had been brought up by savages, and who came bounding upon the stage with the wild grace of a startled doe. In the last act she is supposed to have been sent to Paris and there educated. In this phase of the character she exhibited the wonderful art of showing the fire of the wild Indian girl through the culture of the French lady. I have never seen this transparency more perfectly acted."

Laura had a sharp eye. She saw what made people different and conveyed that knowledge to the stage. When she performed Puck she made clear to the reviewer the difference in attitude "between the droll and scornful devilry of the madcap sprite to all beings . . . and the half-fear, half-affection . . . for Oberon, the master."

To show an actress acting is one of the most difficult tasks an actress can be called on to perform. To show a distinction between her everyday behavior and her stage behavior without caricaturing one or the other tests the performer's skills. The part of Peg the actress in *Mask and Faces,* a story about Peg Woffington, was played by all of Laura's female contemporaries. Speaking of Laura in the part, a Philadelphia reviewer observed, "When she attempts the wild Irish jig she did not dance as others do, in perfect abandonment of self, but wearily and heavily, recollecting that the jollity was but assumed and that while she was acting to rouse the starving family, her heart was breaking . . . and that after all, she was only acting." She used her good eye, her actress's perception, when describing feminine types in the magazine she later edited. A stiff specimen she characterized as "precisely lengthening up her body." A not-quite-lady failed to "occupy her chair." Such ability to see and to describe aided her in coaching the younger members of her company to act with added effectiveness.

Her sharp eye helped her with costuming and makeup as well as teaching. A critic accustomed to seeing her like her portrait with "wavy masses of brilliant hair, and youthful beauty," commented on her skill in makeup, which gave "an incomprehensible coloring to her acting."

In the play *Rachel the Reaper* she relished her creation for the aged grandfather. "We invested several cents each night in a sheep's bladder damped it with alcohol which was stretched over Daddy Patrick's head, the wrinkles of the brow were carried half way up the skull — a few locks of long silvery white hair fell from the almost bald scalp on his shoulders — certainly it was a wonderful *make up*."

iii

Laura's attitude toward acting was eventually reflected by her company. As she could, she employed only responsible and knowledgeable actors. She was praised for showing "a larger amount of self-abnegation than most lady manageresses . . . She was not afraid to surround herself by talented and pretty women. She did not absorb all the best parts herself. Nor did she engage her actresses because they indulged in extravagant displays of dry goods, wore a profusion of diamonds, . . . but simply because *they could act*." Her company was equally remarkable for its men. She employed or trained most of the superior comedians of her time. However, she never had a leading man with magnetism. Theatre is more than competence, it is charm and magic. Laura had it; it was a characteristic that set her apart. Lester Wallack had it. When he and Laura played opposite each other there was electricity in the air. George Jordan did not have it. Laura offered the leading man's place to Edwin Booth when he came East from California, but he wanted nothing of plays in which he would be secondary. He wanted stardom. Laura, of course, would not hear of that.

Two young performers she brought to public attention were Kate Reignolds and Joseph Jefferson. Both went on to stardom. Reignolds joined the company in 1855. Jefferson joined in 1857. Both had trouble with Laura's imperiousness. Theatre management is still one of the autocratic professions, but Laura in her first years as manager carried the regal manner too far. "The sun of the Drama shines gloriously at Laura Keene's theatre," the *Clipper* reported without tongue in cheek, "where the Queen Victoria of theatrical empire sways the sceptre of discrimination over the whole dominion of taste and female elegance."

The fair Laura bullied Kate Reignolds. "All women, I suppose, in girlhood adore some other woman," Miss Reignolds wrote in her book of theatrical reminiscences. "I adored her; I found an excuse for every fault; I waited her bidding, ran at her call, and meekly accepted the scoldings I got for my pains. . . . She was so in the habit of calling me to account for others to take warning that on one occasion when her complaint was a smell of tobacco, tobacco from a pipe, . . . from pure force of habit (she) turned in my direction. . . ."

Other managers thought Laura took a great risk when she hired Joseph Jefferson. He was obviously not yet the most permanently popular actor of the American theatre; instead he was the youngish representative of a third generation in an acting family, American trained, and in the less genteel theatres. Laura was as careful of his debut as Wallack had been of hers. She appeared in two of the plays with him. It was unnecessary. "He is a comedian from his nose to his toes," read one review the morning after his opening. Jefferson acted in the way Laura thought was the only way. He riveted attention when he listened. He became a part of the organism which was the Laura Keene Theatre: he suggested plays which might attract business, he wrote plays to stir up business, he helped in every way he could. He became so valuable that Laura later offered him carte blanche to manage for her. But his destiny led elsewhere. At this time, fall 1857, he was part of her good company. He was a part of that group which she was trying to move not just as individuals but as a whole.

She was striving to be a director as we today use the word. In her time, the stage manager allotted parts, told the actors where they stood and when they sat and through what door they left, and a coach or teacher taught them roles if they were not self-taught. When there was a crowd or scenic effect, the stage manager or his assistant led the mob and kept it in the shadows where it would not be too ridiculous. The theatre Laura dreamed of for herself had a regisseur who gave artistic unity to all aspects of the play. "On the stage, while conducting rehearsals, she was absolute master." Rehearsals were the time for actors to improve acting. The contract that actors signed carried such printed rules as: "The Green Room clock or the Prompter's watch is to regulate time; ten minutes will be allowed for difference of clocks." After the ten minutes, an actor late to rehearsal received a fine. "A performer rehearsing from a book or part . . . after proper time for study, forfeits one dollar." "No stranger, or person not connected with the Theatre will be admitted behind the scenes without the written permission of the Manageress." Even John Lutz, "if on the stage during rehearsal, was brushed away by the wave of a hand." Although the actors scoffed at such tyranny and some defected because of it, many were inspired by it. "Every person in the cast . . . seemed to thoroughly understand the parts assigned to them."

iv

Her work as a regisseur was pioneering. Jefferson and J.G. Burnett wrote a Revolutionary War play, *Blanche of Brandywine*, to end the 1857-58 season. It was full of red-hot conspiracies, blazing haystacks, and the second act was to end with a tableau of the Battle of Bunker Hill, which it was decided should duplicate in every detail John Trumbull's picture. The theatrical problem was to get the actors into the appropriate grouping.

"On the morning the tableau was to be grouped," as Jefferson tells the story, "Miss Keene appeared with the engraving, which she unrolled with a proud air and Sir Oracle demeanor. . . . We the company were assembled.

"Looking over the scroll, which every now and then would keep rolling itself up, much to her annoyance and our smothered delight, she began to place us in our different, and I may say, difficult positions. One would be made to rest upon his elbow while another was arranged to stand over him with an uplifted gun. The next gentleman, a cruel British officer, was then told to be on the point of thrusting a bayonet into the vital regions of some American patriot. The wounded Warren was ordered to lie down in an uncomfortable position and be held by a friend. This was all very well, and for a brief period these attitudes could be maintained; but by the time Miss Keene had got through the militia the regular army was completely worn out. Then she began to badger Warren, telling him to lie with his head a little more that way, or a trifle more the other way, besides requesting him to look exhausted.

"'General Warren, you have got your head all wrong again.'

"'I cannot stand it,' said the hero; 'my head has been in that position for twenty minutes.'

"I do not think that the original general could have suffered more than did his counterfeit on this occasion. By this time every one was exhausted, Miss Keene included, so there was nothing left but to dismiss the army and hold a council of war.

"I now saw that the arrangement of a tableau from a picture with so many figures was a more difficult matter than I had first imagined. Miss Keene declared that it could not be done at all, and I was myself beginning to think we were nonplussed, when Burnett came to the rescue with a simple suggestion which made the way clear at once. His idea was that the characters in the engraving should be cast just as they would be in a play. Thus each figure in the picture was marked with the name of the actor who was to represent it. The engraving was then hung up in the greenroom where each one could look at it and so study the attitude he was to take. This was caught up at once; their names were then marked upon the mount in chalk, and when the word was given to strike the tableau each one took the position, assumed his attitude, and the picture was complete."

Laura thought of directing as a way to correct bad acting. She wrote, "Stage directors are sometimes adroit, and by a timely rush of soldiery or citizens, or with some beautiful grouping, or admirable bit of stage management, they redeem the scene, and secure the applause which acting has failed to obtain."

v

Managing — here was where she knew her greatest excitement and found her greatest joy. "Each day, at an early hour sees her at her post as manager, superintending all the details of the stage, from the ballet-dancer to the man who tends the green curtain," said a reporter.

One of her functions was timeless: meeting the payroll. All theatre persons were paid in cash. An envelope with the individual's name on it was handed out by the treasurer in his office, and the recipient wrote his name in the company book by way of receipt.

J.G. Burnett was a bulwark of the Keene Theatre. Officially he was the stage manager in charge of playscripts and rehearsals, but he also acted older men and even wrote plays when they were needed. He was the villian of OUR AMERICAN COUSIN Couldock his dupe. THOMAS BAKER SHEET MUSIC, LIBRARY OF CONGRESS.

The financial panic of 1857 hit the theatres hard. Lutz and the treasurer of Wallack's agreed that rather than let anyone go, they would cut salaries by a third, with this assurance: "The management of both houses pledge themselves to resume payment of full salaries as soon as the business will warrant it." Banks were suspending payment all along the Eastern seaboard. On Tuesday, October 13, eighteen banks closed in New York City. The following Monday, Laura presented an original play on high finance and family spending called *Splendid Misery*.

Admission prices were cut, and Laura Keene's Theatre ran an advertisement that the box office would take notes of all the broken banks of New York at par.

For the Keene company the panic was remindful of the days of the Varieties, with frequent changing of bill in the hope that something would catch on, and with Laura's jewelry disappearing little by little each week.

Jefferson wrote that the panic "was almost fatal to her. In the midst of financial difficulties she displayed great taste and judgment in making cheap articles look like expensive ones, and both in her stage setting and costumes exhibited the most skillful and effective economy."

As a manager, Laura was also learning how to handle an audience. She allowed the stage manager to make the announcements at the end of performance, but it was her theatre and her philosophy of entertainment and therefore her responsibility when an audience needed controlling. She became adept at judging a crowd's reactions. In a season of forty weeks anything could happen. The *Clipper* reported one extreme incident. During a performance of *White Lies,* when the curtain dropped on the first act, an old woman who was seated in the parquet, "suddenly rose, and in a wild and 'woman's rights' tone of voice, cried out, to the consternation and astonishment of the audience: 'Now is the time! Now is the time! Let's have an old-fashioned camp meeting. Glory to God! I want to serve God and not man! Join in brothers and sisters!'" Only the manager could cope with a situation like that.

There were all the calls on a manager then that there are now. The "thousand little annoyances that beset public people," Kate Reignolds called them, "demands for assistance from those who seem to think an actor owns a mint of his own; stage-struck youths and damsels who implore, if nothing else, entrance behind the scenes; requests for his autograph, photographers wanting a picture, ambitious young play-writers who coolly request the artist to give his brain in criticism of a maiden effort. . . ."

Laura spent much of her time with play scripts and with correspondence about plays received, plays read, plays wanted, plays to be copyrighted and published. A week after an attempt on the life of Napoleon III, Laura received a three-act play on the subject from Augustin Daly, who was trying his fledgling wings in the theatre. Laura mislaid it and could not return the rejected manuscript. She received so many scripts that she ran an advertisement, "Persons leaving manuscripts here can apply at the boxoffice." The minutiae of copyright she eventually turned over to her lawyers, but in the building years she took them as one of her tasks. The new responsibility was twofold: the registration of title by either the author or Laura as proprietor and a later deposit of the work itself, "within three months from the publication thereof, to secure the *copy-right*."

She produced a second play by Wilkins, *Young New York. Mary's Birthday,* by George H. Miles of Baltimore, had its first hearing at Laura Keene's. One of the New York reviewers said the language was remindful of the poet's corner of a country newspaper. *Love in '76* by Oliver B. Bunce, the only parlor play of the Revolutionary War, was tried while the city was still suffering from financial woes, but critics said it was the best written of all new plays and deserving of more than passing notice. During that year of 1856-57 she presented fifteen plays by American playwrights, one by a woman.

Ellie Ellet, the first writer to emphasize the role of women in the development of the United States, through her books *The Women of the American Revolution* and *The Pioneer Women of the West* had a hand in the adaptation of *White Lies,* performed at Laura's theatre in January, 1858. The playbills said the work was that of Cyril Turner, but the reviewers for the various newspapers put Turner's name in quotation marks each time they mentioned him. When having the play published by Roorbach, Laura said in a letter, "Mr. Turner being absent I have requested Mrs. Ellet . . . to represent him." Mrs. Ellet probably took a pen name so as not to jeopardize her other activities by an association with the theatre.

Mrs. Ellet made a success of her life as an independent-thinking female, which always was attractive to Laura. She had entree to the major society homes of America, which Laura envied. As an author, Ellie Ellet might be the particular pet of the ladies' magazines, but she was not cut out for the theatre. One critic wrote, "The dialogue throughout is clumsily written, and 'Cyril Turner' whoever he is, has certainly done his best to spoil the foundations of a good drama."

Laura's taste in new plays was too saccharine much of the time: she let the reformer in her get the better of the manager. She ran an advertisement with *Mary's Birthday:* "Should the public encourage the Management in this step toward advancing American dramatic literature of a high order, it will be a pride as well as pleasure to continue the cultivation of such flowers, which can thrive luxuriantly only under the fostering care of pure and refined public taste." One doesn't need an active imagination to foresee the sarcasm with which the Bohemians greeted that effusion. But Laura always had the barometer of the box office to warn her of changing conditions. The woman who could cultivate such flowers could also serve one show after another, which was reported, "as a vehicle for the introduction of much music . . . many pretty faces, multitudinous legs, and some scenery."

The visual side of her theatre was another area where Laura took great pains and spent much time. She was interested in the scenery not only as easel paintings but as a means of shifting light and background for the actor in the foreground. When she produced *Faust and Marguerite,* her playbills carried a manager's preface concerning the easel painting background provided by Messrs. Hawthorne and Almy. "Great care has been taken to produce the play with strict fidelity to the author," she wrote, "following in the architecture, costumes and groupings the celebrated chefs d'oeuvre of Reizsch, who devoted the best years of his life to illustrate this great work."

For Christmas of 1857, Laura wanted an old-fashioned British pantomime for the youngsters. (It was probably to satisfy some requests at home.) Her staff of resident designers did not think they could do what she wanted done, so she wrote to John Ford at Ford's Theatre, Baltimore, for his permission to borrow C. S. Getz for a month, while the pantomime was a-readying. She then wrote Getz "to know if such an arrangement would be agreeable . . . Mr. Burnett and Mr. Jefferson think that the scenery I want for the Christmas piece would be so entirely pleasing to you to produce that I venture to propose your coming on and shewing the Gothamites one of your paintings. . . . If the matter is deserving of your attention inform me of your terms." Getz and his scenery were a success, old-timers from England enjoyed *Harlequin Blue Beard, or The Good Fairy Triumphant over the Demon of Discord;* it was called a "real fairy triumph." But just as Laura was learning with plays she now had to learn with entertainments. New York was not London. Pantomimes were not successful on Broadway.

A press notice said, "The Lady-Managers of the Shirt-Sewers Union have the pleasure to announce that Miss Laura Keene has in the kindest manner put the entire resources of her beautiful establishment into requisition for this occasion."

Laura saw the theatre as an influence in the highest affairs of life. Her playhouse extended an invitation to General William Walker, the Nicaraguan Fillibuster, who visited New York in the summer of '57. The following year her note of invitation to the Turkish envoy, Rear Admiral Mohammed Pasha, was printed in the papers, as well as conveyed to his hotel: "Desiring to manifest the courtesy due you, personally, as a stranger to our country, and the exalted official position you occupy, permit me to tender to yourself and suite the freedom of my theatre." Both Walker and the admiral attended, giving Miss Keene the opportunity to decorate the boxes in the appropriate flags and bunting and do all the honors with Baker's orchestra and the box-keepers.

vi

She was achieving her dream. Baker and the orchestra had become a part of the desired milieu. "The music," one reviewer said, "is as welcome a feature as the performances." Another noted, "The attention of the ushers to strangers merits special commendation." There was a hint of criticism that the lights over the auditorium were kept too dim and young fashion could not admire itself. This was corrected.

"All strangers should pay a visit to Laura Keene's to see how pieces can be produced in a first class New York theatre," said the *Times*. But the true achievement was that strangers did not feel strangers very long. "This very pretty little theatre reminds us much of a club-room," said another newspaper, "or rather a social reunion of friends, male and female, so pleasant and agreeable is everybody and everything about the establishment."

On Laura's benefit night in her second year in her theatre, there were many who would have said she had arrived. The *Era* reporter told English readers. "The dress circle and front sofas presented a splendid display of beauty and fashion; flowers glowed in the ladies headdresses; feathers waved; scarfs and fans fluttered; ermine and sable gave richness to the effect and the whole scene was rendered more interesting from the fact that almost every third person was distinguished either for talent, beauty, fashion or position." The audience was remarkable for the number of women. Its behavior was unusual in that it had chosen a young lawyer, R.C. Hawkins, to make a presentation speech to Miss Keene and to tender her a laurel wreath and a splendid brooch flashing with diamonds.

"Miss Keene," Hawkins said, "I have been requested by a number of ladies and gentlemen interested in literature and the drama to express their . . . approval of the excellent taste you have displayed in pruning from immoralities and improper language the plays brought out on your stage; and their admiration of the industry and enterprise with which you have kept New York posted up in dramatic literature."

There was more to the speech. There was more to the evening. There was more to the season. Did she ever pawn the brooch? Yes. Did these representatives of beauty and position rally to her when her cause grew desperate? Seldom, except on the stage, does the curtain fall at the dramatically right moment.

Chapter 5

The Long-Run Play

*"I've got a cool head, a stout arm, and a
willing heart, and I think I can help you, just
as one cousin ought to help another."*
TAYLOR, OUR AMERICAN COUSIN, ACT II, SCENE 1

The theatrical season 1858-59 was different. The feel of
New York City was different because Little Old New
York was disappearing with the shade trees. The streets
and the shops and the carriages in the streets showed
the new wealth. Speculation on the stock exchange and in railroads
and land had created a new aristocracy of wealth.

W ashington Irving, promenading along Broadway on a pleasant
afternoon, suggested an age as remote as his own Rip van Winkle's.
His courtly ways of the eighteenth century were historical oddities,
like his essays. Irving was attending plays only occasionally. He did
stop at the Laura Keene Theatre on two occasions, once to see an old
play in which Joseph Jefferson appeared. He was delighted to find that

*Matilda Heron's life touched Laura Keene's many times. They both tried
for California gold. Matilda was the more successful. Her CAMILLE was
more vivid than Laura's. Her emotional brio inspired a reviewer to call
Giuseppe Verdi "the Matilda Heron of composers."* UNIVERSITY OF TULSA
THEATRE COLLECTION

Laura's Jefferson, the third of that name, resembled Jefferson number two "in look, gesture, size, and make."

The theatrical district was changing. Burton's Theatre (formerly Laura Keene's Varieties) was announced for sale or rental. Burton said that after more than thirty years devotion to the duties of his profession, he found that his health demanded "some relaxation from the cares of management." The newspapers bayed at his heels: "It was an unfortunate day for him when he circumvented Sister Laura Keene, and moved from Chambers street to Broadway . . . 'Tis Dimity that shapes our ends."

The theatrical district was different because of the changing styles in entertainment. Minstrels which continued to grow in popularity, had become respectable. The "Saloon Theatres" imported from Britain were the most recent disreputable places of congregation, and the pretty little waiter girls who worked in those places were contributing to the open depravity of the Rialto.

Theatrical fare itself was changing. Matilda Heron had, the preceding spring, presented her own unbowdlerized translation of *Camille*. She was hailed by the Bohemians as the exponent of a new "realism." Fitz-James O'Brien, who led the hailing, was Heron's paid promoter and advance man. He may have been responsible, or Ned Wilkins, for the *Herald's* review of the production.

"The heroine is a bad woman, who seduces a spooney young man, then makes extraordinary sacrifices for him and finally dies of consumption. It is a well written play, dramatically speaking, and affords the greatest opportunity for strong effects. Miss Heron is an actress who deals in strong effects. Miss Davenport played Camille well. She was like a safe, strong ocean steamer, well constructed in every part, carrying just enough steam to make good time, and bring her passengers safe into port. Miss Keene resembled a nicely built beautifully fitted up yacht, gliding among pleasant scenes giving you glimpses of Etruscan vales and Claude Lorraine Landscapes, throwing vivid color over all around. Miss Heron we should describe as a high pressure first class Western steamboat, with all her fires up, extra weights on the safety valve, and not less than forty pounds of steam to the square inch. The effect is fine, but the danger of an explosion imminent."

The theatrical season 1858-59 was different at Laura Keene's Theatre also. It did not begin as all the others; Laura was rested, her cheeks were filled out. She, Lutz, and her family, with the Joe Jeffersons and their two children, had rusticated in the hills of Eastern Pennsylvania outside Scranton.

Negotiations with actors had been successful and Laura might soon have the strongest stock company of her history. She wanted to challenge herself as an actress. One way to do that was to present a season of standard comedies. She had assembled just the company for it. To the comedians of last year she was adding C.W. Couldock, Mr. and Mrs. William Rufus Blake, and Mr. and Mrs. E. A. Sothern.

If her grand revivals were to be a success, she needed Blake. He had no equal as the eccentric old man in eighteenth-century comedy. Couldock, whom she remembered from her first day in the United States, when he played Shylock, added a tragic dimension to her company. Sothern had joined at the end of the preceding season for "juvenile and light comedy business." He had made his reputation supporting Matilda Heron in *Camille*. He was the good actor and the irrepressible practical joker Laura had employed for her short season in Baltimore. She responded to him as to a favored younger brother.

"Before he made any hit, we had a dispute concerning some trivial affair at rehearsal. I became very annoyed," Laura reminisced. "After a brief quarrel on stage, I retired to my office and sent for him. I planned to rate him roundly.

"The scoundrel halted me with his hand, 'Stop! Just a minute!' and advancing to the light, turned it down.

"'What do you mean by that, sir?'

"'Nothing. I can bear to endure whatever you have to say, but I cannot bear to see those beautiful eyes blazing with passion. I cannot bear to see that lovely face distorted with wrath. Now, go on, and say whatever you please.'"

She could say nothing, she reported; he was the most impudent, audacious, good-for-nothing, good-hearted fellow she had ever met.

This brilliantly augmented company of comedians Laura billed as an "unapproachable combination of artistic talent." She was calling herself directress. The announcements said that Laura's theatre was "the most popular place of amusement in the city," that it had "the most proficient orchestra, the most truthful scenic illustrations, the most gorgeous stage appointments." "Miss Keene's company has been found strong enough to galvanize some stupid old plays which ought to have been shelved," an insightful reviewer noted. As the company performed in repertoire nightly, they began rehearsing novelties.

They had a new play from Palgrave Simpson, who had written one of the flowers in Laura's garden of last year; they had a play, *Rosalie*, by an American author, and they had a script that Lutz had recommended Jefferson read. It was a play about a Yankee in England, as yet untitled. It had been written by Tom Taylor and Jefferson responded to the script because it gave him a chance of making a strong character of the leading part. He could exploit his eccentric qualities while also winning the sympathy of the audience in a self-effacing love scene. Laura had little or no hope for the play, but it could keep the theatre open while she readied *A Midsummer Night's Dream,* for which she had high hopes.

ii

As with all new scripts, the company was called together in the greenroom to hear Laura read the piece. As the reading progressed the company assessed the play. No wonder Jefferson recommended it; there was a fat part for him . . . a good part for Laura, but nothing demanding. Nothing at all for Blake, unless he played the butler. Looks of commiseration were directed at Couldock and Sothern because their parts were so insignificant. Blake relinquished Binney the Butler to Charles Peters. Couldock made an opportunity to see Miss Keene in her office, where he respectfully declined the role of Abel Murcot. Sothern followed suit and threw up the part of Lord Dundreary. Laura, who had little confidence in the play, sympathized with the men, but she couldn't permit a rift in her company. Couldock and she discussed his role and eventually they could see ways of making it a sufficiently important and challenging character for a Shakespearean performer. Laura's problem would be to see that Couldock did not make Murcot so serious that he threw the play out of balance and changed its comic mood.

Sothern she left to Jefferson. If the latter thought the play so great, he could persuade Sothern. "I had to beg him to try it. He did it reluctantly," Jefferson said. Only the request from Laura that Sothern oblige her "for a few nights," and her promise that he could do what he wanted with the character persuaded him. Since most of

Casting a tragic actor of the stature of C.W. Couldock in OUR
AMERICAN COUSIN *was a gamble, but a* WILKES SPIRIT OF THE TIMES
*reviewer said, "He brings forward the character from its natural obscurity
to be one of the most prominent and interesting of the play. It is a piece of
correct, faithful, terrific acting that we have seldom seen equalled."*
UNIVERSITY OF TULSA THEATRE COLLECTION

Dundreary's scenes were with Georgina, a character assigned to Sothern's wife, he had an opportunity to develop the part in the way he preferred. "I can master any light comedy or juvenile part in 48 hours," Sothern said, "so far as the language is concerned; but in the creation of a character, every look, tone, motive, that suggests or shades an individual must be the subject of patient practice." He stood to put on his make-up, advancing to the mirror as he put on lines, retreating to see the new character, adopting mannerisms as he changed his appearance.

Laura gave herself two weeks to rehearse the play and ready the scenery. This was the extreme of lavishness. The show could have been done in stock sets; there were after all only the commonest of scenic requirements: three different interior scenes, library, dressing room, and chamber, and one exterior scene, a model dairy. The play's characters were so standard that a good stock company such as Laura's could have readied the script for production within a couple of days. But they had two weeks. Laura was a directress now. Jefferson had ideas of underlining the pathos in the role of Asa Trenchard. It was written as a stock Yankee comedy figure: "I'm about the tallest gunner, the slickest dancer, and generally the loudest critter in the state." Although nothing in nature ever resembled a stage Yankee, all such characters in plays resembled each other. Tom Taylor, the Englishman, knew as much about them as any other playwright, this "piece presenting, in suitable situations, those eccentricities usually attributed on the stage to Yankees." Jefferson had played a number of them. This one he was making different. He was not letting Asa become a buffoon.

Sothern, however, was making Dundreary into a new buffoon prototype, the silly-ass Englishman. The Bertie Woosters of the 1920s were the offspring of Lord Dundreary. The sound substitution of w for r, as in "the wabbit wan away fwom the wed fox," was standard eccentric comedy of the time. But Sothern was irresistible when he said "Iwwesistible." Americans thought the British made such sound substitutions just as the British thought Americans spoke with a nasal twang. The weeping-willow whiskers that drooped from Sothern's cheeks were part of the make-up repertoire of the eccentric comic. But many of the other touches were original.

"During a rehearsal one cold morning, I was hopping at the back of the stage to keep warm," Sothern related.

"'Do you intend to introduce those movements into your role?' Miss Keene asked, while the actors standing around laughed.

"'Yes, Miss Keene, that's my view of the character.'

"Having said that, I was bound to stick to it."

The Dundreary skip, which grew out of this incident, became as famous as the Dundreary whiskers and the Dundreary sneeze, although the sneeze did not develop in rehearsals. What was developing there was a slick, Laura Keene production. Baker had read the script, and although nothing inspired him to write special music, he did select a group of numbers for the orchestra that would enhance the comic mood of the play. The scenic and machinery departments were busy making the richest settings they could manage. Laura's instructions that the visual side of the theatre reflect the best in illustrations led to settings with draperies at the archways and curtains at the windows, and after some rewriting of the third scene, Asa Trenchard is introduced to a shower bath on stage, a scenic novelty.

The pen-written manuscript was receiving pencil emendations at a great rate as the creative processes flowed. Asa Trenchard, who had been from Pontiac, Michigan, in the original, now hailed from Brattleboro, Vermont. More than half of one of Taylor's scenes was

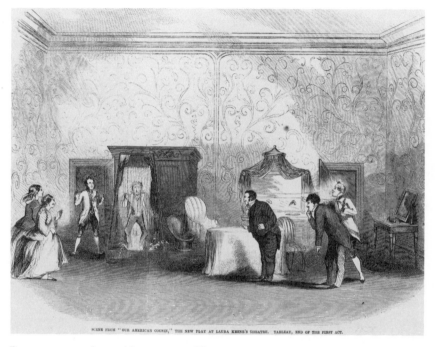

SCENE FROM "OUR AMERICAN COUSIN," THE NEW PLAY AT LAURA KEENE'S THEATRE. TABLEAU, END OF THE FIRST ACT.

DRAWING FROM LESLIES' ILLUSTRATED NEWSPAPER.

cut, another scene lost a fourth. Asa Trenchard lost lines but gained stature. Jefferson was pleased by what was happening. "Too much for any man to speak in one night," was his comment to Laura.

All the while they were cutting and rearranging Taylor's play, they were working without a name for it. Taylor had suggested it be called "Our Cousin from the Backwoods." Laura had copyrighted it, with herself as proprietor, on October 2, 1858, as "Our Country Cousin." As the show moved closer to scheduled performance, she became increasingly dissatisfied with the name. Lutz finally made a suggestion she accepted, so they announced that on October 18 they would premiere a new three-act comedy by Tom Taylor, *Our American Cousin.*

iii

It was this improbably titled play that changed the lives of the principal characters and, not to make too much of it, changed the ways of the theatre in the United States. *Our American Cousin* was the first long-run play at a major house. It was the play which stirred up so much greed that the laws of copyright had to be altered. It was the play — insignificant in itself, but played so brilliantly by Laura's company — that gave the final cachet to the phrase "as performed in New York." *Our American Cousin* made New York the theatrical capital of the United States. It spawned a host of theatrical imitations — second cousins, if you will. It created styles and fads and crazes. It made stars of Sothern and Jefferson. It bored Laura. Had it not grossed well over $500 a night, she would have taken it off the stage long before she did. But since it paid bills and redeemed pawn tickets and, with Lutz's careful guidance, put money into savings, it was allowed to run 140 nights. "The success of the play proved a turning-point in the career of three persons — Laura Keene, Sothern, and myself," Jefferson wrote.

The development of Jefferson was the first wonder. He played the comedy with control, the love scenes with delicacy. It was, he later admitted, the romantic more than the comedic possibilities in Asa that had drawn him.

"A Yankee boy of twenty-five falls in love at first sight," Jefferson related, "with a simple, loving, English dairymaid of eighteen. She innocently sits on the bench, close beside him; he is fascinated and draws closer to her; she raises her eyes in innocent wonder at this, and he glides gently to the farthest end of the bench. He never tells her of his love, nor does she in the faintest manner suggest her affection for him; and though they persistently talk of other things, you see plainly how deeply they are in love. He relates the story of his uncle's death

Jefferson's self awareness made it possible for him to teach others what he did. He corrected an actress who wasn't getting the response she should, saying, "You think you are funny. You know it is a comic speech, but you show the audience that you know it is funny . . . That is the reason you have lost the laugh." THOMAS BAKER SHEET MUSIC, LIBRARY OF CONGRESS.

in America, and during this recital asks her permission to smoke a cigar. With apparent carelessness he takes out a paper, a will made in his favor by the old man, which document disinherits the girl; with this he lights his cigar, thereby destroying his rights and resigning them to her. The situation is strained, certainly, but it is very effective, and an audience will always pardon a slight extravagance if it charms while it surprises them."

The early reviews of the play did not describe the second wonder of the play, Lord Dundreary, because his part developed during the run before audiences; rehearsals had only sketched the outline. To say that Dundreary affected Sothern's career is tantamount to saying warfare affected General Grant's career. From the opening in 1858, Sothern virtually never played another role until his death in 1881. He played it all over the English-speaking world; he was Lord Dundreary in literature and art.

Sothern developed his guying, charming, joking self into a marketable dramatic character on stage. Using the license Laura had granted him, he altered the character. Jefferson remembered, "One night he was trying to keep back a sneeze, and the public perceiving it, thought it a wonderfully funny thing and laughed immoderately." Sothern incorporated the sneeze into his part. It became another hallmark of Lord Dundreary. Baker memorialized it in a novelty composition, "The Sneezing Polka."

He developed the comic effects of the letter from his brother Sam into such a vaudeville turn that he had a play written around the idea. To the criticism that the character was overdrawn, reporters rose in his defense. The *Sunday Times* responded to a cavil that "such a polished idiot as Lord Dundreary could in any conceivable way be connected with the English admiralty" with the chauvinistic comment,

"That is just the place to look for 'polished idiots.' If it hadn't been, how in the name of sense would we, with one frigate to their fifty, ever have thrashed them so handsomely in the war of 1812-14?"

After *Our American Cousin* became the rage in London, Henry Adams reported that "Mr. Gladstone himself went to see Sothern act Dundreary, and laughed till his face was distorted — not because Dundreary was exaggerated, but because he was ridiculously like the types Gladstone had seen — or might have seen — in any club in Pall Mall."

Jefferson recounted that Laura was delighted at Sothern's rising fame because she found that Jefferson was becoming hard to manage.

The tension among them brought constant freshness to an otherwise commonplace play, so that the public was sharing in the creative process and applauding accordingly. One reviewer recommended, "Persons who have not seen the piece since the first week or two of its career might go to Laura Keene's now, and almost fancy it was a different affair altogether. Every week Mr. Jefferson or Mr. Sothern introduces some new 'business' or bit of dialogue, and singularly enough, this 'gagging' process has really had an improving effect upon the original author." As the success grew into a craze, the public applauded a folk creation which by then had developed a dynamic of its own completely divorced from Keene et al., a dynamic which made it a success wherever it was played, no matter who did the principal roles. The play developed such a life of its own that people who would not ordinarily have wanted to see it, or liked it, found themselves forced to see it to be a part of the literate world. An essayist on the esthetics of drama in 1875 wrote what he knew would be a completely understandable sentence. "A public seeks amusement at the theatre, and turns impatiently from dreariness to Dundreariness."

iv

This success at Laura Keene's Theatre brought competition through imitation. About a week after the play opened in New York, Lutz, from his point of vantage near the box office, saw the Messrs. Wheatley and Clarke, managers of the Arch Street Theatre of Philadelphia, in the crowd. He saw them on a second occasion, this time with their leading lady, Mrs. John Drew. When Clarke asked how much Laura wanted for the show, Lutz replied that she would not take less than $1,000 for it. When Lutz and Laura learned that the play was going to be presented in Philadelphia at the Arch, Lutz attended the opening there, where the playbill bragged that the play was "now in the sixth week of its brilliant and triumphant career in New York."

Laura instituted proceedings, claiming an exclusive right through her purchase of the manuscript from Taylor and under the 1856 statute for the protection of general and dramatic literary property. She sought an injunction to restrain Wheatley and Clarke. John Cadwalader, federal judge for the Eastern District of Pennsylvania, before whom the suit was brought, ruled that since the play was in the course of successful performance at both theatres, if the Philadelphians would put up a sum of money equal to the amount for which Miss Keene had been willing to license performance to them, along with sufficient other money to cover costs, $1,500 to be exact, he would hear the case in a more orderly fashion.

Injunctions or threats of injunctions were brought against other imitators. A.H. Purdy at the National Theatre in New York was restrained by law, but Moses Kimball in Boston ignored Laura's protests and the Massachusetts courts abetted him.

Legal bickering was not new; what was new were the problems a long run presented. What do you do with stellar performers who are not cast in your long-run vehicle? What to do with Blake and Mrs. Blake? They were paid; they were not acting.

Why does one present afterpieces with a hit play? They require extra actors not needed for the hit, and the public doesn't care about the afterpiece anyway. Madame Vestris had done away with the afterpiece almost ten years before in England. Wasn't it time to do the same thing in New York?

And what about the building? Why open it in the morning if there was not to be the usual rehearsal at ten?

The box office was coping with new answers to new questions also. For a hit play the box office opened at eight in the morning and balcony seats could be secured one week in advance without extra charge. Tickets could be procured at places other than the box office, at Hall & Son, 239 Broadway, and also from scalpers. Even the mechanics of selling tickets had to be developed. People crowded the box office. No watchful policeman kept the crowd in line. One observer reported: "Three or four fists grasping money were thrust at one time through the tiny aperture in the boarded window. An invisible hand within grasped the fists in turn and released the money from the fingers, which would then indicate the number of tickets required. Tickets and change would by the same unseen agent be then enclosed within the expectant fingers, and the owner would back away after a terrific struggle." The editor responsible for the weekly summary of theatre news in the *Clipper* complained that he had had nothing new to report for "several months. That sounds oddly enough, don't it? Counting the representations of a single play by months — only to think of it."

The first break in the monotony of success was a benefit for the Mount Vernon Association. Laura was a natural target for the ladies raising money for "the hallowed resting place of Washington." She was probably approached first for a private donation. *Godey's Lady's Book* was backing the fund solicitation, printing the names of all individual contributors through the magazine, and they had as many as five names some months, although no one had given more than a dollar.

Laura proposed the use of her theatre, and the contribution of the gross amount of the receipts accruing from a performance of *Our American Cousin,* for the afternoon of December 29, 1858. She wrote, "The ladies and gentlemen composing the company over which I have the pleasure of presiding, embracing every artist, musician, officer and artisan connected with the establishment, . . . made a free will offering of their service for the proposed entertainment."

The ladies who were trying to save the Washington home — it was going to become a resort hotel, if they were unsuccessful — were impressed by Laura's "great liberality" and mightily impressed with a check for $500. And again, in such an offhand way, Laura continued her trail blazing. The matinee was not new, neither was the benefit for a worthy cause — there had been special performances in England to save Shakespeare's home in Stratford. But the charity matinee, now hoary with tradition, was a novelty then.

The benefit matinee served one important function. It was deemed respectable and socially acceptable. Thus a new segment of society could be attracted inside the playhouse on this special occasion. Later, that segment might be enticed to see a play at night.

The one hundredth performance of *Our American Cousin* was another break; an occasion for celebration. There was to be a grand display of fireworks, and every lady who visited the theatre was to be

THOMAS BAKER SHEET MUSIC, LIBRARY OF CONGRESS.

given a copy of Thomas Baker's sneezing polka, now titled "Our American Cousin Polka," with pictures of the principal performers in the play set in a circle around the title. The music retailed for thirty-seven and a half cents at Willson's. There were to be other special activities. "The house was decorated with flowers as artificial as the Cousin in question," a reporter biliously noted.

But another reporter wrote that with the Cousin always in attendance, there was nowhere to go of an evening. "I don't mind the run of a month or so; but when you try the 'every night until further notice,' Miss Keene, I trust you will have consideration for a suffering public, and change the diet at least two or three times during the season. It may be all very well for you, and jolly for your actors, who go over a part until they do it as water runs down hill, rest as well asleep as awake; but for the mass of city play-goers, you might as well shut up shop — they never will come after the third or fourth time, unless like the subscriber, they are afflicted with a storm of country cousins who insist upon being toted around to see the sights, the first of which, of course, are the play-houses. So, when you have made a handsome profit, as I hope you soon may do, just let the boys have a holiday, and give us a change."

Lutz shuddered at the idea of change, business was so good; Jefferson shuddered at the idea of change to *A Midsummer Night's Dream*. Sothern wanted no change. He had taken a long distance flyer in management, on which he lost $1,200. He was glad for his $60 a week salary as Dundreary.

Laura wanted change. Florence Trenchard, her part, was such a mannequin role that a younger member of the singing company took it over to give Laura a day off, and the box office never noticed the difference. Also when she had dreamed of her ideal theatre presenting long-run plays so that there would be time to rehearse other plays properly, she had not realized that you can rehearse only so long or that the play which permits the rehearsal time may be a bore. Also, she was irked with Jefferson.

When she had employed Blake she had intended him for the old comedies, not for A Midsummer Night's Dream. But she had also not intended that he should sit idle for months. She was tired of his complaints about not being used, so with one of her Czarina Catherine gestures she sent Lutz to Jefferson to ask him to relinquish the role of Bottom to Blake. With his George IV appearance, moist dewlaps, protuberant belly and 240 pounds, Blake could make a solid Bottom. When Jefferson learned that Laura was suggesting that he play Puck instead of Bottom, he flatly refused. Although there may have been worse castings of Puck — in its three hundred and fifty year history there would have had to be — it is hard to conceive of one so bad as Jefferson in the role. He was a lanky five foot ten: he was all angles, by design and practice, and enunciated in a slightly nasal tenor (with a sh substitution for the ess sound). All of this enhanced Asa Trenchard but would have played hob with Puck, as he recognized. He told Lutz what he thought of such a casting. He told Lutz that he would not change his mind, particularly because Laura would take it as a sign of weakness, not generosity.

Poor Lutz. He urged the matter. How else could they get both Blake and Jefferson into the same cast? Their salaries were expensive items. Laura was just suggesting that they both be used. "Very well," Jefferson said resignedly, "if that is all, tell her I will play Bottom, and let Mr. Blake play Puck." Lutz, who did not know the play, left, pleased to have a solution. Laura was furious and had additional cause to be irked with Jefferson.

After he rehearsed Bottom for a week, Jefferson realized he had made a mistake, that he would fail in the part. He suggested to Laura that he relinquish the part to Blake and leave the company.

"And what will you do, when you leave the company?" she asked.

"It's my intention to star."

"Star! Bless me! Indeed! And what will you play as a star?"

"*Our American Cousin,* if you will give me permission."

"Which I decline to give," she said as she swept out of the greenroom.

However, it was so arranged. Blake eventually played Bottom. He was unhappy and unsuccessful in the role and revealed his dissatisfaction in childish clowning. A Shakespearean scholar who saw a performance wrote "I shall not forget Bottom. His ass's head would not stay on right, and in pulling the string that opened the mouth to speak, he would pull the whole concern to one side: the applause in the pit was thundering."

Box-office proceeds from *Our American Cousin* were spent on readying *A Midsummer Night's Dream.* As early as the first week in January, a theatrical reporter was commenting, "An immense amount of money has been expended . . . but we are informed that more is still being laid out. It will be complete this week for the scenic artists and costumers have exhausted their powers and despair of making one improvement." The play did not get on the boards before an audience until April 18. Even then the public appetite for *Our American Cousin* was still strong.

The production of the *Dream* was a success also. It ran until the end of the season, June 4. It made money. And Laura finally heard the words she had longed to hear: "The inauguration of a new era, when plays are carefully put on the stage, is a great improvement over the slip-shod style that, until recently, reigned almost supreme in New York."

The success of *Our American Cousin* had given her the time and resources to produce and direct as she desired. Baker had augmented his orchestra so that they could play the full Mendelssohn score during the Shakespearean idyll. The entire scenic department had combined to present a variety of devices that it took a full page of the playbill to describe. Special effects were provided by "Calcine, Drummond and Electric Lights" managed by Prof. Grant and Mr. Scally. Just a few years before, Laura was acting on a stage in California lit with whaleoil floats; now her performance as Puck was picked out by limelight.

v

"I have undertaken with enthusiasm the production of the 'Midsummer Night's Dream,'" Laura wrote in a preface, "not that the range of its female characters present any one which I might make peculiarly my own, but because this play, and that of 'As You Like It,' have been the chief objects of my admiration and study in the Shakespearean Drama — the one abounding in the most exquisite poetical imagery, and the other fascinating by its beautiful pastoral simplicity. It has been my earnest endeavor that the present representation shall be in strict accordance with the text as far as theatrical capabilities will allow, and I trust my endeavors will prove successful.

Her *Midsummer Night's Dream* was antiquarian. Laura had sought help from Fitz-Greene Halleck of Harvard College on Athenian antiquities and from Richard Grant White, author of *Shakespeare's Scholar,* for interpretation of ambiguous phrases. Genio C. Scott, an original if there ever was one, had helped with the costuming. Scott was a fashion publisher. He had come to New York after a successful career in business upstate; he was interested in antiquarian dress, and fishing. He and Lutz could discuss the latter after he counseled Laura on the former.

Laura should have been exultant. Instead she couldn't wait until the season was over. Taking her benefit the closing night of the season, she announced that June 4 would positively be her last appearance on any stage until fall.

She had made herself a hell with the long run of *Our American Cousin*.

No; her suit against Wheatley and Clarke had created a hell in which she was suffering.

The judge had heard sufficient evidence to conclude that "the defendants enabled themselves to represent the play knowingly taking advantage of confidence committed by a person in her employ." In other words, Jefferson was a traitor.

If you played a long run, you first changed the audience's behavior, you next changed the box office behavior, you next changed the profession's behavior.

The long run threatened the actor. Company members would often play parts not to their liking, knowing that the unpopular role would be supplanted by a more popular role with the change of bill. Now with a long run, an actor played an unpopular role with no prospect of relief. Might just as well be a clerk in a countinghouse: no change, no growth, no challenge.

The long run threatened the ways actors learned their profession. Young Jefferson could learn his business by watching his father act. What would an actor learn watching *Our American Cousin?*

After Charles Peters played Binney the Butler, John Ford tried to get him away from Laura for $35.00 per week. OUR AMERICAN COUSIN *made him a featured comedian as it raised Jefferson to Stardom.* THOMAS BAKER SHEET MUSIC, LIBRARY OF CONGRESS.

The long run threatened the way an actor learned his trade. An actor used to learn how to do a funny make-up, or do a funny skip, or restrain a sneeze, or turn a backwards somersault from other actors backstage. He'd say to someone who had done something he admired, "How did you do that?" and be shown.

Jefferson had taken the changes he had made in the script of *Our American Cousin* and given them to Wheatley and Clarke so that the Philadelphia production could be like the New York production. Someone had asked him, "How did you do that?"

In the judge's opinion Jefferson was culpable. "Clarke obtained the principal parts and the language from Jefferson," the judge said. "He did it while Jefferson was in employment as an actor of one of the principal roles in the play. . . . She was entitled, in her competition with professional rivals, to the co-operation and support of every person employed by her within the walls of her theatre."

Laura was bedeviled by that comment. Jefferson was the soul of honor. Was he to be publicly castigated? He didn't realize that part of what made a play popular was the quality of the original production. Wheatley and Clarke recognized it. The judge recognized it. Laura wished it weren't so.

Jefferson eventually recognized it. At his summer place near Laura's in Paradise Valley, Pennsylvania, he was trying to find a role for himself which he could make his own; one which no one could take away. If he could find such a role, he planned to give his life to it and play it long-run forever.

That story is really no part of Laura's story. He did find the role, Rip Van Winkle; he did make it his, and he played it to the delight of every good-humored citizen from 1866 until his retirement in 1900. He outlived Laura by thirty-two years, yet in 1872 she wrote an epitaph for him in the magazine *Fine Arts:*

> Jefferson's most brilliant gift, versatility, is lost, merged in one part, and of the greatest serio-comic actor in this generation, we have nothing to expect but Rip Van Winkle.

Chapter 6

Litigation and Long Runs

Between two hawks, which flies the higher
pitch;
Between two dogs, which hath the deeper
mouth;
Between two blades, which bears the better
temper;
Between two horses, which doth bear him best;
Between two girls, which hath the merriest eye;
I have perhaps some shallow spirit of
judgement,
But in these nice sharp quillets of the law,
Good faith, I am no wiser than a daw.
SHAKESPEARE, *KING HENRY VI*, PART I, ACT II, SCENE 4

There is a contrapuntal movement in Laura's life during the next several years. One theme is the success of Laura Keene's Theatre. A second is the strife in courtroom and press. The sounds of actors quarreling were played against the political passions of the times. Laura's struggles were a microcosm of the nation's struggles: the old ways refusing to give over to the new.

The summer of 1859 she followed the doctor's orders. She took walks after the heat of the day and savored the air of the Poconos, which, she wrote a friend, was "as good as it is in England." She assured that friend that she hoped for complete restoration to health if "nothing occurs to annoy or distress me." She was dubbed the Peri of Paradise Valley, Pennsylvania.

Her theatrical company was complete by July 27. "I beg to inform these artists who have favored me by solicitations for engagements for the ensuing season, but whose letters — in the press of business — have remained unanswered, that their services are respectfully declined," an advertisement over Laura's signature stated. Playwrights sought her out. Charles Reade wrote his agent, "Send out a MS copy of the piece to my friend Mr. Kinahan Cornwallis, Fifth Avenue Hotel, New York, and request him to propose it to the New York Theatres beginning with Miss Keene."

Miss Keene, however, had her plans made. She was going to rely on the tried and successful: Another play by the author of *Our American Cousin,* entitled *House and Home,* was to open the season. Later in the fall, when business slacked off or Laura grew bored, it was to be followed with something she had announced a full year before, *World and Stage* by Palgrave Simpson.

The competition for the spectator's money was going to be intense. Wallack's had re-established itself as the theatre of New York society while Laura was endlessly playing long-running hits. Joseph Jefferson had not found the times right for starring and had been lured by William Stuart to the Winter Garden. Laura joined in the belittling remarks about the potted palms and drooping shrubbery that changed the house which had once been Laura Keene's Varieties, and then Burton's New Theatre, into a winter garden. But she knew that the house was well located, the staging potential great, and with first-rate people the company could affect the success of her own enterprise. William Stuart, who had been a manager at Wallack's, offered co-managership to Dion Boucicault: thus with one move, Stuart had acquired a resident playwright, who was the most vocal and skillful of the emerging directors, as well as Agnes Robertson, Boucicault's wife, the loveliest doe-eyed representative of femininity on the American stage. Added to Joe Jefferson, that combination would be hard to beat.

The Tom Taylor play opened at Laura's theatre to standing room only. As one reporter noted, it was "an extremely good-natured and determined-to-be-happy audience." Although the company lived up to expectations, Mr. Taylor's play did not. Before she had planned to, Laura was presenting the Palgrave Simpson import, *World and Stage,* and although it was put on without curtain raiser or afterpiece, thus achieving one of her ambitions, she could not make it successful.

Laura found herself being criticized for her poor choice of plays. For the first time since her days in California she was receiving the rough edge of the tongue and the blunt tip of the pen from the reviewers. One reviewer wrote: "Miss Keene is a brave, energetic manager, full of ambitious courage and love of adventurous enterprise; but she is also a woman and an actress; in other words, she is mentally unstable and professionally vain; two qualities which are apt to interfere with the profitable working of a theatrical speculation. Last season, those little rocks-ahead of private weaknesses were avoided through the skillful pilotage of *Our American Cousin;* but American Cousins don't turn up every season, and the chance for Miss Keene. . ."

The chance for Miss Keene, she thought, was to revive *Our American Cousin.* Sothern was available and willing. He agreed with her that the play's success depended on her finding a replacement for Jefferson. Sothern suggested that she go outside her company. Instead Laura tried William H. Stephens in the role. An English low comedian, he had joined her company after the season began and had been damned by the New York *Times* as "an actor of merit who will make his way

When Laura read the MSS of OUR AMERICAN COUSIN to the members of her company, the part of Lord Dundreary had 47 lines and E.A. Southern, who was cast for the role, had previously played, according to his son's meticulous count, 681 parts. He virtually never played another after he became Dundreary. THOMAS BAKER SHEET MUSIC, LIBRARY OF CONGRESS.

when he has fairly shaken off the hobnailed shoes of provincial Britain." After a few rehearsals, Laura decided Stephens could not play Asa Trenchard. Sothern concurred, so the idea of a revival of *Our American Cousin* was shelved. At the end of a month she was preparing her third play, *The Sea of Ice,* because the two she had counted on to run most of the winter had lasted only two weeks each.

Laura's life took on a pattern: open a play on Monday with high hopes on the part of the audience and company, run the play two weeks to dwindling business, and at some point make an appearance in a court of law.

While *Sea of Ice* was running, Laura was admitted to American citizenship. It was a step precipitated by the legal point that the copyright law was protection only for American citizens.

Two weeks later, while *Midsummer Night's Dream* was being revived, Miss Ada Clifton peevishly left the company threatening to sue Lutz and Laura for breach of contract; Sothern was suing for unpaid wages.

Her next production, *The Marble Heart,* ran less than two weeks, during which Laura appeared in court to receive the printed copy of her Bill in Equity, *Keene v. Wheatley & Clarke.* While *The Wife's Secret* was running, the courts heard the first pleadings of Pat Hearne's widow for the money which had kept a successful actress's theatre open in the days of great adversity. Pat Hearne, the gambler, who had befriended both Lutz and Laura, had paid the $400 due to LaFarge back on that Christmas Eve when her theatre had been vandalized. She had known nothing of his intervention for her, and as the wags claimed, she would not acknowledge the money's "Pat Hearnity." What was a mere $400 now to a woman whose theatre the newspapers reported took in $950 on Thanksgiving day?

During the run of the same play, Sothern's suit was brought before the jury, which ruled in Laura's favor.

George Jordan withdrew from the cast of *The Wife's Secret*. During Christmas week, 1859, his lawyer brought suit for breach of contract and salary unpaid.

ii

Better things were hoped for the new year. The press of January 1 carried the news that "Miss Laura Keene begs to announce that Mr. Boucicault is now engaged upon an entirely new Drama in three acts, entitled *Jeanie Deans or the Heart of MidLothian*. This work will be produced as soon as the new scenery and the rehearsals will permit. Miss Agnes Robertson will make her first appearance in this theatre in the character of Jeanie Deans." The two-week cycle it was hoped would end and the long run return.

On the legal front, Laura settled the Hearne claim by paying the widow. The *Jordan v. Keene* suit had come to trial and Laura had lost. The proceedings against the pirates of *Our American Cousin* were the only legal entanglements carried over into the new year.

The Boucicaults were the most sought-after performers in the English-speaking theatre at the time. Dion had been of the theatre since his boyhood, and Agnes had been raised in it by the Charles Kean family. Dion, who had always been a playwright or translator or play-doctor, had but recently hit upon a formula for writing success: newspaper headline topicality for plots coupled with injured innocence roles for his wife. The Boucicaults had been part of the competition Laura faced at the beginning of the theatrical season, but they had left the Winter Garden when Dion's demands for more salary had not been met. Since the press reported that his share of the profits the week he quit was $1,363 and that he had never made less than $700 a week, it was assumed that Laura had written a profit-sharing arrangement with him for the pair's work at her theatre.

Whatever the arrangement, it was worthwhile because the Boucicaults made the season in the same way *Our American Cousin* had crowned the previous season. *Jeanie Deans* ran fifty-four performances and then was succeeded by another Boucicault play, *Vanity Fair*. It was not a hit but held the stage while the indefatigable Dion wrote and rehearsed *The Colleen Bawn*, which was.

iii

The lawsuits which had darkened Laura's days and certainly stained her personal reputation were as much a part of the success of her theatre as heads and tails are a part of the same coin. To the uninformed observer, it appeared that actors in Laura's company could not get along with her as manager. Yet what was really happening was a shift in actor-manager relations as revolutionary as the change from bands of strolling players to limited-liability companies in Shakespeare's day.

Taking the lawsuits of Sothern, Clifton, and Jordan as one problem (they were all suits for salary which grew out of disputes over contract), they were *prima facie* evidence of disharmony backstage. Yet . . .

Sothern sued for one month's wages at $65 per week for the time the proposed revival of *Our American Cousin* was in rehearsal. He claimed that he had entered into a speculative agreement with Lutz and Laura and that their failure to find a suitable Asa Trenchard for the revival did not abate their responsibility to him. They in turn claimed that "by custom, theatrical engagements did not commence until the piece was actually put upon the stage before an audience," and that they owed him nothing. The courtroom in which this contention was heard was crowded by the curious public seeking a free look at some of its idols as well as by members of the acting profession. A major point of theatre conflict was being raised, perhaps for the first time. Sixty years later the actor's strike of 1919 finally determined that an actor should be paid while rehearsing.

The Sothern case reached farther into the future than just the single issue of pay for rehearsals. The tryout of Stephens for the part of Asa Trenchard was a precursor of the theatre today. An actor auditions for, or is cast in, a specific role in theatre, cinema or television. But the New York theatre was still committed to the idea of an actor's playing a "line of business." Had the tryout of Stephens been successful, Sothern would probably have signed a contract with Lutz for "juvenile business" as he had done the year before. The point didn't come up but it was moot; would Sothern have been willing to do juvenile business in other plays of the season if *Our American Cousin* had not run? Or was he being given a run-of-the-play contract? Such a contract form had not yet been devised, nor the phrase coined.

Our American Cousin had changed the usages of the theatre. Sothern wanted to revive a long-run success. A specific role needed to be filled. When an adequate performer for that role could not be found, Lord Dundreary had no further interest in Laura Keene's theatre. Such an experience today would not create a ripple. When a replacement is needed for a hit play, actors are called in to read for the role. Once one begins rehearsing he is paid. But no management today expects an actor to play Lysander in *Midsummer Night's Dream* after playing Lord Dundreary, as had been the case in Laura's theatre in 1859.

The Clifton case was similar. Ada Clifton had signed a season long contract to "second lady business" for $36 a week, but when given the part of Helena instead of Oberon in Shakespeare's *Dream,* she threw over the role and sued for her season's wages. William Davidge, an actor of the previous generation, came out of retirement to testify that Laura, as leading lady, should have played Oberon and that Miss Clifton, as "second lady," should have played Puck, but that since Laura had preempted that role, Miss Clifton should have been offered Oberon. He also pointed out that Helena's lines had been cut to such a degree that the part was third-rate, probably fit only for a "singing chambermaid."

Two years before, the suit probably would not have been brought. The company would have acted the traditional version of the play with the traditional assignment of parts clearly known. But Laura was presenting her version of the play with advice from a Harvard don and a Shakespearean scholar and with cuts in the text which shifted the balance of roles. Two years before, the feelings of Miss Clifton could have been mollified by expectation of soon playing better roles in the repertory, but she knew in 1859 what all other actors knew: Laura Keene would run the play as long as she could.

The Jordan case was identical.

The fear which had haunted Ada Clifton was also Jordan's. Suppose the play caught on and Laura did with minor characters what she had done with Lord Dundreary; if she rewrote plays while they were running, no one might have a leading man's role.

The trials loosed paragraphs of vituperation. *The Saturday Press* cautioned, "Ponder, my masters, before you stir up that dangerous wild fowl, the law. Miss Laura Keene is used to it. Like Burton, she would die without her summonses, citations, answers, replications and demurrers."

The trials brought to the knowledge of the public what had only been known inside the profession, the importance of Lutz in the Keene management. He negotiated and signed all actor contracts: Miss Keene selected the performer, but contractual relationship with the theatre was through Lutz. He also was responsible for raising money when it was needed. He was in charge of the front of the house and served as Miss Keene's agent in all matters theatrical.

A reporter could now say, "Laura Keene . . . lives, as everyone, I suppose, knows, with a Mr. Lutz, a gambler. They say she is his wife. I hope so. Her two or three children by other parties live with her mother, whom she supports creditably."

Her success as an entrepreneur was walling her from her associates. She had become "Miss Laura Keene, sole manageress and directress." She did not of her own volition change. Her company was clinging to the past; Laura was relentlessly forging into the future.

Her arrangement with Boucicault was an example of her forward reaching. He was to act or not depending on conditions; no standard contract could denominate his line of business. He was to direct his own plays. He, like Laura, recognized that how a play was done was as important to the audience as what was done, maybe more so; therefore he was solely accountable for the way his plays were done.

Their first collaboration, *Jeanie Deans,* was presumed to be an adaptation and dramatization of Sir Walter Scott's novel, *The Heart of MidLothian.* It was more nearly a series of melodramatic incidents of the Scotch highlands framed in brilliant scenery by Laura's first-rate scenic department, bathed in light by the drummonds and kleigs, and

This action photograph from a production of JEANIE DEANS *shows Laura with Agnes Robertson, about whom a critic said, "She seemed . . . the ideal embodiment of innocence, artlessness, sweetness, simplicity, moving with a grace, speaking with an intelligence, which took captive mind and heart at once."* THEATRE ARTS COLLECTIONS. HARRY RANSOM HUMANITIES RESEARCH CENTER, THE UNIVERSITY OF TEXAS AT AUSTIN.

wrapped in special music arranged by Thomas Baker. The overture was a potpourri of favorite Scotch airs; the play developed to the strains of "descriptive music composed expressly to accompany and illustrate this story." The performance ran without afterpiece and was announced to end at ten o'clock, "thus enabling families to arrive at home in good season, and affording visitors from the country an opportunity of returning by the earliest trains on the same evening." When this mixture of box office concern and production expertness was illumined by the acting of Dion and his wife it was good business; when electrified by Laura, it was magnificent theatre.

Laura may have felt some discomfort in the role of Effie Deans. As she stood in handcuffs in Minard Lewis's courtroom scenery, did she identify Effie with the Laura Keene who had spent so many days in courts in New York City? There may have been a familiar ring to the lines of which Boucicault was so proud:

> Counsel for Crown: *I object to that question.*
> Counsel for Defense: *It is not a question.*
> Counsel for Crown: *It sounded very like one.*
> Counsel for Defense: *Object to the sound then.*

But Laura was a professional. She did not bring the problems of the daytime law courts to her performance in a nighttime theatre, however similar the incidents she acted. Now, freed from the responsibility of direction, she acted superbly. She knew, as she later said, that she had been "sinking the actress in the manageress."

"The performance of the piece is deserving of much credit," a reviewer said. "The cannie Scotch Girl, by Miss Agnes Robertson, was very excellent, but the star of this lady's glory is dimmed in contrast with the performance of Miss Laura Keene. The latter throws her soul into all that she does, and kindles in the heart of every one a sympathetic feeling. She plays to the heart as well as the eye and ear of her audiences, and in Effie Deans holds them under the spell of her finished and touching performance. Miss Robertson, on the contrary, throws no life into the part she assumes. She does what she has to do, and that correctly, but no more. You admire Miss Robertson, but you more than admire Miss Keene. Your whole nature is touched by her sympathetic voice, her powerful nature, and the passion which she throws into the part of Effie. Miss Robertson, for so good an actress seems to be peculiarly unfortunate — for Mrs. Wood overacted her at the Winter Garden, through contrast, and Miss Keene has played her under, by superiority, in her own line."

"In her own line," Laura again was breaking with tradition, inasmuch as Agnes Robertson played the same traditional "line of business" as Laura. The stock company of old could not accommodate two leading ladies, but Laura was initiating the pattern of the future, a company hired for a particular play.

iv

The Boucicault play, *Colleen Bawn,* which ended the season, was the farthest into the uncharted world of the future that either Dion or Laura had so far gone. The genesis of the play is accounted for in several conflicting stories. The need for another attraction was immediately apparent after the opening of *Vanity Fair.* It lacked vigor. The play which followed *Vanity Fair* would have incident, he promised.

Dion Boucicault was one of the wonders of his age. When associated with Laura he was nearing forty. Laura whose theory of play production was to be "ever gay" felt comfortable with Boucicault, who believed that "Art is the Philosophy of Pleasure."

Boucicault had entered the theatre in 1838. His play *London Assurance* was performed by Madame Vestris and her excellent company in 1841. Over the years he achieved success in theatres on both sides of the Atlantic with such plays as *The Octoroon, The Shaugrun, The Poor of New York,* and Joseph Jefferson's version of *Rip Van Winkle.* In all, he was responsible for the writing or adapting of more than 150 plays in a fifty-two-year career. *The Octoroon,* presented at the Winter Garden just before the Boucicaults joined Laura, had been a sensation in every way. It had a steamboat explosion on stage. It treated the sore subject of negro slavery at a time when nothing could be said that did not offend the advocates of free soil or states' rights, the proponents of the fugitive slave act or abolition. In the play, its author tried to walk a path described in the playbills as "nothing extenuate, nor aught set down in malice." He reveled in the ensuing controversy. He loved contention and was to have it, like Laura, in the various federal courts of copyright; in fact, it could be said of him that he was more familiar in the courtroom than in the greenroom.

The playbill introducing *The Colleen Bawn* says, "Miss Keene has received the following letter from the author: —

> 39 East Fifteenth Street,
> New York

My Dear Madam — Here is another Drama — my last for this season. It was written in five days and the labor has overtaxed me, as this makes the seventh I have written within the space of Twenty-eight weeks — one five act play, five three act dramas and a Burlesque. This piece is called "The Colleen Bawn," and is Irish to the backbone. It is the first time I have taken a subject from my native country, and quickly as the work has been executed, I am not the less satisfied with it. 'Twill be found to be, I think the best constructed of any of my works. Whatever demerits it may have, it is my happiest effort in that particular. The public must determine the rest."

As Boucicault tells the story, the night he met with Laura over the disaster that loomed ahead if they continued with *Vanity Fair*, probably Tuesday, March 13, he had no idea of the *Colleen*. This is his account:

"Have you nothing — no subject, no play half written?" he reported Laura to ask. "Can you think of nothing to replace this unlooked-for collapse?"

"I have nothing. Excepting a very poor sketch of 'Little Dorrit' and another of 'Bleak House,' but let us meet tomorrow and talk it out.

"It was a bitter night, [Boucicault continues], and the sleet driven by a northerly blast lashed the author's face as he turned up Broadway. A few doors from the theatre a dim light in a cellar showed that a thrifty little Italian, who sold cheap publications and small stationery, invited the belated pedestrian to buy a home-made cigar. His name was Brentano. Descending into the den, where he knew he should find the usual display of ten-cent literature, Boucicault asked for two novels, over which he intended to spend the hours of night. Brentano pointed to a shelf where a scanty row of cheap novels represented his stock in trade; from these the visitor selected a dozen at hazard, and with the pockets of his overcoat stuffed he pushed his way through the sleet and the darkness to Union Square, near where he resided. The following morning Miss Keene received this letter:

My Dear Laura:

I have it! I send you seven steel engravings of scenes around Killarney. Get your scene-painter to work on them at once. I also send a book of Irish melodies, with those marked I desire Baker to score for the orchestra. I shall read act one of my new Irish play on Friday; we rehearse that while I am writing the second, which will be ready on Monday; and we rehearse the second while I am doing the third. We can get the play out within a fortnight.

Yours,
"D.B."

"Amongst the books picked up at Brentano's was, haply, 'The Collegians,' by Gerald Griffin. Throwing it aside, Boucicault evolved 'The Colleen Bawn.'"

That's his version.

Another and very different story of the play's inception is told by the comedienne Mrs. Barney Williams, which would have no place here were not the ways of playwrights the particular problem of managers like Laura and the federal courts under the new copyright law.

My husband [Barney Williams] and Mr. Boucicault had entered into an agreement in the fall of 1859, whereby Mr. Boucicault was to furnish us with a new Irish play to be ready in the fall of 1860. The Boucicault trademark meant a great deal in those days and carried a star a long way. Well, in January or February we met Mr. Boucicault, who read us the first two acts. The play was "The Colleen Bawn." My husband was delighted with the character of Myles, and although Eily O'Connor seemed a bit too sentimental for my line of business, we were both very much pleased with the play as a whole. At that time Mr. Boucicault was house dramatist for Laura Keene. Along in March he put on a play called "Vanity Fair," which was expected to last through the season. But it failed. Something had to replace it. Imagine our indignation and surprise to find that "The Colleen Bawn," which he had written for us according to contract, had been brought out at Laura Keene's! He was profuse in apologies. He had been caught in a corner, so he said, and having nothing else up his sleeve, had to give them "The Colleen Bawn." He would write us another piece. But my husband said, "No." Mr. Boucicault had broken faith with us, and we didn't propose to give him another chance. There was a little bitter feeling, but when we came to think it over we agreed that we might have done the same thing if we had had the same temptation. We are all of us human, and Dion Boucicault was very human.

Boucicault's reading of the first act to the assembled company was followed by his description of what was to follow. "To hear him describe the plot of the play, his small Irish eye sparkling, and the words all well chosen, pouring out like a torrent and cataract, was to see it acted before your eyes in every detail," an actor recalled. Eily O'Connor, the Colleen Bawn, (Bawn simply means the fair-haired, the part to be played by the golden-haired Agnes Robertson) was secretly married to Hardress Cregan, her better socially but her inferior spiritually. He has continued his suit to Anne Chute, the Colleen Ruaidh (Ruaidh means red-haired, the part for Laura), because her wealth is the only means of saving the Cregan estates. His man servant, Danny Mann, offers to remove Eily should Cregan ever send him his glove.

The copybook containing the first act was given to the copyists for lengths to be prepared for the actors, while Dion took another copybook to write Act II. He also took a suggestion from the scenic crew.

The big moment of the play came with the water-cave scene in which Danny Mann, who has received the glove by cruel accident, attempts to drown Eily O'Connor, who is subsequently rescued by Myles-na-Coppaleen, a part Boucicault wrote for himself. The light blue gauze of the water into which the Colleen Bawn sank did more to make the play a success than any performance of the actors. Myles's dive and the gauze waters were the suggestion of Laura's stage carpenter, who, while building the rocks of the cave, asked, "Why not try a dive for something new? A dive would go better than an ordinary jump, sir." It did.

The water-cave scene affected the theatre from that day forward. It became the staple of the ten-twenty-thirty-cent melodrama of rushing locomotives and logger's saws, and then of motion pictures. King Kong's climb up the Empire State building is a derivative of Myles's header.

Just prior to this big scene, Myles was to hurry across the forestage to save Eily from Danny. The scene must take time enough for the carpenter to set up the water-cave. The third copybook reads in part, "Music, low storm music . . . Myles sings without, then appears upper entrance right on Rock . . . Swings across Stage by Rope. Exit. Music. Boat floats on from right with Eily and Danny. Eily steps on to Rock Center. Danny stepping onto the Rock the Boat floats away unseen . . . Music. Throws her into the water left center. She disappears for an instant then reappears clinging to Rock . . . Thrusts her down. She disappears . . . Shot heard. Danny falls into Water behind Rock . . . Myles sings without . . . Swings across by Rope to R., fastens it up, then fishes up Double of Eily — lets her fall. Strips, then dives after her. Eily appears for an instant in front. Then double for Myles appears at back and Dives over Drum. Myles and Eily then appear in front of Center Rock. Tableau. Curtain."

George Bernard Shaw had vivid memories of the way Boucicault had played Myles. He "had a charming brogue, musical in sound, or irresistible in insinuation — 'sloothering' would be the right word," said the greatest of Irish playwrights about one of his predecessors. Shaw found Dion's Myles a coaxing, bland sort of liar, "to whom you could listen without impatience long enough to allow the carpenter to set the most elaborate water scene behind the front cloth." Boucicault wrote no words for himself in this scene, he ad libbed comments, which could be as short or as long as needed.

Agnes Robertson was never in Laura's class as a performer, just as Laura was never in her class as a popular idol and heartbreaker.

THE COLLEEN BAWN;
OR, THE BRIDES OF GARRYOWEN.
A DOMESTIC DRAMA, IN THREE ACTS.
BY DION BOUCICAULT, ESQ.

The playscript of THE COLLEEN BAWN has a notice that it can be performed in Great Britian without permission. The playscript of OUR AMERICAN COUSIN states 'printed but not published.' Both signs of copy-right litigation. UNIVERSITY OF TULSA THEATRE COLLECTION

Roorbach, who gave the palm for acting during this period to Laura, took time out to describe his first glimpse of Miss Robertson outside a hotel: "An azure blue satin cloak, trimmed with ermine, was thrown gracefully over her shoulders. Her petticoat and body were of white satin, ornamented with real Brussels lace. A short turban, of the same material as the dress, and set off by ostrich feathers, was on her head. Long gloves of white kid covered her hands and part of her arms. She had ivory tablets, and a pencil, gold-cased, and before the carriage was driven off made some memorandums. Then there was a lifting of hats, a wave of the hand, a smile, and the word of action given to the horses." Her beauty, it was claimed, had caused Harvard men to pawn their clothes in order to buy tickets to successive performances in Boston. The red cloak she wore in *The Colleen Bawn* became an item of fashion. She had her moment in the sun as Eily after having been in Laura's shadow as Jeanie Deans.

Only two weeks could be given to readying *The Colleen Bawn*. Boucicault liked working with Laura's company, and on this play he was in his element. She gave him everything he wanted. When Madame Vestris produced *London Assurance* her stage manager was shocked that Boucicault wanted a real carpet laid on the floor of the stage drawing room. "What next?" he complained, "He will be asking for real flowers and real sunlight in the garden." Laura's men were prepared to provide them, if asked. Laura's actors, accustomed to her directions, could accept Dion's. One reminisced, "I can see Boucicault now, holding the book at rehearsals and dogmatically dictating every bit of stage business." His economical turns of speech to aid an actor became the aphorisms of acting schools in future years: "Play to the actor, and not to the audience." To an actor with very little to say or do, "Always put your foot down as if to say 'This spot is mine!'" Even his mistakes became legend. At a rehearsal he gave a stage direction different from his commands of the day previous.

"Mr. Boucicault, I have written the directions as you gave them to me yesterday."

"Ah!" said Boucicault in his Dublin brogue and sweetest manner, "yesterday, certainly, my boy, I told you to do it that way, but the world is just twenty-four hours older, and we have advanced that much; so do it this way today."

The play could have run longer than it did, but Laura was unsettled. The trials with Wheatley and Clarke in Philadelphia and Moses Kimball in Boston over pirating *Our American Cousin* were no closer to resolution than they had been when they were brought, and they kept turning up new areas of unpleasantness. Her theatre gave benefits to Thomas Baker, Agnes Robertson, and Dion Boucicault in the first weeks of May, and she took her own benefit the last night of the season. At the curtain call she turned to Agnes Robertson and said, "This lady and myself have, I fear, greatly disappointed many of you; we have lived together and worked together for many months, and have not fought once, nor scratched each other's faces." Some believed that, if Miss Robertson was the only person who had not fought with her, she was also the only person who had not sued her.

Laura sailed for London on the day Abraham Lincoln was nominated for president by the Republican party, May 18, 1860. She sailed on the *City of Washington*.

This oil on canvas portrait of Laura Keene was painted in 1858 by
William H. Powell (1823-1879). He was better known for historical
paintings such as "The Discovery of the Mississippi by De Soto" which
was hung in the U.S. Capitol only a few years before Laura sat to him.
COURTESY OF THE NEW YORK HISTORICAL SOCIETY, NEW YORK CITY.

Chapter 7

Clutching Our American Cousin

'Twill be recorded for a precedent,
And many an error by the same example
Will rush into the state . . .
SHAKESPEARE, THE MERCHANT OF VENICE, ACT IV,
SCENE I

Keene v. Wheatley and Clarke in equity never became as famous in literary affairs as *Bardle v. Pickwick* or *Sir Thomas Lucy v. William Shakespeare*, or *Douglas v. Oscar Wilde*, but it should have its niche, if for no other reason than its nine long years of controversy, and if for no other reason than its revelation of the ways the theatrical profession operated in the 1860s.

The trial's beginnings were simple enough. Laura heard from Lutz that Wheatley and Clarke said they were going to do a play, *Our American Cousin*, in Philadelphia of which she had the only copy and for which she held the copyright. Lutz went to Philadelphia to see what they were up to.

He had read the manuscript of *Our American Cousin* when it came to Laura's theatre and had recommended that Jefferson read it. He had handled the two payments of five hundred dollars each for purchase of the play. Had someone of the Keene company surreptitiously made a copy of the unique manuscript in the stage manager's possession and slipped it to the Philadelphians? Were Wheatley and Clarke thieves?

They were, as Mrs. Barney Williams said of Boucicault, "very human." William Wheatley, the scion of a theatrical family, had acted since childhood. He had been managing the Arch Theatre since 1853, first with John Drew, then alone, and most lately with Clarke. In the normal course of theatre activity he knew Laura.

John Sleeper Clarke was not so well known. He was a younger man. He had not been born into the profession although he had had a flair for amateur theatricals while a boy in Baltimore, acting with Edwin and John Wilkes Booth. He had made rapid strides in his career, playing "low comedy business." He joined with Wheatley for his first experience in management. During the first year of the long-drawn-out court proceedings in the suit brought by Laura, he married Edwin Booth's sister, Asia.

The Keene forces tried to restrain the presentation of the play by Wheatley and Clarke. The Philadelphia forces admitted that their production very greatly resembled the New York one. Such similarity was inevitable when they were acting from the original script and Miss Keene and her company from a copy made from it.

Where did that script come from? Laura wrote Tom Taylor immediately. He responded as fast as steam could make the round-trip across the North Atlantic.

"My Dear Madam — The following are the precise facts of the case as to the play of 'Our American Cousin.'

"It was written with a view to the principal part being played by Mr. Silsbee, but never sold to that actor . . . it was found that the part did not suit Mr. Silsbee, who wished to alter it, by omissions entirely destructive of my conception.

". . . Mr. Silsbee had no right to be in possession of the play and your right derived from me will no doubt enable you to defeat any claim founded on the surreptitious and unlawful possession of a copy of the comedy by any other person. It is also certain that there was no publication of the piece.

"P.S. — I may add that I do not believe Silsbee was in possession of a copy of the piece. If he should prove to have had a copy, it will, I think, prove to be a mutilated one — i.e. — one with the omissions which he himself wished to have made in it. I do not imagine it possible that the possession of a stolen copy can invalidate your right, nor will I believe that this can be the case till I learn it from the American bench."

Taylor's assumption that the Silsbee copy was a mutilated one was never put to the test. No one ever asked to see the Silsbee script. The Silsbee script was a ploy. The Philadelphians had Laura's script with all its changes, cuts, additions, and development of characters.

"Was the play as represented by the defendants that evening and witnessed by you," an attorney asked Lutz, "similar to the play as represented at the complainant's theatre in New York?"

"Yes, sir, with the exception of one scene, called the Wine Cellar Scene. With that exception it was the same play in three acts. The characters were all the same, incidents and general acting the same."

"On that evening that you visited Defendant's Theatre, had you a manuscript A, or other copy of the play with you?"

"I had the manuscript with me," Lutz replied. (He of course could have followed the words line by line had he wanted since auditoriums were still as brilliantly lighted as the stage.)

"Did you follow the performance upon the manuscript?"

"I did not."

"Did you examine the manuscript at the Theatre on that evening and if so in what part of the house were you?"

"I was in the parquet. I did not examine the manuscript having seen the play very often. I did not think it necessary. I knew it word for word. As the play went along — I also had this bill which gives the scenery and incidents — I could see by that it was the same," Lutz answered.

Actually, anyone familiar with the theatre of the time knew how Wheatley and Clarke had secured an exact manuscript. On their visits to New York they had observed the performance carefully and somewhere in the audience a secretary had taken down the words.

Was not such pirating an infringement of the new copyright law? Not according to Judge Cadwalader before whom Laura's injunction was brought. In fact, he expressed an opinion that "if the defendants had attended the performance of the play and been able to remember it all, he would have dismissed the bill, but they used a manuscript obtained from the widow who did not have a legal claim to it." In other words, had the defense continued to stress the Silsbee manuscript, or had Laura's lawyers stressed its illegal possession, Laura might have won a punitive battle against Wheatley and Clarke but she would have done nothing to protect her valuable property, *Our American Cousin,* from further pirating by other managers.

The suit continued therefore as an action of infringement under the 1856 copyright statute. Judge Cadwalader ruled that placing the play before the public was "publication." He suggested that in regulating the police at her theatre Laura "could have prevented reporters from taking down the words of the play during its performance, and could have excluded persons unwilling to acquiesce in such conditions."

In his opinion, she could not protect the words, but the play had a character outside the words and the judge ruled that Laura had a right "in property."

ii

Her lawyers in Boston did not plead infringement of copyright against Moses Kimball, the Boston manager who had also pirated *Our American Cousin,* but rested her case "solely upon her common law right of property in a literary production." They would use Judge Cadwalader's reasoning. The learned judge of the Massachusetts Supreme Court ruled against them and Laura.

Anthony L. Robertson, judge of the superior court of New York, before whom Laura had brought John Sleeper Clarke on the same old charge, but in a different venue, ruled that "any manager owning a manuscript play and having it acted, must hang prominent cards about the auditorium, and also print on his tickets a notification to each visitor that mere admission to the theatre does not imply any permission to memorize the piece acted, or any part of it, with the intention of representing the same elsewhere; otherwise the manager is not protected."

All had ruled that once an actor has voiced a word of a copyrighted play from the stage before an audience which has paid to hear that word, the playwright's word has been published. The word was now the possession of the hearer who might want to repeat it in the same fashion that the lecture of a teacher in a medical school belonged to his students and in turn to their patients. The federal law and the courts would not protect the performed manuscript of a play.

Laura's dreams of a long-run production were meaningless. Every other theatre manager anywhere could present her play.

She had spent a fortune in legal fees to learn this. Only Cadwalader had given her hope of any protection for her theatre and the preservation of her dream. He ruled that because of Wheatley and Clarke's infraction of proprietary right she was entitled to redress. "The defendants enabled themselves to represent the play by knowingly taking advantage of a breach of confidence committed by a person [Jefferson] in her employ."

Judge Cadwalader ruled that Laura should be paid $1,000. It was the amount of the license her agent, Lutz, had said she would accept when Wheatley and Clarke had talked with him in the theatre lobby in New York City. The defendants would pay court costs. They would also pay Laura some amount to be yet determined based on the amount they had profited from using Jefferson's knowledge of *Our American Cousin.*

Both parties were given ten days to challenge Cadwalader's ruling. If they challenged, then the judge would order a jury trial at which the depositions taken so far would be read in open court. The Wheatley-Clarke forces, protecting Jefferson, did not challenge. Laura, hearing of Lutz's deposition, did not challenge. The Wheatley-Clarke forces contended Laura was incompetent to plead because she was a married woman. The judge said that there was no allegation that her asserted marriage was a newly discovered fact. But wasn't it? Was Laura's connection with Henry Wellington Taylor known to Wheatley and Clarke before Clarke married Edwin Booth's sister? Edwin Booth, with whom Laura traveled in Australia, knew of Taylor's presence in Australia. Did Asia pick up information about a fascinating woman at the Booth family table on Edwin's return east? Had she shared that pillow talk with her newly wedded husband?

The Clarkes were married in April. John Lutz was interrogated in May. Constant Guillott, attorney for Clarke, asked questions of Lutz as if he already knew the answers.

Q. You have said that you attended to the business of the theatre for complainant. Was your place in the box office?

A. Yes, sir.

Q. Are you there upon a salary payable weekly or monthly or how?

A. I am not there on any particular salary. I live by what I get from the theatre. If the business is good, I get more, if bad, I get less.

Q. Has the play of 'Our American Cousin' been published? And if so, when was it so published and where?

A. It has not been published that I know of.

Q. Be kind enough to state, what you mean us to understand when you say that you attend to the business of the theatre.

A. I am about the front of the theatre attending to the business of it in front.

Q. I must trouble you to state what business it is that you attend to.

A. I oversee the front of it to see that it is conducted properly. Sell tickets sometimes. . .

Q. Have you an account in the books of the complainant or is there one in them opened with you.

A. Not that I know of.

Q. Have you not frequently assisted in the payment of salaries with ladies and gentlemen of that establishment.

A.   I do not often pay the salaries.

Q.   Are receipts taken for the salaries as paid?

A.   Sometimes they are, and sometimes not. . .

Q.   Have you not on various occasions provided, and furnished the means for the payment of some of the salaries?

A.   I have raised money for such purposes when it was not there. . .

Q.   Out of your own means, or on your own liabilities?

A.   I have raised money for the theatre on my own liability.

Q.   Where does Miss Keene reside?

A.   In New York.

Q.   Whereabouts?

A.   With her mother at 58 Bleecker Street.

Q.   Who constitute that family besides Miss Keene.

A.   There are various persons living there. Two Miss Taylors, Miss Wells, Mrs. Foster, Mr. Gray stayed there this winter, and myself. . . I believe that is about all.

Q.   I fear that my question, or your answer has been misunderstood by the Commissioner. Do you mean that all of the persons whose names you have given reside there now?

A.   I said they had lived there this winter. The two Miss Taylors, Mrs. Foster, Miss Keene and myself live there now. The mother left last week to go to Europe. Miss Keene thinks of following her when the season is over.

Q.   Please give me the ages of the two Miss Taylors . . . Are they grown ladies or minors?

A. One of them is grown, the other is a minor. I don't know their ages.

Q. How old is the minor?

A. About 10 or 12 years.

Q. And how old the elder?

A. I should think 15 or 16.

Q. How long have you known Miss Keene?

A. About six years.

Q. Did you ever know the father or mother of the Miss Taylors, and if so, where and when?

A. No sir.

Q. In whose name is that house taken from the landlord.

A. Mrs. Keene I think. Mrs. Jane Keene.

Q. Did you never pay the rent for that house?

A. I have for them.

Q. How often ?

A. Time and again for the past year going on two years.

Q. How long since you have been living in the same house with Miss Keene.

A. Going on two years.

Q. You will be pleased to state upon what pecuniary terms you are living in that house.

A. No particular pecuniary terms.

Q. Are you not married to Miss Keene?

A.   No sir, never was.

Q.   Are you not living with her as though you were married as husband and wife.

A.   No sir. I don't pass myself for her husband.

Q.   Are you not living with her as though you were married?

A.   No sir, I never passed as her husband. I never was married — .

Q.   I understand you to mean to say upon your oath, that you are not living with the complainant together as married.

A.   No sir.

Q.   Do you so mean to state.

A.   I do so.

Q.   Do you pay any board at that house? If so, at what rate and times, and to whom have you paid it.

A.   I do not pay any particular board, as I said before. I work in the theatre, and get my living out of it. I never had any positive arrangement as to pay of salary, or pay of my board.

Q.   Did you ever pay any board at that house?

A.   No sir. I have lived just as I said there.

Q.   What business have you transacted for Miss Keene, prior to the commencement of this arrangement that you were to get your living out of the theatre? Had you done? And if so, state what it was.

A.   How do you mean, out of the theatre?

Q.   My question is general and is not limited to this theatre.

A.   I transacted some theatrical business for Miss Keene at another theatre — Burton's Theatre. Previously to that in California. It was general theatrical business, the same as now.

Q.   Was she a Manager at Burton's Theatre and at California?

A.   Yes sir.

Q.   When did you commence living in the same house with her?

A.   I boarded in the same house with her, off and on, during that time.

Q.   Did you pay board then?

A.   Sometimes I have, and sometimes not.

Q.   You will please to state what is the connection or relationship between Miss Keene and the Misses Taylor.

A.   I don't know.

Q.   By what title do they address her?

A.   They call her 'Aunt.'

Q.   Do you fix the 18th October 1858 as the day of the first representation in New York?

A.   It was Monday 18 October.

Q.   Is not the complainant a married woman?

A.   Not that I know of.

Q.   Have you conversed with her upon that subject — and has she not said to you that she was.

A.   We have had a great deal of conversation on that subject. I don't know if she is a married woman.

Question repeated.

A. She has told me that she had been married.

Q. Is that all the answer that you desire to give to that question?

A. Yes sir.

Q. To whom did she say that she had been married.

A. I wish to ask if I must relate the conversations I have heard? She said that she has been married.

Q. Did she mention the name of her husband?

A. Mr. Taylor was the name she mentioned. I don't know the first name. If she told me, I have forgotten it.

Q. Do you know Mr. Taylor, or anything of him?

A. No sir. I never saw him. It was before she came to this country.

Q. Did the two young ladies who call her 'Aunt' come to this country with her?

A. Not that I know of. I don't know.

Q. Do you know how long the two young ladies have been in this country and how long since the complainant came to this country?

A. I do not know how long since either the two young ladies or Miss Keene came to this country. I have known her five or six years, as I said before.

Q. When you procure means, as you have stated, for the theatre, do you take any due bill, note, or other obligation whatsoever, of the complainant?

A. I have done so but I have not received any money recently this year. I have taken due bill, note obligation for money I procured and I have not. This is not recently however it was a year or two ago. I have not procured any money recently this year.

That testimony must never be produced in open court, Laura decided.

How could the woman who had been crowned with a laurel wreath for pruning immoralities from the plays on her stage allow the public to know that the rent on the house her mother and daughters lived in was paid by a man not her husband? Know it from his lips.

By her decision not to challenge, Laura received only the license fee from her legal battle with Wheatley and Clarke. All she received from the injunction against Moses Kimball in Boston was an acquaintance with Thomas William Clarke, the Massachusetts legal representative of her counsel, William D. Booth.

The matter of copyright was still thoroughly confused. Was the public performance of a manuscript drama publication or not? Thomas William Clarke became the Boston attorney for Boucicault when he attempted to stop the pirating of his play *The Octoroon,* but the side issue of the non-citizen alien seeking copyright was raised and the case was dismissed. Boucicault's citizenship affected his rights in England also. The printed copy of *Colleen Bawn* has a prefatory statement that amateurs and others may produce the play royalty free in Great Britain: "In consequence of the production of this drama, and others by the same Author, in the United States of America, with which there is no existing International Treaty of Copyright."

When Boucicault went to law again over copyright, in 1868, Booth and Clarke again were his attorneys. All of the arguments from the first days of the trial over *Our American Cousin* were paraded before the court. But there was a different judge, Samuel D. Blatchford, of the southern district of New York.

He wanted a workable definition of a "play." He finally ruled that a dramatic composition "is not related, but represented by dialogue and action . . . by persons who represent it as real . . . by countenance, voice or gesture." It was a breakthrough! By his definition, pantomime was a part of a theatrical entertainment, and, when it was a part of copyrighted play, it qualified for its own copyright. "Those parts of it represented by motion or gesture, without language, are quite as much a dramatic composition, as those parts of it represented by voice," the judge said.

He went further in defining copyright. He ruled that an idea was the essence of a play or dramatic entertainment and should be as protected as the expression of that idea. By extension, he was saying about *Our American Cousin:* Miss Keene, your way of doing the play should have been protected to you by the courts from such an infringement of your ideas. Judge Blatchford's ruling was relayed to Laura as fast as Booth and Clarke could get the word to her.

On January 6, 1869, Laura took out an advertisement in the *Clipper,* now recognized as the official weekly means of communication with the theatrical profession.

Our American Cousin

The litigation concerning the ownership of the comedy
"Our American Cousin" having terminated, and the
right of the subscriber thereto having been confirmed,
all permissions to perform said comedy not under the
hand and seal of the subscriber, are hereby revoked,
and all persons are cautioned against performing said
play without her consent after this date.
Laura Keene
Riverside Lawn, Acushnet, Mass. Jan 6, 1869

Laura would have taken a wry interest that the copyright law which went into effect on July 8, 1879, owed much to *Keene v. Wheatley and Clarke*. The learned men who drew up the law acknowledged their debt publicly.

NEW YORK, THURSDAY, MAY 16, 1861.

LAURA KEENE'S THEATRE

SOLE LESSEE...MISS LAURA KEENE

Doors open at Seven o'clock.   Performances commence at a quarter to Eight o'clock

One Hundred and Sixty-nine Nights!

276,000 PEOPLE!

TO-NIGHT, THURSDAY, MAY 16th, 1861

AND EVERY NIGHT,

Will be presented, the great three-act Burletta, the

Seven Sisters

New Scenery..............................by..................Mr. James M. Roberts
National Music, arranged expressly for the New Tableaux.......by...... Mr. Thomas Baker
Uncle Sam, with the American Eagle under his arm : : : : : : : : : : Mr. B G. Rogers
Diogenes, as great a cynic as ever : : : : : : : : : : : Mr. T. B. Johnston
Columbia, an interesting female, who must be seen to be appreciated : : : : : Mrs. J. H. Allen
Arthur Stunner, a dramatist and artist in crayon : : : : : : : : Mr H. F. Daly
Catchem, a phenomenal policeman, always in the way when wanted : : : : : : Mr. Martin
Pluto, King of Hades, the Elysian Fields, and all low countries generally ; a monarch by no means so black
    as he is painted, though probably not nearly so good as he will appear by the representation of : Mr. Barton
Demonos old friend with a new face, and a striking likeness, hoping to impress the public favorably : Mr. Levick
Cuffee, one of the original sable brothers, an unmitigated nuisance, in everybody's way, and never accom-
    plishing anything good—in fact, so very bad that his black father, Pluto, won't have him in Hades at any
    price : : : : : : : : : : : : : : : : : Mr. Burnett
Diavoline, first of the Seven Sisters raising a revolt in Hades and a breeze on earth, afterwards the Angel
    —— afterwards Tom Highboy, afterwards the Murderous Mother, afterwards Flora, Goddess of Flow-
    ers, afterwards Captain il ghboy, of the Feminine Zouaves, which disguises she assumes in the vain en-
    deavor to mislead Arthur : : : : : : : : : : : : : Miss Laura Keene
Flutelia, the second Sister, a chip of the old block, out for a holiday, afterwards the Angel ——, afterwards
    Bob Highboy, afterwards Psyche, afterwards Lieut. Highboy, of the Feminine Zouaves, afterwards
    the unterrified South, afterwards a Bootblack, always assisting her sister, and occasionally speculating
    a little on her own account : : : : : : : : : : : : Miss Ione Burke
Tartarine, the third Sister, another ligneum vitae chip, also out for a holiday, afterwards the Angel ——,
    afterwards Jeremia Highb'y, afterwards Lieut. Highboy, of the Feminine Zouaves, afterwards the
    irrepressible North, afterwards a hot corn girl, following in the footsteps of her illustrious predecessors
    in all particulars : : : : : : : : : : : : : : Mrs. Lotty Hough
Sulphurine : : : : : : : : : : : : : : : : : : Miss Everett
Farcinella : : :   : : Miss Couldock
Satanella : : :   who, in the most subtle manner, assist the diableries of   : : Miss Sutherland
Cantabil : : :   their sisters, assuming a variety of characters for that   : : Miss Richmond
                   purpose.
Mrs. Pluto, formerly called Proserpine, the one fair daughter of Ceres, originally borne to her by Jupiter,
    and subsequently borne from her by Pluto, which fact sufficiently accounts for her appearing in this
    connection : : : : : : : : : : : : : : : : : Mr. Peters
Ceres an estimable lady, considerably younger than her daughter above alluded to, and introduced solely for
    the purpose of introducing the last scene : : : : : : : : : : Miss Secor
Spirit of Arthur's Sister : : : : : : : : : : : : : : Miss Frances
Cupid, afterwards Young Sam, afterwards the Sprite of the Chrysalis : : : : Little Mary Bullock
Puffles the Statue Father : : : : : : : : : : : : : Mr. Goodrich
Premiere Danseuse, with a grand Pas from "La Sylphide" : : : : : : : Mlle. Helens

SYNOPSIS OF SCENERY AND INCIDENTS:

Act I.—Scene I.—A Breakfast Room in Hades. The female head of the Plutonian family; Pluto himself;
Matrimonial Felicity in Tartarus slightly analogous to the mundane institutions; The Seven Sisters; A strong
minded nuisance; Summer to be passed on earth; A Warning Picture; The Miseries of Mortal Love;
New arrivals at the infernal regions; Municipal and legislative spirits below par; THE INEVITABLE NIGGER;
A dutiful wife never allows her husband to say she's't; THE ESCAPE OF THE SEVEN SISTERS. Scene 2.—
THE POOR AUTHOR'S HOME; A lucifer match highly recommended to sugar venders; the Poor Author and his
Friend; Pluto, as usual, raises a breeze; sleep; the dream; The PICTURE of the SEVEN SISTERS; Diavoline's
resolve to ensure the success of the new piece; Pluto's influence thrown the other way; the waking; AFTER
A PHANTOM; Snail again; TWO NEW YORK BOYS; wheat and rye; billiards; fascination and diablerie; IN
THE TOILS; The WARNING of the SISTER'S SPIRIT. Scene 3.—AT A NEW YORK HOTEL; Our old
friend s all his Tiger; Letter R; A slight error. Scene 4.—BEHIND THE SCENES at LAURA KEENE'S. The sen-
sation Drama looking up; Brimstone in the air; a Stage Wait and beauty not in distress; A SHERRY COBBLER
FOR MR. PETERS; GRAND COMBAT with REAL SWORDS; EVERYBODY FOR THE LAST SCENE; A
difference of Opinion; The Yankee Girl; The Statue Father slightly intoxicated; The Ballet Nonplussed and the
Denouement Knocked into a Cocked Hat. Mrs. PETERS PLUTO AS CUPID. GRAND PAS FROM LA SYL-
PHIDE GRAND MYTHOLOGICAL GROUP SERIO-COMIC TABLEAU. Scene 5.—A STREET IN NEW
YORK. The colored individual once more; A NEW SONG TO AN OLD TUNE. Scene 6.—The PALACE GAR-
DENS. The Nigger Again; THE CORPS DES ZOUAVES; ZOUAVE'S SONG; GRAND MARCH AND DRILL
BY A FEMININE CORPS OF ZOUAVES.

Act Second.—UNCLE SAM'S MAGIC LANTERN. Tableau First—COLUMBUS. Tableau
Second—THE FOUR SECTIONS OF THE UNION. Tableau Third—WASHINGTON CROSS-
ING THE DELAWARE. Tableau Fourth—COLUMBIA AT WASHINGTON'S TOMB. Tab-
leau Fifth—THE THIRTY-FOUR STATES :—Massachusetts, Mrs. Lotty Hough; Maine, Mrs.
Richmond ; South Carolina, Miss Ione Burke; Kentucky, Miss H. Mosley ; Ohio, Miss Martin ;
Virginia, Miss Florence. Tableau Sixth—The HAPPY PLANTATION HOME. Tableau Seventh.
—CALHOUN'S DREAM, and WASHINGTON'S ARMY at VALLEYFORGE. Tableau Eighth.
—THE PICTURE OF DESOLATION. Tableau Ninth—APOTHEOSIS OF WASHINGTON
AND THE UNION.

Act 3.—Scene 1—CANAL STREET. Apples and songs; a boot black ; a glimpse of returning affection ; Mrs.
P. wants to go home ; salutary punishment ; hot corn ; working out in a new place ; our old friend has his boots
polished ; a general row. Scene 2—THE POOR AUTHOR'S HOME. Stunner and Snail; the Yankee Girl again ;
"Where's them gals ;" she calls her mother. Scene 3.—A CHAMBER IN HADES. Pluto's family safe ; Mrs.
Pluto's affection revived ; a plea of guilty ; the inevitable nigger once more; BANISHED TO CONEY ISLAND ;
the punishment of Diavoline and Satanella; INVOCATION TO CERES; Diavoline's banishment; the protection
of Ceres; I WISH I WAS IN DIXIE. The piece to conclude with the

GRAND TRANSFORMATION SCENE OF THE BIRTH OF THE BUTTERFLY
IN THE BOWER OF FERNS.

Chapter 8

War-Time Theatre

Tell me where is fancy bred,
Or in the heart, or in the head?
How begot, how nourished?
SHAKESPEARE, *THE MERCHANT OF VENICE*, ACT III,
SCENE 2

The next three theatrical seasons are Laura's last in her own theatre in New York. The lease expired at the conclusion of the 1860-61 season, but she renewed it for 61-62 and again for 62-63. At one time, she managed the only legitimate theatre to remain open in New York.

Her plan for the first of those years was simple: avoid all the acts which had brought her into the law courts. She was going to have an American citizen, Thomas H. De Walden, for house dramatist. There was going to be no confusion about copyright and ownership: he was to be paid a salary of fifty dollars a week to write plays especially for her. Her theatre was to have a brilliant machinist and scenic artist, James M. Roberts, from Covent Garden Theatre, London. The *Herald* applauded, "As the success of a play has come now-a-days to depend more upon the scenery and stage effects than upon the ability of the authors or the cleverness of the actors Miss Keene has done a wise thing in bringing out from Europe the best painters and machinists."

After mixed success with the first three plays of the season, Laura's theatre premiered on Monday, November 26, 1860, *The Seven Sisters,* which had the longest unbroken run known up to that time in New York. Two hundred and fifty-three performances were given before the summer break on August 10, 1861. During the first hundred days of the play's run Abraham Lincoln was elected, South Carolina seceded, the constitution of the Confederate States of America was adopted, Jefferson Davis was sworn in as provisional president of that republic, and president-elect Lincoln arrived in Washington. Lincoln was inaugurated, Fort Sumter fell, volunteers were called for a Northern Army, and Colonel Ellsworth of the New York Seventh Regiment was killed, all in the play's second hundred performances. The Battle of Bull Run was fought and bloodily lost by the North during the play's concluding days.

Firing on Fort Sumter was the signal for many of the theatres of the country to close. *Wilkes Spirit of the Times* editorialized, "The provincial theatres are closing everywhere, and the followers of Thespis, instead of strutting their brief hour on the mimic stage, will soon be compelled to take up arms against a sea of troubles and by opposing end them." The *Herald* reported, "Those [theatres] which still remain open do so in face of the most discouraging circumstances. It is not so much that people have become pinched in pecuniary matters, as that they have lost all present taste for artificial excitements. . . Then there are few families of position in society from which one or more members have not gone to take up arms in defense of the national existence . . . Add to these causes of decline among the theatres the fact that many of our ladies of taste and fashion are devoting their time and money to the high duty of providing necessaries and luxuries for the soldiers, both in camp and hospital, and there will be no surprise felt at the depressed condition of our places of amusement."

How did Laura keep her theatre open?

She had a hit. The production was typically Laura.

It isn't often that one can get a certificate of the facts of conception of a new play, but C. Young, treasurer of Laura's theatre, wrote an account of the birth of *The Seven Sisters* which he was "willing to verify by my affidavit if necessary." The company's resident dramatist, De Walden, began work on an adaptation of a German play, *The Seven Daughters of Satan,* some time after October 7. It was presented to Laura for approval, reading to the company, casting, and rehearsal. "Fearing it would not go, Miss Keene, at the last moment wrote a piece herself, which I sitting at her side, copied as she wrote it," Young stated. "This was the piece produced under the title of the Seven Sisters — very little of Mr. De Walden's piece was used — with the exception of one scene, and that even had to be altered. Mr. De Walden was engaged five weeks in the construction and composition of his work. The week following Miss Keene wrote her piece."

De Walden's part in the final script was so minute he never made a claim for further recompense when the play was an acknowledged hit, or challenged Young's story of the play's inception. The copyright title page for *The Seven Sisters* names only Laura as the author. It calls the piece "A Grand Operatic Spectacular, Diabolical, Musical, Terpsichorean, Farcical Burletta, in Three Acts."

The one scene that had been in the play from the beginning was the scenic climax, "Grand Transformation Scene of the Birth of the Butterfly in the Bower of Ferns." This particular wonder was the "finest specimen of scenic art ever witnessed upon the English stage," her advertisement read. "In order to present this splendid scene to the American public in an appropriate manner, Miss Keene was induced to bring from London the only scenic artist capable of producing it."

Actually the play was *Camp at the Union,* or *Novelty,* those other revues Laura staged across the years. Like them it would change with the changing headlines: the longer it ran the more different it became.

This hit show told the story of Diavoline, a daughter of the lord of the underworld, Pluto, who disobeyed him by falling in love with a playwright. Diavoline [Laura] helped this poor mortal get a play of his produced. For this she was punished by her father: she was banished to Coney Island. However, deeming the punishment too harsh, Diavoline makes an invocation to Ceres, "I Wish I Was in Dixie," which is the lead-in to the grand transformation scene.

More than four hundred thousand spectators witnessed this play. Few, if any, went to hear the story of Diavoline. Most of the men and women who filled the theatre for eight months went to find delight.

Over the years theatre-goers had come to expect gaiety and excitement at Laura's theatre. They found it first in the advertisements. Laura, with her willingness to spend money, bought inches in the press. "Instead of a brief and inhospitable announcement of the evening's play conveyed in the most dreary language, with no blessed relief of capitals . . .," a perceptive reporter commented, "a more luxuriant and refreshing document was submitted to the curious in such matters." Audiences felt an anticipatory excitement for Laura's theatre after reading the advertisements.

Laura's "rapturous use of an exceedingly ornate" language was called oriental.

Friendly pre-opening announcements in the theatrical columns added zest to the spectator's interest. Although the tone was sometimes patronizing, it served Laura's ends. "Miss Keene produces tonight a string of stray and sparkling beads of various hues and forms, entitled *The Seven Sisters*. The piece can hardly be more disconnected than the advertisements which announce it, poor little verbs and substantives being thrown upon the world without the smallest provision for their support, with all that charming but careless affluence which distinguishes the style of the fair lessee."

The aficionado had his expectancy given a final fillip by an advertisement that seems to have been run first at Laura's theatre: "Laura Keene's theatre was closed on Saturday in order that the new piece [whatever it might be] might have the benefit of a full rehearsal by gaslight." Such a notice meant a theatre could afford the loss of one night's revenues. But to the reader it also meant that a theatre was going to serve up a finished article on opening night — not a penultimate practice for the paying public. Laura was so prepared for the audience on opening night that she invited the press to attend her final dress rehearsal for *The Seven Sisters*.

Going to Laura's theatre was intended by her and her staff to be gala. When you entered the lobby you were apt to see John Lutz, "the sprightly and jocund agent of the house, with that amiable smile, which is peculiar to his good-natured face." The auditorium was brightly lighted. Laura's theatre used programmes as well as playbills. The programme was part "fan magazine" and part bill of the play.

The spectator knew the play would stay within time, because Laura's theatre was noted for concerning itself with commuters. To accommodate a change in ferry schedules, the theatre responded,

Notice Change of Time

Doors open at a quarter past Seven o'clock;
to commence ten minutes before Eight to meet
the wishes of many Ladies and Gentlemen who
reside at Newburg, Brooklyn, Jersey City,
Williamsburg, Newark, etc. The Performance
will end at half-past Ten o'clock.

You might not get to the theatre when the doors opened, but you did try to get there early enough to hear the orchestra of Thomas Baker. He was a contributor to the habitué's delight. "They applauded when Mr. Baker came in," the *Times* reported, "cheered when he sat down, and fairly yelled when he made that peculiar bow which exposes the excessive baldness of his musical cranium to the gaze of a delighted public." Another paper called him "the most popular conductor we have in this country." It claimed that "when persons have been in doubt as to which theatre they would patronize . . . Baker's orchestra has frequently given Laura's theatre the choice. This she knows full well, and hence its excellence, Baker having *carte blanche* to make it all he wants it to be."

His theatricality and his emphasis upon elegance matched that of Laura's. He introduced the use of the baton in conducting a theatre orchestra in the United States, and under the elegant ebony and gold baton presented to him by the Laura Keene orchestra, his overtures were a skillful blend of familiar entertainment with mood-setting, story-telling preparation for the play. Each year he could be counted on for original compositions which either enhanced the play or enhanced the reputation of the manager. Over the years he wrote "Laura's Linnet, A Polka" (1857), "The Laura Keene Waltz" (1861), and "The Laura Keene Mazurka" (1862). "Our American Cousin Polka" was joined in the ranks of hit tunes by the New Ibernian Quadrilles played for *Jeanie Deans*.

Baker was just right for Laura and her theatre. She, who could play the piano well enough to appear in public as a pianist, was

In this silverprint by Charles Fredericks, Laura resembles the woman of the MIRROR'S *romantic retrospective of 1887, "Her figure was good, and but for a rather pronounced nose, her features were regular; clear, deep blue eyes, hair inclined to auburn."* THE NATIONAL PORTRAIT GALLERY, SMITHSONIAN INSTITUTION remarkable for her interest in what music could do. In a time before radio, television, and the phonograph, she had acquired a knowledge of music that ranged as widely as her knowledge of art. She made use of folk songs and balladry in the plays of her theatre, she performed burlesques of opera favorites, she approved Baker's selection of music from church to concert. She used music every way she could to enhance the spectator's joy. For a theatre with a motto "ever gay," Baker wrote an extremely popular polka, "Bobbing Along." He also wrote "Laughing Galop," which he used as his benefit song at Laura's theatre:

> *Laugh and be gay*
> *Drive dull care away, ha ha*
> *Come fill the sparkling cup*
> *Let's have a merry day, ha ha.*

The members of his orchestra were chosen for their ability to intensify the spell. A reporter related, "The clever clarinet imitated the intoxicated bagpipe, the house rang with thunders of approbation, as though the imitation of a bagpipe were the acme of human happiness." Baker's ebony baton, inlaid with gold, was a familiar sight to the playgoer. It was, to state the obvious, a magic wand.

ii

A ringing of the prompter's bell, and Baker's hands signaled quiet: the lights of the orchestra dimmed, lights in the hall were adjusted to the scene to be viewed on stage, and the curtain rose on what the spectator hoped was further enchantment. It was November 26, 1860, and the new play at Laura Keene's was about to begin.

The format of *The Seven Sisters* was that of British burlesque. Men took older women's parts; thus, Charles Peters, who had come into his own as Binney the Butler in *Our American Cousin,* played the part of Mrs. Pluto. Most of the time the language was in heavily accented rhyming couplets. And like all burlesque, what was visualized was far more important than what was said. Laura and Polly Marshall changed costumes for every scene.

The show-stopper in the first act was a mechanical miracle. Laura had somehow learned of a patented device which could ignite gas burners simultaneously. All the gas lights in the auditorium and on the stage dimmed completely out. Then in the darkness Laura's voice in her character of Diavoline was heard invoking the spirit of light. At the climax of her incantation all the lights burst forth simultaneously. Quite a stunt. Today, with electricity and switches, the effect is commonplace, but in Laura's day, when gas was still lighted in the home with a taper, the effect was magical. People in Laura's audience could see the lamp lighters in the streets, and, when they came early to the theatre, they could watch one of the stagehands lighting the chandelier and other stage lamps with a long pole.

Act II was climaxed by a distaff Zouave drill. No miracle, but a pleasing display of legs and precision movements. The sneer, "Many a dull play has been saved by a judicious and liberal display of nether limbs," could have been expected but it missed the point. The United States, which had reveled for years in military pageantry, was on the brink of hostilities. Feminine Zouaves doing a manual of arms added to the patriotic ferment and contributed nothing to war's alarums. "In these times of military excitement, we think we discover some of the whys, and wherefores of the popularity of this extraordinary performance," an editor commented two months after opening night. Later, when such drills became a part of the lives of most of the young men of the nation, there was amusement in seeing them so well done by women, the members of "the Laura Keene radiant Regiment," as it was called. In May, Colonel Ellsworth's New York Regiment of Zouaves was presented with a banner inscribed, "From Captain Laura Keene to her Brother Zouaves." Then after the North knew defeat, the disillusionment of the press could find outlet by reporting: "The Zouave corps there is so excellently drilled that it is proposed to transfer . . . officers of the company to our volunteer army at Washington."

The big moment of the evening, of course, was *The Birth of the Butterfly*. Blasé New Yorkers applauded the scene on opening night until the curtain was raised again and they were permitted to view the scene to their fill. "Emerald light, water clear as crystal," a reviewer rhapsodized, "water lilies, fern leaves, revolving pillars, in short everything which could increase the grace of the lines or the luxury of the colors, were welded by the genius of the scene painter into one brief and delicate vision of fairy land." Uncertain reviewers commented that the water scene was achieved by a piece of plate glass or a mirror, but how it was done was as much a part of the delight at Laura's as what was done. And for that age, much of the delight was the cost of the illusion. Laura advertised, and the press reported, that the glass cost $2,000 and the whole scene $1,000 more. To exhibit the illusions, the theatre employed forty stagehands. Once it was a hit, and belatedly thinking of infringement by competitors, Laura published an announcement the first week in December:

Miss Keene takes this method of informing
the public and the profession generally that
the final scene of the Seven Sisters has been
patented as a mechanical invention. In ad-
dition to which the piece has been copyrighted
in the usual manner. Managers out of the city
wishing to produce the piece may apply in
writing to Miss Laura Keene at the Theatre,
624 Broadway.

*Milnes Levick had
been a younger
member of Laura's
company since
Varieties days. He
continued to act with
her off and on until her
death. He played
Laura's sailor beau in*
OUR AMERICAN
COUSIN. THOMAS
BAKER SHEET MUSIC,
LIBRARY OF CONGRESS.

With such a display, what did people matter? But there again the New York play-goer could expect delight. Laura's theatre, as a stock company playing no stars, worked for balance among the actors. It might discover a person capable of stardom and send him out to future success — Laura's theatre was a highly regarded finishing school — but the public was led to expect proficiency throughout the ranks. The public was also prepared to accept as commonplace Laura's exploitation of actor skills which had hitherto gone unnoticed. Actors were used as singers, dancers and variety performers to the advancement of their careers and the complete enjoyment of the spectators. In *The Seven Sisters,* J. G. Burnett, who was really a stage manager, became a deeply moving singer in his role of Cuffee, the slave. Milnes Levick did such a takeoff of Sothern as Lord Dundreary that he later played the Dundreary role in Broadway performances. The women were all beautiful. This was attested to by nearly every reporter. "Mrs. J. H. Allen, whose pretty pout has grown more saucy than ever." . . . "Plump and pretty Mrs. Chanfrau" . . . "Miss Melvyn, with golden ringlets, great blue eyes, and a sadly saucy way of putting her head always on one side" . . . "Miss Sara Stevens . . . a timid, sweet-spoken, gentle creature" . . . "Mrs. Lottie Hough is a terror as well as an attraction. She has made a specialty of that vile abomination, the stage Yankee Girl, and is probably its best representative. Smart, quick of apprehension, with snapping eyes, and a voice that goes through one like a rapier. . ."

Leading the company in *The Seven Sisters* were Polly Marshall and Mrs. W. H. Leighton. Miss Marshall, who had been on the stage since a child of two in 1815 — it is now 1860, remember — played one of the sisters and did a shadow dance. She was thought to be indelicately dressed in one scene. Mrs. Leighton eventually took over

Laura's role. "The lady more than fills the part," a *Spirit of the Times* reporter wrote, "Not because she is a size or two larger, but because she throws more life into the part, and enlivens it with a dash and aplomb."

As critic after critic said, the various parts added up to "just what the Public Taste wanted — glorious scenery, pretty women, patriotic nonsense." "Pretty women, low neck dresses, finely shaped legs," — "the hidden mysteries of alabaster bosoms." There were matinees on holiday afternoons to help accommodate those eager to see the scintillating production.

"All the time," the *Clipper* said, "Mr. Lutz stands in a happy condition — ready, on one side, to disburse the needful, and on the other, astonished by the daring spirit of the fair one with the golden locks."

iii

One of the play's conceits was the introduction of Diogenes with his lantern looking for a hero who could save the Union. When the run began James Buchanan was president, and his efforts to keep the peace were described as "boot blacking and whitewashing, kicking the bucket and turning a little pale." As the political climate worsened the dialogue of the play improved.

Enter in my magic glass
Demagogues of Dissolution,
Face the shades of Revolution.
For union, cheer with cheer sublimely blending.
From heath to hill, from hill to heaven ascending.

The part of Diogenes, played by T. B. Johnson, was constantly rewritten and diminished as secession became a fact: it was finally eliminated from the script when Johnson became fatally ill. The device of the incantation was substituted for Diogenes to help hold the various parts of the production together.

The changing scenario reflected the changing times. A successful Yankee performer, Ben Rogers, was added to the company, and a new second act, "Uncle Sam's Magic Lantern," with Rogers playing Uncle Sam, was added on February 11, subsequent to a convention of the seceded states in Montgomery, Alabama, on February 4.

This melange of tableaux and newspaper-inspired dialogue eventually evolved into an entertainment form like the Ziegfeld's Follies, with Ben Rogers playing the sort of role for Laura that Will Rogers played for Ziegfeld. Speaking of letting the Southern states go with nothing but regret, as many a Northerner was suggesting, "Uncle Sam" says that to accept secession is to submit.

> Shall it be forgotten
> That King George failed to make us submit, and so shall
> King Cotton?

Elsewhere in the same act, South Carolina is chided for calling itself a sovereign state but still using United States postage stamps.

The changing temper of the times can be read in manuscript revisions of the play. By late March the damsel representing South Carolina talked of the Palmetto flag which waved over Charleston harbor. She was answered by the Goddess of Liberty,

What a nice figure you'd cut in the seas
When the stars and stripes float no more in the breeze;
When instead of the pennant that sheltered Decatur,
From the trembling masthead hails the bloodless Palmetto.

The *Clipper* reported that this verse was the signal for a storm of hisses, then a burst of applause, "to be succeeded in turn by hisses, the latter, in the end, carrying the day. Yet amidst the war of the factions there were no harsh words used . . . Could the same have occurred, and with the same results in South Carolina or any of the other seceding states?"

After the firing on Fort Sumter, the *Clipper* editorialized, "Secessionists will not be allowed the same latitude to perfect their treason in the North that they heretofore have had. They will now have to carry civil tongues in their heads, and the gang who have been in the habit of attending Laura Keene's Theatre, to applaud secession sentiments, will do well to 'hold their hush' in future. Miss Keene has been compelled, in deference to change in public sentiment, to change her tactics. On Saturday evening last, she found it necessary to omit certain inflammatory passages in the text of the 'Seven Sisters.' It was well, perhaps, that she came to such a conclusion. It would be better were she to dispense with the entire second act as now given. The conflicting sentiments and tableaux in that act cannot but have a tendency to excite the worst passions of men already excited by the fearful news from Charleston." A week later the same writer noted that "Laura has curtailed some of the disunion sentiment and taken on a little more of the present Northern sentiment."

Even though Fort Sumter fell to the Confederacy and President Lincoln called for volunteers, the war continued to partake of the musical comedy atmosphere of Laura's Zouave drill. Then that all changed. Col. Elmer Ellsworth, who had received Laura's flag, as from one romantic figure to another, and who was the president's good friend, attempting to remove a Confederate flag which tauntingly waved in view of the White House, was killed by an Alexandria, Virginia, hotel keeper carrying a shotgun. Ellsworth's body lay in state in the White House. The war no longer could be rhymed and sung.

Laura decided to keep the house open and play her show. Business was as variable as the headlines. Bad news from the South meant bad news at the box office, but she kept the theatre going, partly as a service to the home front. Many wars later, American society now takes for granted the need for USO, Army shows, combat-zone entertainers, and benefits for war-derivative causes. These uses of entertainment had to be discovered. Laura began to make free seats available to soldiers in uniform. She gave a benefit for the families of New York volunteers. It did not provide very much, but in the early days of the war it looked large.

Few people had time for entertainment in the hot summer months of May and June, but those visitors to the city who were unhappily stranded there, or those countrymen in uniform waiting to move out, could spend an evening at Laura's theatre if they so desired. No other legitimate theatre was open.

But after Bull Run, on July 21, 1861, nothing could draw. Laura finally closed on August 10.

iv

September 27 Laura was back with *The Seven Sons*. "This incomprehensible mass of dramatic nonsense has been arranged in three acts, without the slightest attempt at cohesion of plot or continuity of action," Laura's candid advertisements for the *Sons* read, "for the sole purpose of furnishing amusement and provoking laughter." She achieved her purpose, and although the *Sons* never had the run the *Sisters* had, it lasted until December.

During the run of *Sons* the transcontinental telegraph was completed, and Mason and Slidell, Confederate commissioners, were surrendered to the British.

Those events, and others as they occurred, were commented upon in *The Seven Sons,* where the formula which had proved so successful before was being repeated. "The applause which followed every telling hit announced that Miss Keene had not only selected popular subjects for her dialogue, but had hit to a nicety the current public opinion upon these subjects."

The build-up for opening night was the same. This time, however, the stories reported that Laura had spent over $7,000 for the grand, novel effects. Baker's music included a fairy minuet written for the occasion and a new military galop.

"But, hark!" a reviewer described opening night. "The prompter's bell, the audience settle like a church congregation after the text is read and prepare to see and hear; another tinkle, and up goes the curtain, disclosing a 'Dell in the Catskills.'"

The curtain rose at various other times to reveal "A Skating Scene in Central Park," "A Lake of Lilies with Fairies Rising Through the Waves," a mock drill of a collection of awkward recruits, a dance of polliwogs on the great looking glass, and a coral cave with a spiral staircase and even more pretty young women. There were the expected takeoffs of successful plays and burlesques of songs and people, the whole ending with a great "Watteau scene of Arcadian Nymphs reclining among their flock by the Mountain Torrent of Real Water!"

Our American Cousin was re-revived and lasted over a month. A new play was not added until February 22, 1862, when the theatre opened a play by Laura Keene herself, *The Macarthy.*

During the spring and fall, theatrical columns carried notes that Laura was indisposed. Her absence from *Seven Sisters* did not affect business; Mrs. Leighton had filled in capably. Her absence from *Seven Sons* was noticed, but her replacement was acceptable. Lotty Hough played Florence Trenchard in *Our American Cousin.* During those absences, Laura wrote *The Macarthy.*

This stock Irish play of spies, betrayal, arrest, courtmartial, pardon, and ultimate happiness kept the theatre going until May. Laura's triumph was in her directing. Since her version of the Battle of Bunker Hill, she had been improving her ability to duplicate actuality to such an extent that, in *The Macarthy,* "The fight represents the appearance of reality, from the ways in which the shillelaghs fly around, cracking a head here, disabling an arm there, and distributing 'ballyhoo' everywhere. There must be sixty or seventy faction men in the melee at once, and more exciting stage scrimmage we never saw upon any other stage. It's a beautiful row, and does one good to see it from a safe stand point," said a spectator.

v

In the days of *Our American Cousin,* when Rufus Blake had sat around doing nothing, Laura had nibbled at the problem of the unused stock actor during the long run. She thought she had a solution for it for the 1862-63 season: hire two companies and tour one.

Finding actors was simple. Most of the profession still in the United States was out of work. Some of the actors had entered service North and South, and others had left the country. Boucicault, Agnes Robertson, and Sothern, British citizens, had returned home; Jefferson had gone to Australia. So, although Laura might have difficulty finding persons of proven ability, getting two companies would be comparatively easy. Touring might be just as simple. To take a company to Ford's Theatre in Baltimore, as she proposed doing, would be possible because Ford could transfer his company, while Laura was in town, to the theatres he managed in Washington and Philadelphia. Taking a play to a theatre which had no resident company might be equally simple, if John Lutz could work out the leasing arrangements on a short-term basis. In short, what Laura was proposing for 1862-63 was multiple company production. It was a surprisingly successful innovation.

The season, 1862-63, began with old comedies suitable for touring with company one: *Old Heads and Young Hearts, She Stoops to Conquer, School for Scandal, Masks and Faces, Rachel the Reaper;* all standards, all challenging roles for her, all speaking of a simpler, more innocent time. Laura won an accolade any actor would be happy to receive for her production of *Masks and Faces:* "At the fall of the curtain I doubt if there was a person who didn't feel, in his enthusiasm, that he had witnessed one of the best performances that ever was given."

Before the season began, Laura had announced that the public might "look for a fairy spectacle got up in a style far exceeding anything . . . yet done. For this piece only, Mr. Lewis has been three months at work on scenery." *Blondette* was offered the public on Tuesday, November 22, after some nights of rehearsal.

The play's lineage could be read like a coper's stud book. Sired by *Seven Sons* out of *Seven Sisters*, out of *Novelty*, out of *Camp at the Union*. Its difference was cost. *Blondette's* scenery was advertised as having cost $10,000. It followed the familiar formula: the first act ended with the Grotto of Love, the second act with the Palace of Lace, and the third with the Kingdom of the Magic Watch. The story was about a magic watch which the fairies could permit no one but the rightful owner to wind. "There are about thirty very pretty women among the *dramatis personae,* and about half a dozen funny men also," the *Herald* reported, "there are tricks and transformations and very nice songs."

Blondette was Emma Brougham-Robertson's responsibility. Emma would manage the company in New York, while Laura would head the touring company. Yes, Laura's teacher in England was again with her and putting her managerial skills to work. The *Clipper* waxed eloquent: "About a dozen years ago, Mrs. Emma Robertson (then Mrs. Brougham) first introduced to the public at Richmond Theatre, near London, that admirable actress since known as Laura Keene. The other evening, Mrs. Robertson appeared at Laura Keene's theatre in the city. With both ladies Old Father Time has laid his hand lightly and kindly, and although Mrs. R. was cast for a mother-in-law etc. we were glad to witness such a pleasing conjunction, for

Is all the counsel that we two have shared,
The sisters' vows, the hours that we have spent,

When we have chid the hasty-footed time
For parting us, — O, is all now forgot?
All school-days-friendship, childhood innocence?"

Laura's plan of two companies worked. Playgoers in the provinces knew about the contemporary New York theatre. They wanted to see popular successes. For her third week in Baltimore, Laura had extensive paraphernalia shipped down from New York in order to present *The Seven Sisters* with the original New York company and scenery.

She treated play-goers in Philadelphia, Brooklyn, Boston, Providence, New Haven, and Washington to some first-rate New York stock company productions. She found the provincial audiences — as she characterized them — responded to her dream of a theatre to which ladies of taste and refinement could repair; different from those of New York where, as the *Clipper* editorialized, "Burlesque and Burletta are Laura's Safe Cards."

It would be rewarding to play for them . . .

If she could get away . . .

If she could find a lessee for her theatre . . .

The week following the January 1 release of President Lincoln's Emancipation Proclamation, John Duff, of the firm of Crook and Duff, made an offer to buy the Laura Keene Theatre. She permitted him to pick up the lease immediately, so long as he let her complete her theatrical season.

Her eagerness to be gone is shown by the manner of her going. She discharged half of her double company. Two of the group bought an advertisement to protest the action. Laura tartly responded. Again the problem was the inadequacy of the old contract form for the kind of theatre Laura was pioneering. A contract was for the length of a season, but how long was a season? The courts finally ruled, about

Mathew Brady, the renowned Civil War photographer, made this studio likeness of Laura Keene sometime in 1864. She is shown in outdoor costume, VIDE her gloves. Contemporary etiquette books stressed that a lady never walked or drove abroad without them and that they must be buttoned before she stepped out of her door. THE NATIONAL PORTRAIT GALLERY, SMITHSONIAN INSTITUTION

fifteen months later, that a season was 40 weeks. How many matinees could a manager schedule? The disaffected actors had played matinees on Thanksgiving and Christmas, but had "refused to act on New Year's afternoon — that day conceded as a universal holiday even by the most exacting task masters."

Her staff speeded her departure, advertising, "Specialties which must be produced in rapid succession to enable Miss Keene not only to oblige her New York patrons but to furnish herself with novelties for the great Provincial Starring tour."

The final novelty was *Tib, or The Cat in Crinoline.* It was said that the authors "had purr-puss-ly" written a play about a cat so that there could be "loud cat-erwauling and loud mews-ic" from Thomas Baker. The play was like its advertising, a cat-astrophe. No one could resist the compulsion to pun. The *Clipper* called it the "veriest mass of Tom Foolery that we have ever seen presented. We were really annoyed to see Laura Keene in such a position and trust never again to see her take such a part, so utterly unworthy of a lady of her talent. . . ."

The *Programme* for May 4, advertising *Tib*, carried this note: "— Miss Laura Keene, in presenting this her last production in the scope of all her former triumphs, begs to assure her patrons that no expense has been spared in placing it upon the stage in a manner worthy of their patronage, or of that reputation, which she has studied so hard for seven years to obtain, and which, she is proud to add, has been so liberally accorded to her. The piece can be played but a few nights, Miss Keene being already due to Philadelphia, where she will commence her farewell engagements in the provinces previous to her departure for Europe. This will, therefore, be most positively THE LAST WEEK OF THE SEASON."

Laura closed *Tib* after opening night. The Laura Keene Theatre closed the next day.

"Thus passed," George C. Odell wrote in his *Annals of the New York Stage*, "from the New York theatre one of the most talented, energetic and delightful actresses ever concerned in its history. A poem of epic proportions should have marked the exit; so far as I can see, hardly a ripple disturbed the placid waters of the bay."

vi

Why did Laura give up her theatre? She never said.

Most of her intimates suggested poor health. Her family had a history of consumption. Her regimen, everyone agreed, was enough to try the strongest physique. She missed a great many performances of *Seven Sisters*. The following year, during *Seven Sons*, she was in and out of the company from November through April. She would get up, go back, then suffer a relapse. It was reported at one point that "her recovery was deemed improbable."

Her health on occasion had affected her performing. The writer who welcomed Mrs. Leighton to the Diavoline role in *Seven Sisters* did so because she "enlivens it with a dash and aplomb which Miss Keene parted with several years ago." Each year she sat for a new photograph to satisfy the suppliers of "pictures of your favorite actress." When placed in chronological order, they tell a story of increasing bone-weariness, or perhaps to a more practiced eye a story of developing illness.

Death was never far away those months of 1862. A friend, Matilda Pullan, named Laura co-executrix of her will, leaving at her death in February a ten-year-old son. Laura and Lutz and their lawyer, William Booth, were responsible for him for years.

To make it possible for Matilda Heron to accept a road tour in the spring and summer of 1862 when there weren't too many jobs, Laura and Jane, her mother, took Matilda's four-year-old daughter into the Keene home. While she was with them, the youngster contracted and succumbed to one of those nineteenth-century childhood fevers. Jane with Laura's help was responsible for the melancholy arrangements and eventually for consoling the distraught mother.

The melancholy events of this war-time spring caused John Lutz to rethink his responsibilities to the Keene household. His relationship with Laura was the good fortune of her life. When the reviewer spoke of Matilda Heron as a western steamboat with an explosion imminent, and Laura as a graceful yacht, he was describing the difference Lutz made. Laura could have, and would have, overfueled the boilers of her creative life and might have ended as physically and financially wrecked as Matilda Heron. With John Lutz's loving concern she ended quite differently. The major decisions of her career were hers: she chose the plays, she was responsible for the theatrical and mechanical creations, she coached the rising stars, she conceived the innovations. But he found the funds and kept the whole enterprise on the ground. He was the perfect executive officer.

He was concerned from the first with Laura's extravagances. When they had the funds, he raised little objection to her expenditures, but when they didn't have the wherewithal, Laura spent just as freely. They had bought an insurance policy on Laura as soon as they had any surplus, and John Lutz saw to it that it was kept in force and that payment for it fell to her lawyer, William Booth, if anything should happen to him.

He needed something like that to assure Laura of an income, spend as she might, if he should not be around to rescue her. He had no status legally, therefore he needed the lawyers, and they in turn said he needed his brother.

Lutz's relations with his brother were as remarkable as all the relations of the Keene melange. Francis A. Lutz, a pillar of the Methodist Church of Washington, D. C., a successful dealer in leather goods, a wealthy man of substance and influence in the nation's capital, accepted Laura Keene into his home, knowing her profession and antecedents. Such broad-mindedness was unknown in those days. Further, he was amenable to the idea advanced by the lawyers that he and his wife, Mary Ann, help in the establishment of a trust for Laura, Emma and Clara; a trust so set up that should Laura's husband, Henry Wellington Taylor, appear, he could not make a claim on Laura's estate; neither could John Lutz's daughter, Adelaide, now a ward of her uncle Francis, make a claim upon the trust as part of her father's estate. The trust avoided all the difficulties about relationship of Laura to the girls or Lutz to Laura.

The first asset placed in this trust was a four-story brick house, Number 34 Bond Street, valued at $17,000. The deed was signed the same day the trust became effective, December 18, 1863. Or, signed just three weeks before John Duff made an offer for the Laura Keene Theatre.

vii

Would Laura have left her New York theatre because she had been ill? Because she had been brushed by mortality?

Two of her biographers suggested that she left New York because she had grown tired of managerial labor. This could be true. She did wear herself out each season. But the responsibility and labor of keeping a touring company going is only slightly less taxing, and she continued with this for the next ten years.

More to the point, Laura may have grown tired of her particular kind of management. She may have viewed the continued production of spectacular burlesque with dismay. She who had wanted to be a force for refinement had made her national reputation as a purveyor of mindless amusement. For the rest of her life, she played the classic comedies and domestic dramas she tried to make successful in New York. Bayard, who had written about her theatre for years, said, "When she began in this city as a manager, at the Metropolitan, her inclination for 'legitimate drama' was liberally manifested in the selection of a company unrivaled even by Mr. Wallack, and the production of regular comedies in the most excellent style. But the public taste was rapidly setting in favor of Sensational play, and, after struggling a long time, at the loss of much money, she gave up the fight, and went over to the new style. It was too bad to see her ranting the wretched trash of the 'Seven Sisters', etc.; she who is so true an artist in the very best characters of high comedy and pathetic drama. But she was not much to blame; the public would not have Legitimacy at any price; while they would trample each other in struggling through her doors to see some flimsy spectacle; and as that, and that only would pay, she made virtue of necessity."

Laura may have come to question the morality of what she was doing. Was she comfortable with a reputation for exhibiting flesh?

Her production of *The Seven Sisters* had inspired some magnate to name a popular brothel Seven Sisters. The rumor was widespread in the early 1860s that the hotel over the front of Laura Keene's Theatre was a house of assignation. Was she with her extravaganzas contributing to the atmosphere in which the brothel's existence was accepted? "At this moment it is not very respectable to be a woman at the head of a theatre in New York," she wrote to her lawyer, William Booth. "That state of things will pass, and then I may be allowed to enjoy life (not exist in slavery as I formerly did)."

Laura's feelings went much deeper. She had been recently accepted into the Roman Catholic Church, a convert of Archbishop Hughes, according to her daughters, who converted with her. The depth of the experience can be inferred in her later actions. When her skill — as represented by *Seven Sisters* — might have given her a vehicle capable of competing with and financially profiting from the popularity of *The Black Crook,* the money-making burlesque of 1869, Laura ignored the possibility.

And always, she ached with the hurt of war. As a woman, there was little she could do. She had no sons or brothers in service. Although only a few actors were in uniform, countless young men she had known in all the walks of life her theatre touched were in the lines. No sensitive person could read the printed lists of casualties in the papers — bloody rosters from Antietam, Fredericksburg, Manassas, Chancellorsville, Shiloh, Donelson, Vicksburg — without crying out. When man is so dreadfully mad, how can one frivol in a play? When playing is all one knows to do, or when one feels that art is important, one conceivably could — as Edwin Booth was doing — play Hamlet, but *Seven Sons? Blondette?* There was no philosophy of escapism during the Civil War to comfort the entertainer; there was, instead, a strong Puritanism that flayed the wanton. Did Laura dream of the dead Ellsworth with his banner "From Captain Laura Keene . . ."? The times were such that she might. Her temperament was such that she could.

A touring star would know that Ford's New Theatre was new as of August 27, 1863 and that its capacity was 2,500. What no one could have known was that it would be closed as a theatre from April 14, 1865 until its restoration one hundred years later, or that it would become an historical shrine. COURTESY OF THE FORD THEATRE.

Chapter 9

Other Theatres, Other Ways

. . . see the players well bestowd . . . they are
the abstracts and brief chronicles of the time . . .
SHAKESPEARE, *HAMLET,* ACT II, SCENE 2

Touring is either a series of performances interrupted by travel, or continuous travel punctuated by theatrical performances. It is a series of impressions of the same thing in different and confusing arrangements. The train is the same but the locomotive heads in a different direction and it is on a different track. The hotel room one week is on one floor and the next week on a different floor, up a different flight of stairs, which is carpeted in a different color, and around a different corner, with the potted palm over there . . . but the room looks depressingly like the room of yesterday . . . or was it day before yesterday?

From December 1, 1862, until July 4, 1873, Laura spent only a few hours a day, on the days she acted, in the theatre. The rest of her time was spent in depots, trains, boats and hotels.

During her first year of traveling, the winter and spring season of 1862-63, she played with her own company and she played long stands: three weeks in Baltimore, two separate visits of two weeks in Philadelphia, two weeks in Boston and Washington, and stops of from one to ten days in Providence, Lowell, Albany, Hartford, New Haven and Brooklyn. She presented a varied program of plays, six of the old comedies, four domestic dramas from her own theatre's repertoire, and two spectacles.

In those days, every town in the hinterland had a resident stock company which could fill all parts except one, the part of the visiting star. The star journeyed across the United States playing a limited repertoire of roles, supported by everything from blanket Indians, to enlisted army troopers, to actors. The spectator paid to see Edwin Booth or Matilda Heron or whoever the star might be, and cared little what else happened. Frequently the spectator scaled the heights with the star and plumbed the depths with the supporting company. Early managers were full of stories about producing tragedies with supernumeraries. Sol Smith, father of the Mark Smith in Laura's company, told of presenting the tragedy of Rolla — all about the Incas — with "twenty-four Creek Indians (to furnish their own bows, arrows and tomahawks) at fifty cents each." Every town with a stock company could also report the fiascos of drunken or overwrought or worn-out stars.

Star appearance had everything but aesthetic considerations to recommend it. The traveling star had only herself to get to the train. She was encumbered by her own luggage only. She could adapt to special situations. If the actress had always made her entrance through an archway center, and the stage in the army camp was only eight feet deep, she could adjust to come in from either side. She could, by a hand under the elbow, push or steer a leading man about the stage, keeping him out of the way and herself in the limelight.

If your ideal of theatre was different, as Laura's was, the audience might get more, but the local theatre manager and the touring manager would work disproportionately hard to achieve it. A full house is a full house, however secured. The local manager is always looking for the one-man-show which fills his buildings. There is a maximum profit for the performer and the manager in such an arrangement. The next highest profit is to be made in the visit of the star who doesn't care about his support or its appearance so long as it "stands back out of the way." The riskiest proposition is bringing in an entire company acting in plays no one ever heard of. The manager who ran a star theatre could claim he presented the world's greatest actors in the world's greatest drama. The manager who booked a traveling company took a chance even on the suitability of the play.

Laura attempted the high-risk, low-yield tour. Laura believed in the ensemble; in the interplay of seasoned performers familiar with every aspect of the production. To achieve this effect on the road she toured her company complete with costumes, properties, and scenery. She immediately began to encounter difficulties. To get her scenery in and out of theatres, it had to be rebuilt. When she attempted *The Seven Sisters* in Baltimore she used local dancers in the Zouave drill. They didn't measure up to her New York company. Call them what you would, they were supernumeraries brought into the theatre to play a particular show. She was back to the gaucheries of feathered Indians in the tragedy of *Rolla,* only she had just brought along more scenery and more supporting actors. The result, unfortunately, was the same.

Few of her difficulties were anticipated. Her first arrangements with local managements were typified by this memorandum, "Miss Laura Keene & her company of six people agree to play at the Howard Theatre Boston commencing on Monday Jan 19th 1863 for two weeks and Miss Laura Keene to receive one half the gross receipts nightly."

The problems which arose from such an agreement can be inferred by a similar contract between Miss Keene and a theatre manager seven years later. Laura, then, was to supply the company and to receive one half the gross receipts, but what the local manager was to do was specified: "The party of the second part agrees to furnish house, gas, heating and cleaning — the regular daily advertising — usher and door keepers — carpenters and night hands — orchestra — one three sheet poster — & programmes for day and night — also to pay for all posting and distributing of the same."

Each of those items might make a story of Laura's painful discovery about the road. Her bitter-won experience became the commonplace of theatrical business in later years.

"Mr. Lutz walked miles and miles Friday and Saturday endeavoring to learn where you were," she wrote to an actor in 1865. Lesson — from now on, every actor must tell us where he is going to stay in advance and if he changes locations he must, *must,* let us know.

"If you had given us a warning of the slightest nature on Friday we could have been prepared but getting your letter only one hour before starting. . . ." Lesson — a letter loses at least twenty-four hours; a telegram permits us to know immediately.

"Will you kindly telegraph *we* will pay here. . . . Should you be able to come — still telegraph. . . . Well, telegraph, telegraph." Lesson — impress on the actors how important it is to keep us informed.

She and John Lutz early learned that they must buy the tickets; otherwise actors could be left behind at the ticket windows when the train pulled out. As late as 1870 she had to delay her opening in St. Paul because her leading man missed the train in Chicago. They learned to move the baggage and not leave it up to the individual performer. Within a few years, neatly lettered notices appeared on call boards:

Kindly give all hotel addresses to the stage
door-keeper during this Evening's Performance
so that the baggage will be all collected on
Sunday.

The Co. leaves on Sunday morning by the Fall
River Line boat. Anyone desiring staterooms
can reserve same themselves.

The members of this Co. will please have the
Hotel baggage READY and DOWNSTAIRS
at 10 o'clock
Sunday, A. M. Theatre Baggage, after performance
Saturday night.

They did learn. Each experience became a part of the *modus operandi* of the future.

Scenery once rebuilt and many times moved looked so shabby it could not be used again, the Lutz-Keene touring company learned. They also learned that every theatre had stock sets more or less adequate and that local scene painters would prepare special effects if given the information in advance. Most theatres could provide painted drops and cutout wing pieces. As Laura and her associates became familiar with the accommodations at the theatre, they could plan better what and how to do the next time they played there. She probably sent little pencilled diagrams ahead to local managers, showing where she preferred doors, archway, and fireplace. Dion Boucicault did, so it is safe to assume that Laura did.

No one can travel far with responsibilities at home. Although Laura had taken Emma and Clara with her when she had been on the road with the Keene company on other occasions, it was deemed inappropriate to take them now in wartime. Also, the girls were getting on; Emma was eighteen and Clara fifteen: if they were to have any formal schooling, it should be now.

Boarding school was the answer. The cordial relationship between John Lutz and his brother Francis helped. The only place for the girls, everyone agreed, would be the Ladies' Academy of the Visitation, Georgetown. Francis Lutz's daughter Mamie, would be entering along with Laura's children. Francis's home would serve as a second home for Emma and Clara in case of an emergency. For Laura, the Academy had an additional virtue it did not have in Francis's eyes. He, a good Methodist, thought of the academic and social value of the experience; Laura, the new Roman Catholic convert, thought of the spiritual value as well. To be admitted, the girls must be recommended, and Francis would take care of that; there would also need to be, if possible, an interview with a parent or guardian.

Laura probably made the application while her company was performing in Washington in March. The drive from downtown across Rock Creek Bridge would have been beautiful at that time of year. The Academy would have impressed her. It was described in a city directory of the time, as being "upon the declivity of one of the beautiful heights of Georgetown. The handsome range of buildings appropriated for the ladies' academy is of brick. The buildings occupy part of the side of an oblong square, an area of four or five acres, a portion of which is a play-ground for the scholars, and the remainder a botanical garden.

There are other large edifices on the same square, the Bishop's residence, an elegant church, the convent, and charity schools."

Laura could have been nervous as she stood at the entrance door, waiting to be admitted. Once she was inside the main entrance, the nervousness would increase, because she then stood in an entry with a closed door to the right, another to the left, and the door she had come through behind her. An eye at a peephole in the door before her acknowledged her presence, there was the far-off sound of a bell, and the door to her right clicked open. Laura knew that the Nuns of the Visitation were cloistered, but still it must have come as a shock never to see the person talking with her. In the reception room. Laura sat at a table-high shelf with the headmistress on the other side, separated by a wooden grill covered with cloth that reached to the ceiling. On later occasions, Laura would use the rotating wheel set in the wall to leave packages for the girls, she would learn to call it a *tour*, but on this first visit, as romantic as she was, she must have had memories of novels in which a foundling was placed on the turning wheel and left for the nuns to rear. She surely felt overdressed and overindulged. The simplicity of the reception room was an earnest of a way of life.

Emma and Clara were admitted as "private pupils," so that they could elect subjects rather than take the prescribed curriculum. Emma took dancing and both girls studied piano, harp, drawing and French, as well as religion and literature. Since it was wartime, the girls could remain throughout the year, although the regular session was supposed to end in mid-July.

It is interesting to speculate on the girls' acceptance in such a school. Laura, when she enrolled them, was not their mother but their guardian. But how did Emma and Clara account for their connection with the theatre? "One didn't know stage people, one couldn't speak to them, nor shake hands with them, nor even look at them except from a safe distance across the footlights," a schoolgirl of that era wrote. Surely young women of the Academy were shocked by Emma, who left on occasion to act with her mother and then would return to the serenity of the Academy's chaste halls.

With the girls safely at school, Laura and her company went west the second year of touring. She was going to do without her own scenery. She had been told that it was expensive to take a full company when local actors could fill in adequately. But she remembered so vividly what it was like playing with stock actors in California that she carried a nucleus company which could support her and establish the ensemble effect she desired. She would experiment with the small company in Albany, Cincinnati, Nashville, Louisville, St. Louis, and Chicago.

When she started on the road with her "New York Company" she had to learn about boxcars for scenery, baggage cars for costumes and personal possessions; and the types of passenger cars. She also had to learn about connecting lines, layovers, and transfers.

She learned about the railroads as she had earlier learned about the theatre, by hard-won experience.

That first year, 1862-63, the company traveled to cities near enough New York that day coaches could move the company Keene. Laura's troupe was not big enough to fill a single car; therefore she was thrust into cars with others who couldn't be intimidated by her imperious sniffs at "Tobacco!" or be bullied by her fastidious withdrawing of the hems of her garments. Day coaches in America were awash with chewing tobacco spittle. The experienced traveler learned never to put anything under his seat. The men sat either with their feet on the seat of the empty chair ahead, or their knees pushed into the back of the chair ahead if it were occupied. Women wrapped their skirts around them and brought boxes or bricks or some object that would lift their feet above high tide. An English theatrical associate remarked, "Even in the event of dropping money on the floor, no decent person could venture to wade through the stream of saliva floating thereon, unless he put on an old glove."

Filth was a commonplace of the times. Virtually no streets were paved; horses and men stirred the roads to dust in the dry weather, balled it into mud in wet, and achieved clean going only on the frozen snow. Locomotives burned wood or coal and there was a constant shower of sparks, ash, soot, clinkers, and dust falling on the cars. In the summer when the windows were open, the careful traveler tried to keep the blinds drawn to deflect the stream of dirt. In the winter, the dirt from outside sifted in through the rattling windows, but it was never noticed in the fume and reek of the coal-burning stoves set in each car.

Travelers relished the opportunity for constant refreshment. Butcher boys sold gum drops, fruit, and mints. The trains stopped frequently for the convenience of passengers who were given time to eat in the restaurants or lunch rooms in the stations. The train New York to Boston stopped at Berwick for habitués to have sponge cake. In all seasons but winter the railroads furnished free ice water to passengers. A boy brought around a pitcher and glasses. Experienced travelers not only took a drink but could manage a sponge bath with a second helping. Experienced travelers, and Laura soon became one, learned in winter time to move about the car. The stoves were filled at the beginning of a journey, but no one had time to stoke or replenish them en route, so they glowed white early and died out completely before one's destination was reached. To avoid catching a cold, the wary actress would move forward in the coach as the fire burned down, thus approximating a constant temperature.

Her theatre traveling covered the period in which sleeping car berths evolved. Her first sleeping accommodations were made up by a brakeman. He turned over every alternate seat-back, dividing the car into a series of compartments or near-compartments. Then in each section he fitted from seat to seat a base of boards thinly upholstered, and arranged thereupon the sheets, blankets, and pillows. A slightly longer platform, similarly padded, rested on the backs of the car-seats and formed the upper berth. He hung around three sides of the sections flimsy and dingy curtain of some cotton stuff; and lowers and uppers were ready. Laura found what rest she could on what we would call the most primitive of pallets.

Boat travel was more pleasant. From her second year on, she never played a season without some journey by boat. Down the Ohio from Cincinnati to Louisville, down the Mississippi from Memphis to New Orleans, or upstream to St. Louis. Across the lakes from Cleveland to Detroit and down the upper reaches of the Mississippi in Iowa and Illinois. She traveled the southern circuit sailing from New York to Savannah or Charleston.

Other travelers give accounts of discomfort and frontier crudeness; there is no hint from Laura that she took anything amiss. Mosquitoes, the plague of some visitors, she never mentions; the verminous hotels are treated like the others, places to spend the night; the jolting railway cars, the damp cabins, the soot and sparks from train and steamer engines draw no mention from her. Her strongest comment is about mid-western summer heat, "The weather is enough to drive one to become a fish."

The touring actress had an array of trunks, boxes, and baskets. Surely Lutz saw to it that Laura had the finest matched sets of leather luggage family influence could provide. How much luggage? Olive Logan was moving about with nine trunks. Laura would have had more.

The piano photographed here was displayed in the now defunct Chickering Historical Piano Exhibit as Laura Keene's. Whether it was or not, Chickering & Sons President said no one could attest. This piano was destroyed by fire. AUTHOR'S COLLECTION.

Laura on tour must have been as terrible as an army with banners. To her luggage she added a piano: one of her indulgences was the purchase of a Chickering upright. The initial cost, if she paid the advertised price was $500. It must have cost her many times that over the years as she had it moved with her from one town to the next.

Once arrived, the traveling company went through the ritual of collecting bags; registering at a hotel; settling into the room; going to the theatre; checking on the delivery of costumes, playbooks, lithographs and posters; finding the dressing room; learning the name of the doorkeeper; meeting the manager.

All towns were laid out on a similar plan: hotels were close to railroad stations, and theatres close to the hotels.

Playhouses were not alike. The Pence Opera House in Minneapolis was on the third floor. The dressing rooms in New Orleans dripped with water; those in Columbus, Ohio, were universally praised for roominess and comfort. Memphis was notorious for dust over everything backstage because the streets were laid with gravel. Pittsburgh was maligned for its soot. "Managers are warned against visiting Evansville, Ind., where they will find expenses very large and receipts small, with a stage so cold as to produce rheumatism and sore throat."

Most important to the touring company was the quality of the local manager. What kind of actors did he hire? Did he keep good performers and discipline bad ones? Did he keep them up to the mark? A star's rehearsal, or, as in Laura's case, a nucleus company's rehearsal, was valuable only if the local company had professional pride. If the parts had been cast in advance, the lengths distributed, the lines learned, then the time from ten in the morning until early afternoon could be profitably spent. With a good company, Laura claimed she barely had time to dine. "Rehearsal til two and three — costumes to arrange — etc., etc., to theatre at six." When the manager was derelict, the burden was proportionately greater. Some companies were so limited as to render the casting of pieces impossible. "I sent you my manuscripts and books, and was assured of full support. You know the number of people required; why are they not here?" She soon learned as much about local managers as she learned about local actors. Some were ineffective, some crooked, others able.

A crooked manager was a curse to the business. A manager who cheated the public gave the profession a bad name, but a manager who cheated actors destroyed the fabric which bound the profession together. A manager served as an intermediary between actors and the outside world. An actor used the resident theatre as his post office and his bank. He collected his mail from the doorkeeper, or treasurer. The manager cashed checks, wrote checks, or provided cash for the traveling performer.

Laura quickly had a roster of superior managers with whom she liked doing business and with some of whom she liked to perform. R. M. Field in Boston and John Ford in Washington were high on her list; James McVicker in Chicago and Ben DeBar in St. Louis were actors as well as managers, and they looked forward to her coming as she looked forward to her visit. Audiences had a treat on the occasions when McVicker played Asa Trenchard to Laura's Florence or DeBar played Sir Peter to Laura's Lady Teazle.

She observed the difficulties of managing in the hinterland and she tried to help those managers she liked. She became a play broker. She owned the rights to various plays; the managers needed new or varied bills. *Seven Sisters* and *The Macarthy* were hers by authorship and copyright. *The Elves, The Overland Route,* and *Rachel the Reaper* were hers by purchase and copyright. *Our American Cousin* was hers, but common property by confusion of the courts.

With these properties and the free time traveling provided, she attempted to consult with the managers she admired. She wrote them of the plays she had, suggesting specific plays for their individual needs. She negotiated by mail, she advised by mail. *Seven Sons* went to a theatre in San Francisco complete with drawings and models of machinery.

She made suggestions on how to get best results; she shared the thrill of success at long distance and then extended congratulations by mail. To the manager of the theatre rehearsing *Rachel the Reaper,* she wrote, "You must get your actors imbued with the spirit of the novel. [Charles Reade's *Clouds and Sunshine.*] They must read it tearfully, and understand Reade's meaning. The alterations I ventured upon, Mr. Reade saw and told me that for dramatic effect they were admirable." After the performance, she wrote, "I am glad 'Rachel' did so well."

She worked at increasing her stock of plays. She had much correspondence with Augustin Daly about plays he was sending for her consideration. Then she wrote another play of her own, to capitalize on the craze for scenery pieces and to enrich her play-broking business. It was *The Workmen of America.*

The Workmen were from wherever Laura was or the leasing manager produced. When she sold the rights to R. M. Field, it became *The Workmen of Boston;* when she sold the rights to P.T. Barnum, it became *The Workmen of New York.* She took out the copyright with multiple titles. She herself performed *The Workmen of Harrisburg, Cincinnati, Pittsburgh, Baltimore.*

A playbill was expected to serve two uses: act as an adjunct to the performance of the moment, and act as a notice of performances to come. For the current production it could be a simple list of cast, or cast and scenes; or it could be an elaborate description of scenery, plot development, and even production philosophy. As an announcement of coming attractions it was seldom more than a news item. University of Tulsa Theatre Collection.

FORD'S NEW THEATRE
TENTH STREET, ABOVE E.

MAX MARETZEK'S GRAND
ITALIAN OPERA!

POSITIVELY LAST NIGHT!
AND CLOSE OF THE FASHIONABLE SEASON.

THIS SATURDAY EVENING, APRIL 1, 1865,
Will be presented DONIZETTI'S MASTER-WORK,

DON SEBASTIAN!

Which will be presented in the most Superb Style, with New and Brilliant Costumes, Gorgeous Mise en Scene, New Properties and Appointments, Porcessions, Grand Ballet, and the

FOLLOWING GREAT CAST:

Zaida—the African..Carozzi Zucchi
Sebastian—King of Portugal..Massamillianni
Camoens—the Poet..Bellini
Giovanni—Grand Inquisitor..Susini
Abaialdo—an Arab Chief...Lorini
Ben Selim—Governor of Fez..Muller
Don Antonio—Brother of Sebastian...Reichardt
Don Luigi—Ambassador of Spain..Ximines
Don Enrico—Sebastian's Lieutenant..Lancione
Ladies and Gentlemen of the Court, Soldiers and Sailors of Portugal, Arab Soldiers and Women, Judges of the Supreme Court, Citizens, &c.

CONDUCTOR...Mr. CARL BERGMAN
Leader..Mr. Henry Appy
Stage Manager (Italian Opera).............................Signor Dubreul
Doors open at 7 o'clock.   To commence at 8 o'clock.

Mr. FORD takes great pleasure in announcing an engagement with

MISS LAURA KEENE

The Distinguished Manageress, Authoress, and Actress, on Monday Evening, April 3, when will be produced her New Sensational Play, written and adapted by Miss Keene, to the American stage, in three acts and twelve Tableaux, entitled

THE WORKMEN OF WASHINGTON

Will be produced, with New Local Scenery, by James Lamb: Novel and Peculiar Mechanism, by J. J. Gifford ; supported by John Dyott, Harry Hawk, and the Entire Stock Company.

She adapted the play during the months of December and January in the 1864-65 season, after she had concluded a successful engagement in Cincinnati. To the managers with whom she had dealt in the past, she gave first choice. To Field in Boston she wrote,

> The Workmen of Boston
> Or the Curse of Drink

> . . . It can be played with or without myself and company. It is now the sensation of London and Paris. It has been carefully rewritten by myself to suit America. All my stage knowledge has been employed to give the two grand scenic effects the elements of such a success as will create a genuine sensation. The story is simple, yet thrilling, the piece full of good parts, incidents, and fun. . . It must be played immediately in your city and I give your house the preference therefore an early reply will oblige.

The good news from the Union armies before Richmond gave the entertainment world bigger business, so Laura was happily buried in correspondence. She signed a typical contract with Grover & Sinn in Philadelphia for *The Workmen of Philadelphia*. It stipulated one hundred dollars for the first week and fifty dollars for each succeeding week until the sum of $500 had been paid, which gave them the sole right to the play in their city. What was untypical in such arrangements was Laura's solicitous attitude. She wrote from Baltimore: "In rehearsing the play here, one or two additional effects have suggested themselves to me, a stirring tableau for the end of the piece, etc., etc." A favorable letter from a spectator claiming that the play would "snatch you from the probationary list of irretrievable drunkards," was supplied managements who had purchased the play. To her own performances in Baltimore Laura added matinees for school children, announcing that "A note from any of the Teachers will be received at the door and admit the Scholar Free of Charge." She probably shared that ploy with managers too.

The only interruption of manic interest in *The Workmen* was a hurried trip to the lawyers while in Boston, to sign the deed for the purchase of another property for the trust Lutz had set up. It was a farm, Riverside Lawn, on the Acushnet river. A place suitable for spending the summer months, although they were still ahead. Now it was spring. The property looked full of promise, and so did the times.

The Northern armies were poised for the final blows in North Carolina and Virginia. Laura rushed back to the theatre to continue to promote *The Workmen*.

Typical of the arrangements with play-broker Laura Keene were those John Ford made for his theatre in Washington. He had James Lamb, his scenery painter, prepare drop curtains for "The Machine Shop at the Navy Yard," "The Seventh Street Wharf," "A Moonlight view of the Steam Ferry to Alexandria with view of the Capitol in The Distance," and "Brady's Gymnasium and Guard House." Typical of the arrangements with touring-company-star Laura Keene were suggestions incorporated in his letter to J. B. Wright, his stage manager: "I have just written a note to Miss Keene, stating that the 'Workmen' may not go advantageously more than one week. In that case I would like to do *She Stoops to Conquer, Rivals, School for Scandal,* etc. next week."

Laura the touring performer had learned to depend on the local manager's knowledge of his clientele. In Boston, *Workmen* ran two weeks, the only change of bill being Laura's appearance in *Our American Cousin* for her benefit on Friday. If Ford, who knew his business, thought *Workmen* would run only a week in Washington in April, he was probably right. She arranged with the stage manager to perform the plays Ford suggested, finishing off the second week with her benefit in *Our American Cousin*. Since that second week in April 1865 was Holy Week, business for something like *Workmen* might not be very good anyway.

Chapter 10

Good Friday, 1865

Confusion now hath made his masterpiece!
Most sacrilegious murder . . .
SHAKESPEARE, *MACBETH,* ACT II, SCENE 3

What happened next to Laura has been often told. The hours of President Lincoln's assassination and death have been ticked off minute by minute. The crime occurred during her appearance in *Our American Cousin.* It was an event in her life as unvolitional as her birth, but it became a part of the past with which she had to live as surely as if she had created the moment.

Good Friday morning at Ford's Theatre was like all such mornings when the touring star was presenting a different play for the evening. Harry Hawk, leading man and company manager, was conducting a rehearsal of *Our American Cousin.* Laura's skeleton copy of the play had been sent ahead to the stage manager, when the booking had been completed. He had made it available to the actors who needed to copy out their parts, and Hawk was now working from it with the actors grouped around, running through their lines. The actor assigned the part of Lieutenant Vernon was ill, so W. J. Ferguson, the callboy, was thrust into the role. More work for Hawk at rehearsal. Other than familiarize the company with the differences in Laura's version of the play, there was little to do at the run-through. Virtually every actor in

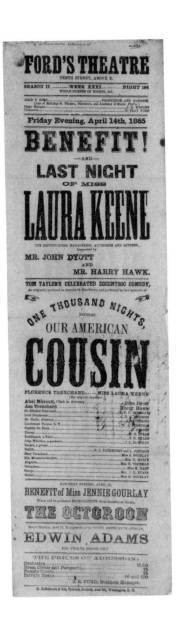

Such a playbill as this was included in the invitation to the Lincolns, if Dick Ford followed custom. A revision with the words of "Honour to Our Soldiers," was distributed at the theatre that night. After the assassination, there was a brisk trade in these bills and arrant forgeries. This authentic bill is from SPECIAL COLLECTIONS LIBRARY OF CONGRESS.

the United States had played in some version of the show; virtually every stagehand had worked it. The property man could recite, "In the third act of the 'American Cousin' there are seven scenes, the way Miss Keene plays it."

The leisurely routine was abruptly accelerated by news that the Lincolns and Grants were coming to the play that night. Young Ferguson was subjected to new pressures,

Harry Hawk needed to get word to Miss Keene of the president's visit, Professor Withers wanted to rehearse the company singing his patriotic song as soon as Laura's piano arrived at the theatre.

Dick and Harry Ford were in charge of the theatre in the absence of their brother John, who, since the fall of Richmond, had been in that city handling personal family matters. Dick Ford, hoping to impress John with his managerial skills, had invited the Lincolns for that night. He had left the invitation with a maid he knew would direct it to Mrs. Lincoln. He didn't know that the Lincolns had already reserved a box at Grover's Theatre or that "some time during the day Mrs. Lincoln learned that Laura Keene was to have a benefit and last appearance at Ford's and she requested Mr. Lincoln to change his destination."

A military equerry engaged the presidential box for the Lincolns stating that General and Mrs. Grant would be of the party. Dick Ford immediately busied himself writing notices for the afternoon newspapers. The two o'clock edition of the *Star* carried a series of advertisements hopefully calculated to arouse the public's interest in the evening's performance. One of them read, "'Honor to Our Soldiers,' A New and patriotic song and chorus has been written by Mr. H. B. Phillips, and will be sung this evening by the Entire Company to do honor to Lieutenant General Grant and President Lincoln and Lady, who will visit the Theatre in compliment to Miss Laura Keene, whose benefit and last performance is announced in the bills of the day. The music of the above song is composed by Prof. W. Withers, Jr."

Dick Ford also sent revised copy to the playbill printer and a copy of the words of Withers's song to be included on the bill.

Harry Ford was told of the White House reservation when he returned to the theatre after breakfast, about eleven-thirty. He and others stood around on the theatre steps in the warming thin sunshine

Ford's Theatre stage area as it looked on the night of April 14, 1865. The stage is set for Act III of OUR AMERICAN COUSIN. *The stage box is prepared for the Presidential party. This reconstruction is part of the historical exhibit of Ford's Theatre by the United States Park Department.*

of spring, desultorily talking about their unlooked-for good fortune. No one had expected much business at the theatre that night. After all, the *Cousin* was an old property, it was Good Friday, and the town was wildly rejoicing over General Lee's surrender to Grant at Appomattox. When Tom Raybold, the box office manager, saw John Wilkes Booth coming down the street to collect his mail, he went inside to get the fat letter left there to be picked up the next time Booth was in town. Edwin's younger brother was familiar with all the staff at Ford's, since he had played there often. He joined the group on the steps, sitting to read his letter, laughing and talking with the other loungers. They shared the news of the Lincoln-Grant theatre party with him. As an actor he would appreciate Laura's good luck.

Rehearsal on stage ended about two o'clock. Harry Ford then began to get the presidential box ready. A couple of stagehands helped him to remove the partition between boxes 7 and 8 so as to throw them together into one large sitting room. The furniture came from the stage and Harry's bedroom, where the rocking chair President Lincoln liked was kept between his visits to the theatre. Harry nailed the decorations in place along the front of the box, facing the audience.

Young Ferguson, the callboy, was the only member of the acting company still around. He was seated on stage busily copying the instructions for the mechanic handling the gas lights. It was after three o'clock, the time when theatre life was at its lowest ebb: actors gone, box office quiet, stagehands relaxing. The crew of Ford's was in the saloon next door having a drink with Wilkes Booth, who, the story goes, had only a few more preparations to make in the presidential box before he would attempt murder.

By this time the Grants had made their apologies to President Lincoln. The General didn't like to be pawed over by the public. He knew they would want to touch him and clap him even more now that he was the victor over General Lee. Mrs. Grant did not want to endure another evening with Mary Todd Lincoln, whom she had last seen in a jealous rage at City Point. Secretary Stanton, when he heard the Grants had reneged, urged Mr. Lincoln to cancel. To replace the Grants, the president agreed to take a competent guard and settled on

Henry R. Rathbone. Young Rathbone was a major of volunteers from New York, engaged to his step-sister Clara Harris, the daughter of the Senator from New York. Lincoln encouraged Rathbone to bring his fiancée. Later that afternoon President Lincoln, in one of his mercurial changes in mood, was talking with William Crook, one of the four men of his bodyguard, of the impossibility of preventing an assassination. He mentioned the theatre party for the evening. "It has been advertised that we will be there, and I cannot disappoint the people. Otherwise, I would not go. I do not want to go."

ii

Laura arrived at the theatre around six o'clock, as was her custom. She and Peanut John exchanged a word of greeting at the stage door, and then her practiced eye swept over her effects in the star dressing room. There was water in the ewer, there was a fresh towel, there were the costumes on the rack, and stacked in the corner were the trunks for the evening's packing. She didn't need to check backstage. John Ford ran a good house; he kept the passageway from the dressing rooms to the acting area remarkably clear. He recognized that ladies in full dress, as Laura would be in the last act, needed all the room they could get. It was a misfortune if a skirt caught on a splinter or a nail. She would, of course, take a look at the decorations of the presidential box. Her eye could tell her the best spot for her curtsy when he arrived.

It was six-thirty. The building began to take on life. Joseph Sessford opened up the box office, checked his box-book for notes of reservation — other than the president's party, the boxes would be empty — saw that his stacks of tickets were ready to hand, the orange fifty-cent ones to one side of the dollar tickets. He could see through the window in the back of the box office how the president's box had been decorated. Actors began coming in the alley door and climbing the stairs to their dressing rooms with the casualness of habit. The orchestra was gathering down under the stage. It was decided to postpone the singing of "Honor to Our Soldiers" until after the play, and Laura was asked to write a note to the president asking him to stay after the *Cousin* curtain call.

Outside, people were gathering to see their heroes. As the crowd pushed along Tenth Street from Pennsylvania Avenue they ran a gauntlet of enticements to Ford's Theatre: tar torches stuck in barrels along the road, with barkers at each barrel yelling, "This way to Ford's."

The play began without the honored guests. The president had refused to be hurried or badgered that night. Ford's stage manager had held the curtain as long as he could in fairness to the audience; then Withers and the orchestra had played as long as was deemed fit, so that the play was still in the first scene when the noise outside signaled that the presidential party was at hand. Laura and the man playing Lord Dundreary were on stage at the time. They continued with the scene since the path from the street entrance at Ford's to the presidential box was long and awkward, and there would be no time for the audience to give the Lincolns an ovation until they reached the box front in view of the full audience. There were scatterings of applause and cheering as the Lincolns climbed the stairs from the lobby to the dress circle level.

On stage, Dundreary and Florence were talking about the medicinal draught Georgina has been prescribed:

Dundreary: You see I gave her a draught that cured the effect of the draught, and that draught was a draft that didn't pay the doctor's bill. Didn't that draught —

Florence: Good gracious! What a number of draughts. You have almost a game of draughts.

Dundreary: (laughs)

Florence: What's the matter?

Dundreary: That wath a joke, that wath.

Laura, ever the newspaper reader, at this point, interpolated a line that reflected the actions of Secretary of War Stanton the day before, which had been reported in the morning's press. The enlisted men's draft was to be suspended as the result of the capitulation of Lee's army.

Florence: The draft has been suspended.

Dundreary: I don't see the joke.

Florence: Well — (catching sight of the president, and indicating him to the audience) — anyone can see that!

The applause reached its crescendo. The orchestra played "Hail to the Chief." Laura dropped her curtsy. Major Rathbone and his fiancée, Clara Harris, took seats forward in the box, Mrs. Lincoln took one less in-view of the audience, and the president slouched back in comfort in a roomy silk covered rocking chair with arm rests. The president was further hidden from the spectators by the Nottingham lace curtains that draped the box. It was his custom to draw back into their shadow.

Those who glanced at the box when a laugh rumbled through the audience or who, just because they wanted to see the president, looked in that direction, could not see his reactions, although the others in the party seemed to be enjoying themselves. The audience certainly was. Harry Hawk said, "The company and the audience seemed in the best of humor." They were now into Act III. Asa's using the will to light his cigar had touched the right note of mingled shock and amusement in the audience; Laura, as Florence, had energized the conclusion of that scene, and Ford's crew had shifted the scenes with dispatch. While the second scene ran, Laura took a moment on the prompter's side of the stage to give additional coaching to young Ferguson.

He had done acceptably in his earlier appearances. He had one more scene, only a matter of four speeches and about eight lines, with a gesture of hitching up his breeches sailor fashion which could get a laugh as he made his exit. Laura and he stood back from the prompter's desk in the space between it and the gas table. She was listening to him say his lines. The gas engineer was standing by, alert to take the lights down at the conclusion of the scene in readiness for the wine cellar scene which followed. The prompter was away from his desk, calling actors for the next scene. Augusta had just left the stage for the greenroom, Asa (Harry Hawk) and Mrs. Montchessington were on stage, pretty far down front. She scored off Asa and exited with a flourish through the curtained archway in the center of the stage, while Asa said:

"Don't know the manners of good society, eh? Well, I guess I know enough to turn you inside out, old gal — you sockdologizing ole man-trap."

That line always got a laugh. It could be used as a cue by Laura, since the laughter plus the rest of the speech gave her sufficient time

They . . .
Went to the theatre in their flag-draped box.
The play was a good play, he liked the play,
Laughed at the jokes, laughed at the funny man
With the long, weeping whiskers.
The time passed.
The shot rang out. The crazy murderer
Leaped from the box, mouthed out his Latin phrase,
Brandished his foolish pistol and was gone.
So, Stephen Vincent Benet described events in his
poem, JOHN BROWN'S BODY. THIS PHOTOGRAPH OF THE
ACTOR JOHN WILKES BOOTH FROM THE UNIVERSITY OF TULSA
THEATRE COLLECTION.

to get from anywhere in the backstage area over to the left side of the stage, pick up the paper which served as the half-burned will from the property man, and be ready to enter — on this occasion, from an entrance closest to the presidential box. But she didn't start. . . .

Withers, who had been backstage near the alley loading doors talking to the stage manager about whether or not the principal singers should be costumed for the patriotic air, had started back along the stage behind the scenery toward the dressing room stairway to return underground to the orchestra. Wright moved away, observing without being aware that he was doing it, that the stagehands were all in place for the next scene shift which was a quick one.

The laugh came on cue.

John Wilkes Booth had chosen the moment of the sure laugh to cover the sound of a pistol shot. . . .

iii

Harry Hawk, in a letter to his father written two days later, reported, "The old lady of the theatre had just gone off the stage and I was answering her exit speech when I heard the shot fired; I turned, looked up at the President's box, heard the man exclaim *Sic semper tyrannis,* saw him jump from the box, seize the flag of the staff, and drop to the stage. He slipped when he gained the stage, but got upon his feet in a moment, brandished a large knife, saying, 'The South Shall be free!' turned his face in the direction I stood, and I recognized him as John Wilkes Booth. He ran towards me, and I, seeing the knife, thought I was the one he was after, ran off the stage and up a flight of stairs." In a later account of his actions, Hawk put the seal of truth on his story by saying further, "I did not know what he had done or what his purpose might be. I did simply what any other man would have done — I ran."

Major Rathbone had risen at the sound of the pistol shot and grappled with Wilkes Booth. He was slashed twice before Booth broke away and dropped to the stage. Rathbone called out, "Stop that man." The audience was shocked. It did not know what was going on. Some thought the cry and the jump a part of the play. Booth caught his spur in the decorations of the box, landed awkwardly, but quickly limped off. He angled across the stage heading for the passage between the scenes and the dressing room area, where he collided with Withers. "I could not get out of his way," Withers recounted, "So he hit me on the leg, and turned me around, and made two cuts at me, one in the neck, and one on the side, and knocked me from third entrance down to the second."

Laura and young Ferguson stood stunned. The audience began to surge like a many-headed beast, with questions, shouts, movement. There was a pushing back of chairs; everyone stood up, almost as if on cue; there was a crowding into the aisles, a movement into the lobbies, a swelling chorus of What happened? What was it? Who was he?

From the box came the sounds of tragedy. Mrs. Lincoln's deep moaning when the president's head could not be raised; the half-formed words; Clara Harris saying the irrational things we all say at a time of crisis; Major Rathbone trying to be a bodyguard while his wounds bled frighteningly, grabbing at his arm to staunch the flow . . . The noises from the box ceasing to be dumb brute moanings and become words . . . "The President" . . . "Get a doctor" . . . "Oh, God . . ."

Comprehension began to come to the audience. There were those who wanted to do something. Withers, backstage, dramatizing his scratches, squealing . . . Cries in the auditorium of "murder" . . . A seething back and forth . . . This Laura knew about. This was an audience on the verge of panic. With this she was prepared to cope.

She went to the front of the stage, raised her hands to get attention, and in a voice that all could hear, said, "For God's sake have presence of mind and keep your places, and all will be well."

Wright ordered the lowering of the lights in the auditorium and then their raising, the usual signal to an audience to leave the hall. Persons at the back began to move into the street with their fearful news. Dr. Leale forced his way into the passageway to the box by vaulting over the intervening seats. Major Rathbone managed to remove the obstruction Booth had placed to bar the door, and Leale made his way past the major who was begging for attention to Mrs. Lincoln and the president. He placed a guard at the passageway, asking those crowding around to bring brandy and water. Miss Harris came to the front of the box and called to Laura still standing below, "Miss Keene, bring some water."

Laura and young Ferguson made their way from the stage, over the footlights down the stairs to the parquet level. He handed her down, as she clutched at her skirts. Although the aisles were filled with milling, distressed, desolated humanity, a way was made for Laura. She reached the lobby and ascended the stairs, people on the stairs drawing back to give her room. Across the back of the dress circle and down the passageway she and Ferguson moved and then hesitated at the door.

Mrs. Lincoln was cowering at one side of the box, weeping piteously. The president was stretched out on the floor, his shirt and coat cut open for Leale's better examination. Leale gently fingered the wound behind the ear, and removed the clot of blood.

All the while the occupants of the box were engrossed in this central concern, the activities of crisis were spreading outside. Soldiers in the audience and from the street were beginning to close up around the box to be of service if needed. Spectators who had rushed into the street and down Pennsylvania Avenue, were telling all they met of what had happened. Other medical men made their way to the theatre and to the box. Those who had come to the theatre to see the president or just to see a play began to move away, some in fear. The gas engineer continued alternately to dim and raise the lights.

Leale tried mouth to mouth resuscitation. Mrs. Lincoln was helped into a chair. Finally Leale, rising, stood before her, with the words, "His wound is mortal; it is impossible for him to recover." He was joined by other doctors who agreed it would not be possible to move the dying man to the White House. The possibility of further attempts on the life of a president of a nation at war argued that he be moved out of the box and out of the theatre. While they waited for Mr. Lincoln to gain sufficient strength to be moved, Laura asked Leale if she might hold the president's head. He granted her request. She sank to the floor of the box and, pillowing the head in her lap, she bathed the temples with the water she had brought. Leale on occasion would check the wound with his fingers, to break the clot to remove any possible pressure on the brain.

Eventually, they felt it imperative to move the president. Leale organized a carrying party, himself taking the president's head. Laura unobtrusively left the box to return to the stage. Soldiers in the dress circle cleared a pathway out of the building and across the street. When they reached the Petersen House and had the president stretched out on the bed, then, and only then, did they give a thought to Major Rathbone's wounds. He had bled all over the box, its fittings, and the hallway of the Petersen house. He fainted from loss of blood and was sent home, where he revived.

Seaton Monroe, a Washington attorney who later wrote an account of his activities that assassination evening, met Laura at the foot of the staircase. "Making a motion to arrest her progress, I begged her to tell me if Mr. Lincoln was still alive," Monroe wrote. "'God only knows!' she gasped, stopping for a moment's rest. The memory of that apparition will never leave me. Attired as I had so often seen her, in the costume of her part in 'Our American Cousin,' her hair and dress were in disorder, and not only was the gown soaked in Lincoln's blood, but her hands, and even her cheeks where her fingers had strayed, were bedaubed with the sorry stains!"

Laura must have responded to a drum-fire of questions from spectators and fellow actors as she worked her way back to her dressing room. Less than twenty minutes had passed since Hawk had called Mrs. Montchessington a man trap.

iv

Laura washed the stains from her face and hands. She moved about backstage as a hastily detailed guard from the army came to take over. Harry Hawk was "requested to walk down to police headquarters and give evidence." Young Ferguson returned from the Petersen house with the latest news and rang the curtain down. The gas was turned off, the building locked. By midnight some of the stagehands who regularly slept in the building were abed.

v

How did Laura get home? She could not have passed unaccompanied through the alleys behind the theatre; they were unlit, unpaved, and a part of what was then called a shantytown. She could not have passed down Tenth Street without being besieged on all sides by questions. Physically it would have been difficult; emotionally it was impossible. The sensation seekers could not have been borne. A carriage sent to bring her home would have needed an escort to get along Tenth Street. It was jammed with humanity from the time the first word of assassination was shouted until early the next morning.

There is a question which, if it could be answered, might tell us how Laura reached home. Was Laura Keene interrogated? She was the reason for the Lincolns' changing their plans to go to Ford's Theatre rather than Grover's. A note from Laura was in the president's coat, or on the floor of the box, or in the possession of one of the Fords — the note asking him to stay to hear "Honor to Our Soldiers."

She had been in the wings when Booth limped across the stage. Harry Hawk was interrogated, first at the police station and again at Petersen's house. He was arrested. Eventually every actor in Washington was arrested. Word went out to arrest those known to Booth or related to him. The Fords were arrested. John Sleeper Clarke was arrested. Laura was not.

Was she interrogated?

Had she been, she would have given evidence at the hastily assembled command post at the Petersen house. Taking evidence were a cabinet member, a judge, the attorney general, and Gen. Christopher C. Augur.

Cpl. James Tanner took down the testimony. "Somewhere, stowed away in my boxes, I have the original shorthand notes which I made . . . and the longhand copy which I wrote out before leaving the Petersen house. We had Harry Hawk, who had been on the stage; Laura Keene and various others before us. No one said positively that the assassin was John Wilkes Booth, but all thought it was he. It was evident that the horror of the crime held them back. They seemed to hate to think that one they had known at all could be guilty of such an awful crime."

That account squares with Harry Hawk's story that he was called by an aide to the president about half-past three to "go to the house where he was lying to give another statement before Judge Cartter, Secretary Stanton, and other high officials assembled there."

But . . .

If Laura gave testimony as Tanner claimed, it did not survive in his papers, although much of the other testimony did. If she gave testimony, it did not appear in the official record of the case. Years later she bought an advertisement in a Mobile newspaper to say she had not identified John Wilkes Booth, that she did not know him. She did not say whether she or Lutz had been interrogated.

Where was Lutz? His place should have been in the theatre box office. Most particularly, his place was there on Laura's benefit nights. The only way a traveling star could be sure that the resident ticket seller did not shortchange her or that a resident treasurer did not falsify the accounts, was to have a member of her personal staff check the local staff. Lutz should have been in the box office watching the orange and purple tickets. At ten o'clock he should have gone with house manager Raybold into the auditorium to count the house. After the house count, which — allowing a margin for human error — would jibe with the ticket sale count, there should have been a financial reckoning in the office. Raybold and the Fords should have totted up the gross for that night and computed Laura's half-share. If there were any deductions they should have been settled then and Lutz given payment. There also should have been a settling for Laura and her company for the balance of the week just completed. There would probably have been a few last-minute details about getting Laura's belongings out of the theatre and down to the train station for departure the next day.

Lutz should have been there for other duties. Friday was Laura's last night at Ford's Theatre after a two-week run. On such a night every person backstage expected a tip. The property men, the stage hands, the dressers all would stand around with their hands carefully curled at their sides.

The stage doorkeeper, the callboy, the prompter would find things to do around the stage until Lutz appeared. Even actors who had done something outside the line of duty would not be insulted if remembered. This routine of tipping was as much a part of touring as

This could be a photograph of "The Lincoln Dress" as worn by Laura Keene before that fateful night in Washington. The dress appears to be of gray moiré and it is worn with cuffs. Like so many old photographs it has no date or identification.
UNIVERSITY OF TULSA
THEATRE COLLECTION

lumpy mattresses in hotels. It was one of Lutz's functions. Laura never had done it. Laura never did do it. After Lutz's death it became Emma's responsibility. Was he where he was supposed to be? So much a part of the background to be never mentioned? If he were there, he would have escorted Laura those four blocks to their hotel, the Metropolitan.

On Saturday he is present in the background, as usual. By Saturday the nation knew that President Lincoln was dead, that the cabinet had declared a period of national mourning, that all communication between the nation and the capital had been temporarily suspended — all exits from Washington had been closed by the military, one telegraph had been mysteriously interrupted — and that there was a hue and cry to apprehend John Wilkes Booth and his accomplices. On Saturday Laura's daughter Emma came downtown to comfort her. By Saturday Laura had made the decision to continue performing, and they were busy trying to get in touch with Wood's Theatre in Cincinnati where she was scheduled to perform *Our American Cousin* on Monday night. She and Lutz must also have been busy using all their political influence to get Laura's belongings out of Ford's Theatre where the military was now in charge.

Laura could not perform *Our American Cousin* in Cincinnati. Putting aside all emotional considerations, she could not perform it because she had no costume for Act III. What she had worn the night before, the pale gray moiré silk, had telltale rusty bloodstains among the bunches of roses. As did the detachable cuffs. Her other costumes were immured in her dressing room. Her piano was locked away in the orchestra pit.

Strings were being pulled to secure Hawk's release and to get travel passes for the Keene company. Those strings must also have pulled open the stage door of Ford's Theatre. While the country was excitedly contemplating the capture of John Wilkes Booth, people who had been on stage with him and who could identify him were permitted to leave Washington. We hear of them through the newspapers of Monday, April 17.

"Harrisburg. Miss Laura Keene was arrested at the depot this morning, on the Northern Central train from Baltimore. Lieut. Gresh took charge of her as she was alighting from the cars. She was bound west to Cincinnati, accompanied by two actors named John Dyott and Harry Hawk — She said she had given bail to appear at Washington, and had left owing to the excitement there incident to her position with relation to the affair at the theatre. The whole three are held by the military authority as a mere matter of precaution until the facts can be ascertained from Washington when she will probably be discharged."

Lutz, who was ignored by the reporter sending the story of the arrest, was immediately busy in the telegraph office, and shortly Louis H. Pelouze, an assistant adjutant general, is inquiring of Col. LaFayette Baker, the head of the secret service, why Laura and her party should be arrested. Baker endorsed the request for a release that same day: "I know of no reason why Miss Laura Keene should be detained." But that wasn't sufficient. John Lutz on April 18 wired Maj. J.A. Hardee, at the War Office: "They will not release Laura Keene Mr. Dyott & Hawk & others Order you gave last night unless they receive official telegram." That did it. They were released.

John Lutz did not have such ties with the military that he could send wires which brought action. Logic dictates that John Lutz's brother, Francis, was the man who had the contacts that gained freedom for the Keene party in Harrisburg. He might have had such contacts that Laura was spared interrogation Good Friday night, and granted a pass to pick up her belongings at Ford's Theatre on Saturday.

Laura's determination to play in Cincinnati was compulsive. She would be a prey to her nerves if she did nothing, so it was probably wise, however heartless, to go on with her tour. With the temper in Washington as it was, it was probably good sense on the part of the military to let her go on to Cincinnati. There, she and her company were one less security problem.

Laura's outward calm was dearly bought. Her daughter Emma wrote two accounts of her visit with her mother on the Saturday morning following Lincoln's death.

"The first intimation I had of the assassination came from a servant of the family where I was visiting in Georgetown," Emma wrote. "She had been to the theatre the night before, and most distinctly spoke of seeing Miss Keene in the box after the firing. On receiving this news I hastened to Washington to see Miss Keene. As she held cut her hands to me I saw they were trembling and that she had lost the self-control that had enabled her the previous evening to quiet the audience and prevent a panic. She told me that on hearing a voice from the box saying, 'For God's sake, Miss Keene, get some water,' she procured some and made her way with difficulty to the box. As she entered and saw the President pale and wounded, the thought passed through her mind how much he resembled a picture of 'The Dead Christ.' She also showed me the stage clothes she had worn; not only her dress, but even her underskirts were bespattered with blood. . . .

"I took her in my arms to embrace her, she shook all over like a leaf. I tried to give her courage, by saying, 'Where is your old-time courage?' but the frightful calamity of the night before was too much, and it seemed as if grief was breaking her heart."

Chapter 11

Many Openings, Many Closings

The chiefest action for a man of great spirit
Is never to be out of action
The soul was never put into the body
. . . To stand still.
JOHN WEBSTER, *HONORABLE EMPLOYMENT*

L aura's life for the three years following Mr. Lincoln's death was a meaningless making of motions. The immediate public reaction to the president's murder was predictably violent. According to political speakers and the Northern press, Lincoln was the latest sacrifice upon the altar of union. His death was the senseless result of the nation's dedication to violence. A later reaction suggested by the clergy and echoed by persons both North and South was that his death was a chastening for an interest in the sinful theatre, as the war had been a chastisement for the country's sinful greed.

A Methodist minister of Brooklyn, the Rev. E. Sands, on May 7 "sounded the keynote of the impending pulpit war against the amusements of the people," the *Clipper* noted, "with malice toward all and charity for none." The Rev. Phineas D. Gurley, Lincoln's own pastor in Washington, preached the most frequently quoted attack.

"It will always be a matter of deep regret to thousands that our lamented President fell in the theatre. Multitudes of his best friends

— I mean his Christian friends — would have preferred that he should have fallen in almost any other place. . . . The theatre is one of the last places to which a good man should go, and among the very last in which his friends would wish him to die. . . . For my own part, I have always regarded the theatre as in the main a school of vice and corruption — the illumined and decorated gateway through which thousands are constantly passing into the embrace of gaiety and folly, intemperance and lewdness, infamy and ruin. I have always hated and avoided it, and taught my children to avoid it, . . . but henceforth it will be more odious to me than ever before. . . ."

Laura would have been sensitive to the public mood had she renounced the theatre and retired from the public gaze. Edwin Booth, by forsaking the theatre because of his brother's actions, raised himself in the public's estimation. "When a nation is overwhelmed with sorrow by a great public calamity, the mention of private grief would under ordinary circumstances be an intrusion," Booth's statement to the public read in part. "It has pleased God to lay at the door of my afflicted family the life blood of our deservedly popular President. . . . For our present position we are not responsible. For the future — alas! I shall struggle on in my retirement bearing a heavy heart, an oppressed memory and a wounded name — dreadful burdens — to my too welcome grave."

Laura could no more take such an action than she could play *Hamlet.* She was a private person, and the public was allowed to see only that part of her that appeared on stage. Never could she have let them see her hurt, her horror, her despair. And she could not give up the theatre. She did not need the public adulation. She did not need the income. She did not need to prove the ministers wrong and the actors traduced. She continued to act because she needed always to be busy.

She was unprepared for the active role in the assassination in which the public and press cast her. The *Herald* of New York reported on Sunday morning, April 16, that Laura Keene and the leader of the orchestra had identified the assassin. "They recognized him as J. Wilkes Booth the actor." That she did not was immaterial. Her identification of Booth was part of the growing folk legend of the event. After she was threatened with bodily harm while playing in Mobile in 1867 — "You are requested to live [sic] our city. if you don't you will get hurt. . . You are nothing else but a Yankee" — she made her first public announcement about the assassination. She bought space in the Mobile newspaper to say: "I could not be the enemy of John Wilkes Booth, as I never saw him in my life. I was never called on by the authorities to identify Booth, never gave any testimony against him, or any other person whose name was associated with the assassination."

Spectators went to the theatre to look at her, not to watch her perform. She was an object of curiosity. She became the subject of a story that only approximated truth and which strayed ever further from the facts as the years passed.

Laura's third-act costume for Florence Trenchard became part of the folk-myth. The public, who believed Laura held the dying Lincoln in her lap, believed that her dress was soaked in his blood. It would have nothing of the story that it was Major Rathbone's blood, or that cranial wounds do not flow but merely seep.

Laura had her first hint in Cincinnati of what was to come. One of her fellow actresses wanted to be shown "her gown." Official mourning was observed in Cincinnati until Thursday. That night Wood's Theatre reopened with Laura and her support in *She Stoops*

Laura's infatuation with lace continued no matter what her financial condition. She used real Honiton lace in the stage setting for the Palace of Lace in BLONDETTE. *Emma said a point lace flounce worn by her mother as part of a costume was probably worth $6,000 and the lace was over four hundred years old.* THEATRE ARTS COLLECTIONS. HARRY RANSOM HUMANITIES RESEARCH CENTER, THE UNIVERSITY OF TEXAS AT AUSTIN.

to Conquer. The *Enquirer* reported that "there was a large audience who were vividly impressed with the part she played in the great national tragedy recently enacted in Washington, and the reception was most enthusiastic. The greeting was extended to each of her companions, and it was evident the romance of horror which surrounded their last appearance upon the stage was vivid in the mind's eye of all present."

When it was realized that she had the dress on which the president had bled his life away, she received offers to sell it, to exhibit it, to capitalize on each browning spot. Her refusal made no difference to some. They simply exhibited dresses they had and claimed they were hers. Pieces of cloth with stains on them were sold to the public and letters attesting their authenticity were forged in Laura's name. Mark Twain in reporting the auction of the Thomas Nast collection of autographs and drawings, listed "A letter written by Lincoln, and which was laid over a piece of white silk bearing a faded red stain, sold for $38. The attached certificate stated that the silk was from the dress of Laura Keene, worn on the night of Lincoln's assassination, and that the stain was made by his blood."

At some unspecified time the dress was placed in a closed box and left in Chicago with its creator, Jamie Bullock. Not until he received a letter from Laura written on August 11, 1873, did he know that he had the "Lincoln dress." He assured Laura, "My wife says that she will not lone your Dress because it would get Destroyed but will take good Care of it until you send." Emma took charge of the dress after her mother's death, and on her death she willed it to her daughter. It was a part of what Emma called her personal estate and was listed as the "Lincoln" dress in her will. Emma died in 1882, so that all the dresses exhibited around the country before that time were fakes.

Emma's daughter, Clara Rawson, is supposed to have distributed panels of the dress to friends sometime around 1890.

ii

Laura cut the touring season short. The last days of May she sought sanctuary at Riverside Lawn, her new place. It had all the associative romance she found so appealing and all the nineteenth-century luxuries she would not do without. The farm was on the eastern bank of the Acushnet river about two miles north of the New Bedford Bridge, in Fairhaven.

On the property was a studio built on piles driven in the river. It gave a view upstream to a wooded world and downstream to an ever-widening tidal river to Buzzard's Bay and the far Atlantic. Westward, Laura could point out King Phillip's Bay; downstream, Fort Phoenix, Fish, Pope's and Palmer's Islands in the roadstead, and the shipyards on shore.

Laura cherished the studio and the view; Jane and the guests enjoyed the house. Set back from the river, it could be reached either by boat or stage from New Bedford. It was a rambling, twenty-room frame building complete with bath. It became Jane's home while Laura was on the road; Clara claimed it as her residence when filling out enrollment records at the Academy; Laura used it as her fair haven during the summer months.

Part of the charm of Riverside Lawn was the journey to it. Laura most often approached it by water from New York City northward through Long Island Sound. The ships *Bristol* and *Providence* of the Fall River Line and the *Wamsutta* and *Acushnet* of the New Bedford Line boasted every luxury; clean linens, cut flowers, music. A distracted Laura could be calm by the time she had made the overnight journey. If she took the Fall River Line she left from Pier 14, North River. After a night's rest, she had a short ride on the railroad cars and then a last few miles by stage across lots from Fall River to New Bedford and home. If she took the more direct New Bedford Line, she left from Pier 13, and had no train or stage — however the New Bedford sailed only twice a week. Once divested of her luggage and parcels by the steward at the gangplank, Laura could sit on the "verandah" aft in the warmth of the late afternoon sun before going below for supper. Then she could talk or read in the "drawing-rooms" before claiming her berth.

She poured her love back into the property by keeping forty acres in active cultivation. She planted fruit and ornamental trees and had a kitchen garden. She had a small milk herd of Ayrshires, Alderney, and Jerseys, and a barnful of rolling stock, hay wain, and a carryall gig. For her guests she put in a curving driveway from the county road. For them she also added bathing houses on the bank of the river. For the family and herself she took a hollow close to the river, enlarged it, diked it, and planted it as a duck pond. She experimented with a sugar cane brake. She had fun.

Jane and the girls loved the refuge. Clara sang with the choir of St. Mary's Church, located at the corner of School and Fifth Streets in New Bedford. Jane went to Grace Episcopal Church.

Laura could leave the family Keene there when she went on the road.

iii

Word from New York was that Edwin Booth had purchased the Winter Garden and put his brother-in-law, John Sleeper Clarke, in charge. Clarke offered himself as a starring attraction in September 1865. He would present *Our American Cousin.*

Laura, who was off in Pittsburgh, beginning another touring year, erupted. She had suffered at the hands of the Booths all she would bear. Edwin Booth had almost ruined her chances in California; John Wilkes Booth had linked her name with murder and treason; Asia Booth's husband, John Clarke, had been robbing her for the past seven years. Clarke was now in New York — her town. He was playing *Our American Cousin* — her play. The critics were applauding his comedic invention — her invention, her adaptation, her ingenuity. Hers. Hers.

Hers. She was probably incoherent; she was certainly unwise. The anger, the frustration, the tension, the nightmares of the past season all combined in the public letter she wrote Clarke.

To J. S. Clarke, Lessee of Winter Garden

Sir — I see by your advertisement in the Herald that you purpose playing *Our American Cousin*. No one in our profession is better aware than yourself that in all honor, honesty and fair dealing the said play is my sole property. I gave the author a large sum for it when it was an unacted manuscript. By my enterprise, industry and expenditure, I made the play a great success. You then being one of the managers of the Arch street theatre, Philadelphia, determined to act the play. You obtained a copy of it, which was proven on trial to have been stolen from the author, Tom Taylor. I brought a suit against you then and it was proved you had obtained all the original matter which had been written by my stage manager and myself from an employee of my theatre. Judge Cadwalader decided against you, and under whose decision you were compelled to pay damages. You ultimately apologized for your share of the transaction and wished to shift all the blame on others. You had made many thousands of dollars, however, while the suit lasted. Since then you have played it in Washington, Baltimore, etc., knowing full well that my professional engagements would prevent restraining you by law from so doing. In these places you have again made large sums from its production. Should not the money you have already made from my property content you? You know well this is not a case of copyright it was my personal, private property, and should have been held sacred to me by every respectable member of our profession; but now, while I am absent from New York, you take advantage of that absence to play *Our American Cousin*. I am so identified with that play that I consider it one of my most valuable possessions. Why seek to deprive a woman of her honestly acquired property? Why not take the Veteran or Rosedale or any other play owned by a man?

The bad taste of seeking to deprive me of the use of this play is only equaled by your ever appearing in a comedy which ought to have only a memory of shame and horror for you and every member of your family. You cannot lift the cloud which has fallen upon our whole profession by acts which set at naught all regard for principle and right.

LAURA KEENE

Clarke's lawyers treated her with patient condescension. She was a lady, therefore incapable of such a letter. If she were capable of it, she was no lady.

There is a hectic quality to Laura's actions. Time and again, she forms a company, goes out on the road; pays off the company, and returns to Acushnet. She finally runs to England.

When she returns in May of 1868 she is more nearly the Laura of old.

iv

Riverside Lawn
Acushnet
Mass.

My dear Sir
I want a comedy!! I have the plot — situations etc., etc. — all sketched. It would not be a task of any great length for you, and would certainly not diminish your rapidly growing reputation as an author.

Will you undertake it? And what terms per night; for U. S. and England, will you want?

I have given the subject a great deal of thought, and have been collecting matter for it, for the last three years — Boucicault, and Tom Taylor are willing to do it, but can not see it as an *American* Comedy, I can not see it as an *English* one for it is of *us* most essentially, and will I am convinced go better in England for being American.

I need not tell you that I want a *fine part*, I played so much bad business in my own theatre (ever sinking the actress in the manageress) that I have refused every offer for New York awaiting the time when a role that suited me, should present itself, that would enable me to do justice to myself.

Will you give me your views at as early a date as possible?

Very truly yours
Laura Keene
August 1868

With that letter begins one of the tantalizing "might have beens" of the American theatre. Augustin Daly, to whom it was addressed, was just getting his start in management that summer of 1868, a field he was to dominate for the next thirty years. He and Laura shared the same ideals for the theatre, so that a collaboration between them could have been dynamic. Laura had known him since he had sent her a play about Napoleon III ten years before. His melodrama *Under the Gaslight* went *The Colleen Bawn* more than one better. It had that famous scene of the onrushing railroad engine from which the hero tied to the tracks is saved in the nick of time by the heroine. He believed in the balanced stock company as the foundation of successful management — no stars

Augustin Daly (1839-1899) was all that Laura strove to be. He was the successful manager of a well-trained, closely-knit company with his own playhouses in New York and London. He played a classical repertoire relieved by novelties. He admired her and she him. Not to belittle him, but he may have built on her experiences. UNIVERSITY OF TULSA THEATRE COLLECTION.

for him. He believed in the necessity of a single guiding artistic idea. The storklike figure of Daly seated at a table by the footlights, his hat pushed back on his head, became the symbol of the new force in the theatre — the director.

Daly's reaction to Laura's letter we don't know. As her letter shows she returned to the United States eager to be active, but her partner, John Lutz, was a sick man, incapable of the rigors of the road. Laura accepted a few bookings at theatres near New Bedford. She would go out for two or three days to Taunton or Springfield or Providence and then return to the haven of Riverside Lawn. It was a relaxed, footling time, but Lutz's health worsened.

His condition may have influenced her to take a company to Washington for General Grant's inauguration. Lutz could be with his family, Laura would be active, and business should be good while visitors, particularly political visitors, fed the box office.

They announced a season to begin on March 1 and for it Laura had an exclusive vehicle, *Hunted Down*, or the *Two Lives of Mary Leigh*. It was another of Dion Boucicault's adaptations from the French. It was a hydraulic drama. In 1866 Dion sent it to Laura, who made changes as she tried it out. She must have discussed those changes with the author while she was in England, because she purchased the exclusive rights for the United States.

The role was a major change in her acting style. She was best known in high-comedy roles: Kate Hardcastle, Lydia Languish, Lady Teazle, Lady Gay Spanker. When it was announced she would try Mary Leigh, a reporter shook his head: "We have always thought Miss Keene nothing else than a fine comedienne and to see her in drama would be seeing her in a new role." Laura may have felt such a change in her style was necessary, not only to meet changing audience taste but to accommodate her flagging energy.

She knew she was not capable of what she once had done. She no longer attempted breeches parts; no Shakespearean heroines for her any longer. She could still manage to dance the jig in *Mask and Faces,* but the balletic movements she had performed in *The Elves* were beyond her. She was forty-two, with the tensions of the last fifteen years in America showing in the lines of her face. *Hunted Down* made few physical demands; it served her purpose sick or well.

Since Lutz seemed better, although not able to go on the road, the troupe moved into upper New York State in the lovely month of April, 1869. In Utica, Laura received a telegram saying that John Lutz had died, suddenly.

> Lutz. On the evening of the 18th inst., John S. Lutz, in the 54th year of his age.
> His funeral will take place from the residence of his brother F. A. Lutz, corner 4½ and C streets, Tuesday afternoon, 20th instant, at 4 o'clock. The friends of the family are invited to attend.

Francis Lutz was a truly remarkable person. He abetted his scapegrace brother in his relationship with Laura, a relationship that others of his circle could only reprehend. That relationship may have been a reason for the funeral being from the home rather than from the Methodist Church of which Francis was such a pillar.

Train schedules permitted Laura to arrive in Washington for the funeral. The kindliness of Francis Lutz and his family permitted her to have a farewell moment with her partner. But Southern custom dictated that John Lutz be interred in the family plot in Oak Hill Cemetery, Georgetown next to Malvina, his legal wife.

Laura nursed her grief that summer at Riverside Lawn.

iv

She was offered the lease of the Chestnut Street Theatre in Philadelphia for the theatrical season 1869-1870. Here was a way again to lose herself in work. Here was opportunity.

It was the Laura Keene Varieties of 1856-7 over again. The theatre had a reputation of failure. The acting company was too large. The herculean labors of Laura and her associates could scarcely keep the enterprise solvent. It was the Varieties again with differences: There was no Lutz; Philadelphia was not New York.

When Laura took over the Chestnut she already had an acting company employed for her annual tour; the management of the Chestnut also had an acting company. She combined them. Although the actors were not of the caliber of her best New York companies, they were better than the usual ruck of performers, and under Laura's direction they improved. The house, when she leased it, was in the process of internal renovation and redecoration, and she added some touches of her own. She later advertised that the theatre had the largest seats in America and that her selection of "Crayons and chromos, pendant shells and trailing vines, natural flowers and ferns serve to give an air of Beauty and Refinement with Home-Like Comfort."

Laura poured a demonic energy into the season. She acted all the leading female roles, thus appearing on stage every night save Sunday. She tutored her company. She conducted rehearsals. She handled business affairs with Charles Day, her company representative, and her daughter Emma. She conceived plays!

On Friday, September 24, the Federal Treasury intervened in the stock market to prevent the corner on gold attempted by Jay Gould and Jim Fiske, Jr. The bold outlines of the swindle were quickly known to newspaper readers. They suggested a play to Laura.

Bogus was copyrighted on October 18 by Mercer Morris as proprietor and co-author with Charles Day. It was called a comedy adapted from "Boucicault." Laura's company premiered it on November 8, just six weeks after "Black Friday."

Jim Fiske, Jr. saw it and called it fun. When he came backstage to congratulate Laura, they talked of presenting the play in New York. He said he might see about its production himself, if he could get it on "before the Gold Panic would be forgotten."

Fiske was proprietor of the Grand Opera House and the Fifth Avenue Theatre, both in New York. Augustin Daly was lessee of the Fifth Avenue. Laura could not allow a chance for *Bogus* to be passed over. She wrote Daly, suggesting he produce it.

"Now it is a presumptuous thing for one manager to suggest to another, but I give you my word as a woman of honor, and a directress — I see for any house in NY thousands of dollars, if produced while the talk is of Fiske and his Gold financing, after it has passed — worth nothing.

"Try it!! . . . you will want to know my motive . . . I want to forward the interest of an American Author . . . Not have to depend for ever on the London Men."

Laura peppered Daly with letters. She sent him the prompt copy of the play. If it would speed production, she offered to come to New York and "direct one or two rehearsals . . ."

Daly could be forgiven for drawing back in fear of such an elemental force let loose in his theatre, but he claimed the truth. He could not attempt *Bogus* because he was too involved with the translation and pre-production details of *Frou-Frou,* another of the hydraulic dramas. The role of the wife had been created in Paris by an actress of great emotional power. Daly paid Laura the compliment of thinking she would be ideal for the role. He offered to star her at his Fifth Avenue.

But she could no more respond to him than he to her. The Chestnut Street Theatre needed her.

She was stimulated by the similarity of her work at the Chestnut Street Theatre to the early days of the Varieties. But the similarity was insidious. Since she had emerged triumphant from those days she assumed she would so emerge in Philadelphia. When her associates counseled caution, she believed she knew better.

The theatrical year 1869-70 was a financial disaster — at least that was the way the girls viewed it. Clara, writing after her mother's death, said, "You know that ill-fated Chestnut Street Theatre was a terrible failure. Aunt lost heavily on that. . . It makes me sad to think of all those things. She really killed herself — and for what?"

Laura would never have asked for what. The excitement of a production well done, the thrill of an emotion well expressed, the exhilaration of an audience surging toward the stage in high good humor were what she lived for. Laura would have agreed with Thoreau that the cost of a thing is the amount of life one is willing to exchange for it. She paid heavily for the Chestnut Street Theatre. She mourned only that she was not as successful as she deserved to have been.

She did some things exceptionally well. She began to cater to children's audiences. She presented two shows during Christmas week and a series of Saturday matinees for younger spectators. She did versions of *Beauty and the Beast, Little Red Riding Hood, Bold Jack, Babes in the Woods,* and Dickens's *Christmas Carol.* She and Emma must have had a large hand in writing the scripts as well as in composing the advertising.

"Everybody knows that all study and no afternoon at the play makes dull boys and girls," one such advertisement read. "Besides a real wolf and a real wood-chopper, with a real axe, are not to be seen often. . . As for the wolf no one need be afraid of that animal . . . it gets its head chopped off in the last scene every afternoon. It don't mind that, though, having got used to it at rehearsals."

Laura tried those things which had brought success in the past. She lavished attention on the actors and technical staffs of the theatre. As one reviewer put it, "Who ever knew her to produce anything badly?"

She next tried splitting the company, as she had done in New York. She went south with one part, the remainder continued at the Chestnut Street supporting touring stars. In 1870 she played Washington to enough business to encourage her to continue, but not enough to stay solvent.

While Laura was in Washington, Francis Lutz suggested that the trust instrument John S. Lutz had made for the girls and her be rewritten. He probably went over Laura's finances with her, because a few weeks later her attorneys turned the Bond Street home into rental property.

On February 15, the Washington *Star* reviewed Laura's production of *Hunted Down* of the evening before in column three of the first page, and next to that story, in column four, was this item: "Mr. F.A. Lutz made the return of his son, Mr. John A. Lutz, and his

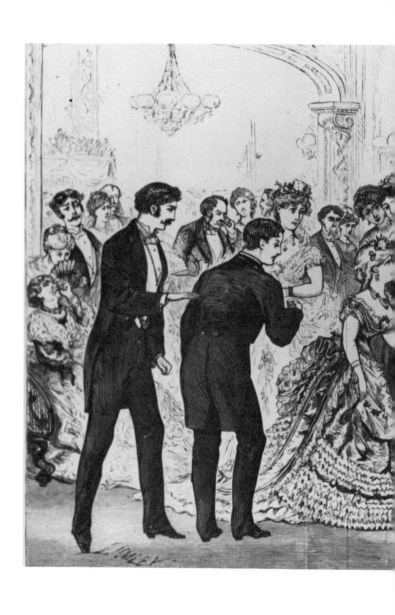

This two-page spread from Laura Keene's magazine, FINE ARTS, *pictures
the public to whom she directed her magazine, as well as the public from
which her profession barred her.*

wife from their marriage tour the occasion for entertaining a very large number of friends at his hospitable mansion on C street last evening." Did Laura arrange replacements for Emma and Clara in her company that night so they could attend the reception?

All the while the company played Baltimore and Norfolk and Richmond, Laura was preparing her version of *Frou-Frou*. It must have been during the rehearsals for this production, when Laura's nerves affected her sense of humor, that she told her leading man, "Mr. Mordaunt, you must learn to act up to me, as it is quite impossible that I should act down to you. I come on the stage, and strew it with my exquisite scraps of oil-paintings. You come along after me with a whitewash brush, and daub all over my oil-paintings! This will not do, sir! You must learn to act up to me!"

During that run, Laura went to the money lenders. Such a visit hadn't been necessary since the season of 1858-9, but it was now, with two companies and one expensive theatre. She again left part of the company in Philadelphia, and with Charles Day going ahead and Emma working the front of the house, she went farther south on the seaboard than she ever had before.

After Lutz's death, Emma took over the onerous task of representing her mother in the business offices of the theatres they toured. She did the work, yet she hated it as few people have hated anything. "I would give ten years of my life," she wrote, "for the health I lost through the hard work and mental care our business entailed after Mr. Lutz's death. There is not a gift on this earth like a light heart and good health." She remembered one dismal spring when the Keene fortunes were at low ebb, how she had envied three little black contrabands "that went whistling through a street in Norfolk. Had I been a millionaire I would have given thousands for the power to whistle in that way."

Emma did not approve of her mother's financial ways, but she did not question them, nor did she criticize them to her. She dutifully did all she could to make her mother's way easier. She acted when Laura's company needed someone in a hurry; she wrote when it needed a script; she took over whatever was being done badly by someone else.

As she always did, Laura responded favorably to new situations and new sights. Charleston, South Carolina, had an English look about it. It wasn't built in the stiff parallelogram of most American cities, and the people used the city. The Battery was an esplanade for babies and nurses, as the Battery in New York had been when she had walked it with Lutz. There was a lifting of the spirit to watch the carefully dressed men and women strolling on the seaward strand of the peninsula in the evening. There were still signs of the war, but they were more apparent in such matters as the absence of horses and carriages. She played two weeks in the Academy of Music there.

Savannah she was unprepared for. She had expected something exotic, instead it was buried among trees. Nor was she prepared for the view of the audience from the stage — the women garbed in a highland style, with tartan plaids, tartan ribbons, and brightly striped mantles; the men in plaid shawls which they wore in smooth folds round their shoulders. The theatre was run-down, needing fresh upholstery and decorating, but it felt familiar to her because Joseph Jefferson had often talked about his days of management there.

The train ride to Augusta was interminable. One didn't begrudge it the time, no smoking was allowed! The ladies' car was the choice part of the train which the conductor guarded from male intruders as

CHORES.

Albert Rawson, Emma Taylor's husband, was the delineator of "Chores" after a design by J.R. Robertson. One can conjecture that Laura's accounts of her adventures travelling through the mid-west inspired the drawing and determined its use in FINE ARTS, *where it was given a full page.*

well as smokers. Only men accompanied by their wives might enter it. Augusta was the strictest town in outward behavior she had ever visited. Even the blue laws of New England paled before Augusta's Sunday strictures: all business of all kinds closed, only an occasional street car for persons going to church.

She met the Oates family troupe down south. They were heading toward New York, bemoaning the lack of a showcase in the big cities. Laura offered them the Chestnut Street Theatre. They had commitments west and north; would Laura go to Minnesota for them if they took the Chestnut Street Theatre?

Just as she had never been seaboard south before, she had never barnstormed. She was due to take up the Oates's commitments in St. Paul in late June. Her advance man, Day, worked her there by way of Wheeling, Columbus, Indianapolis, Bloomington, and points in between. She played a succession of two-night stands. *Hunted Down* was given one night and *Our American Cousin* the next.

They stayed two weeks in Minneapolis, then a country town, and the last week in July they began a float down the Mississippi River. Laura knew the Mississippi from New Orleans to St. Louis; she now learned it from the Twin Cities south through Minnesota, Iowa, and Illinois. She and her company played such villages as Winona, LaCrosse, Dubuque, Davenport, Clinton, Lyons, Muscatine, Rock Island, Burlington, and Quincy. They played on the days they were scheduled, or a couple of days later if their boat hung up on a snag. They played in union halls, odeons, Germania buildings, opera houses, and theatres.

Laura knew she was seeing a part of American life that was rapidly disappearing. When a constable tried to serve papers on her in Clinton, Iowa, she sat like a spectator, while the steamboat captain claimed that only a United States Marshal could serve papers on the seas or inland waters; she watched him shanghai the constable, and calmly sat back and applauded the denunciations heaped upon the hapless constable when he was put ashore at as dismal and desolate a place on the river as the captain could find. She perched on her luggage while her property man and the landlord in Muscatine, Iowa, quarreled over who would put the luggage in the respective hotel rooms. The landlord claimed that circus people always carried their own luggage, but Miss Keene's property man was not going to have their company compared to a circus: they were legitimate. He had all their many effects piled to block the hotel entrance until the landlord changed his mind.

Muscatine was the place also where Laura admitted she did not know how to get a play before the public without scenery. The hall where they were to play had not a stick of scenery or a patch of cloth. Savage, the stage manager, who was called in counsel, explained so readily how the thing could be done that Miss Keene sat down on the floor of her room convulsed with laughter. "Playing without scenery, Miss Keene, is nothing. I've acted in my time without salary."

She knew she was again being privileged to observe America growing. She had ridden muleback to visit California. She had taken stage coaches before the country was laced with railroads, just as she had taken sail before it was replaced by side and stern wheelers. She had acted in military outposts. She had seen the last days of Little Old New York.

All the while that she and her compact little family of a company were moving through the north and west, as the long-tasseled corn ripened in the fields, she was maturing a plan that would take her back south and east.

What if . . .

Chapter 12

Southern Circuit; Fine Arts

Age cannot wither her, nor custom stale
Her infinite variety.
SHAKESPEARE, *ANTONY AND CLEOPATRA,* ACT II, SCENE 1.

That summer, 1870, Laura conceived her boldest theatrical venture. Again she moved far ahead of her generation. A few seemingly unrelated events gave Laura the inspiration for her dream. We can watch her mind working.

When Col. T. Allston Brown announced to his readers in the *Clipper* that he was starting a theatrical agency, Laura was one of the first to enroll. She and Lutz had long realized that some kind of central agency was needed to coordinate the activities of a widespread theatre. Someone, not with any theatrical company but with nationwide connections, was needed to bring actors and managers together.

The development of the telegraph during the war made instantaneous information about the movement of goods and armies possible, why not actors? Such an agency had to have authority, experience, and integrity. Colonel Brown had those qualities in his own person. His agency was soon the clearinghouse for the actor wanting work and the manager wanting a performer.

What if Colonel Brown's services could be enlarged to accommodate touring companies? Owners of buildings being told of companies; acting companies notified of vacant houses? All requisitions and supplies expedited by the telegraph?

Laura had noticed that many of the Southern cities, where once stock companies had flourished, now had no actors; theatres stood vacant. Since visiting stars could not appear without a resident company, those towns had only circuses for professional entertainment.

The major cities were drawing the actors away from the hinterland. Four-fifths of all the actors in the United States were in seven northern cities, according to the recent census. The South had always provided support to the drama. Charleston had one of the oldest theatres in the country; Savannah had one that was built in 1822. When Laura had been south, the ravages of the war were being rapidly cleared away. Business was booming.

Here it came.

What if a theatre manager . . . (strike the term "manager" — there was no word for the person she was thinking of. Yet. John Lutz would have been able to do what she was dreaming . . .) what if a theatre "somebody," like John Lutz, booked, leased, or owned a whole chain of theatres?

Then theatre towns could be as close as circus towns and a touring company could move easily from a Saturday night closing to a Monday night opening with time for rehearsal and make-ready. Such a scheme was possible down South where the towns didn't yet have resident companies.

Laura must have searched for a geography at this point. In every company there were always two or three men who made it their responsibility to see that she was protected, assisted, and cosseted. They gathered her mail at the post office, carried her valises to the hotel, picked up prescriptions at the pharmacy, and dropped off her costumes at the theatre. Now one of them, surely, borrowed an atlas from the nearest school. The finished form of her grand design gives proof of the intensity of her map study.

Laura knew it was better for a theatre to be open three or four consecutive weeks than to be open a week and closed a week. Play-goers are creatures of habit; visitors to a metropolis for wholesale buying or legislative sessions, county fairs, or conventions are in town for a concentrated period of time; and heating, lighting, cleaning are all better done, if done daily.

Laura must have discussed her developing brainstorm with the members of her company. She sent George H. Tyler, her company manager, back to New York to talk to Colonel Brown. She wrote letters sounding out theatre owners.

Laura's letterwriting style deserves notice. Her handwriting became more slapdash and her letters freer of punctuation as she grew older. Virtually every letter ended with a scrawled "in haste" or "very hurriedly yours." Mistakes were seldom if ever corrected, and if she came to the end of a page before the end of the idea, she continued writing at right angles to and over what had been previously written. Only occasionally did she indicate an addressee's name or location, and more rarely did she include a date. She wrote on anything that came to hand. Some stationery had her monogram worked on it in purple, some seemed torn from pads sold by novelty stores. She wrote on old business letterheads and paper furnished by hotels and steamers. Some of the correspondence having to do with her big idea was on black-edged, four-fold stationery, since it was written within her mourning period for John Lutz.

She missed him. She turned to Colonel Brown for the type of advice and support Lutz had given. The colonel was intrigued with her big idea and added suggestions and personal contacts. As early as July they began articulating the plan. The first week in September the results of Laura's thinking, the outcome of her experience, the expression of her theatrical faith, reached the profession in this advertisement in the *Clipper*.

Cotton Is King
Laura Keene's Southern Circuit.

The following theatres will be under the exclusive control and management of Miss Laura Keene, a sufficient guarantee to stars that their pieces will be admirably mounted, correctly costumed and the support and scenic and mechanical effects such as would reflect credit upon establishments in the metropolis.

Academy of Music, Charleston, S. C.
Theatre, Savannah
Opera House, Norfolk
Opera House, Atlanta
Theatre, Macon

In cooperation with R. Dorsay Ogden, Esq. of the New Richmond Theatre, and Messers Barton and Sanderson of Wall's Opera House, Washington, Miss Keene offers advantages to Stars and organizations equaled by no other circuit in the country, the cotton and other crops warranting the most flattering prospects for the coming fall and winter. Dramatic, Pantomimic, Operatic, Minstrel and Variety combinations of decided merit liberally treated with. For the support of stars two full companies will be maintained. Applications for time should be made to Chas. H. Day, business mgr. or Col. T. Allston Brown.

After the form of her grand design was announced she continued to elaborate it. She was able to assure performers that she had made cooperating arrangements with "six adjacent towns, where parties can fill three or four weeks most profitably." She also worked out an arrangement with some of her manager friends, Ben DeBar of New Orleans and St. Louis, and Spalding and Bidwell of Memphis and Mobile, so that she could promise an actor bookings from Washington south to New Orleans and then north through Memphis to St. Louis. As Laura put it, actors could "fill up the entire winter in this delightful climate and highly lucrative field."

Her plan was doomed to fail. It required the sort of logistical skills the Northern armies took nearly four years to achieve, skills not yet available in the theatre. But the idea was sound, and it later worked. It worked so well that touring circuits became the way of the theatre, the commonplace of vaudeville, and eventually the distribution system of the motion pictures. The inescapable good sense of utilizing the railroads, guaranteeing employment to the performer, and a certain level of entertainment to the theatre-goer would be picked up by men of business and made profitable beyond John Lutz's wildest dreams of avarice. Laura's scheme was capable of being turned into a monopoly of buildings which the theatre syndicate later achieved, and a monopoly of talent, which the William Morris agency later accomplished.

How did it work in Laura's day? Surprisingly well. She had built in some safety-valve features. Laura had arrangements with the train and steamer people for discounts to the actors and their luggage. Another safety valve was the use of two acting companies so that even in the smallest cities the theatrical season would be at least a month long. One company, under Emma's management, would support stars like Edwin Forrest in his repertoire of Shakespearean tragedy while the other played ensemble stock. Her conception foundered on the rock of poor scheduling. None of the people associated with Laura had the skill of railroad division superintendents.

Colonel Brown assembled the companies, but Laura made the decisions. One of her many letters in preparation for the Laura Keene Southern Circuit has to do with a man she wanted for the acting company. He had asked Brown some very practical questions about living costs. Laura wrote, "He is mistaken about high rates of hotels — South cheaper than west. . . His board will average $1.50 per day or $12 per week — get him at 34 or 40 for my company."

Some of the causes of her failure are implicit in that letter. Laura was careful of every detail: therefore she felt she had to be everywhere. On a circuit as extensive as hers she could not be. Her multi-city responsibilities needed a full-time manager, not one who managed while acting every night. She was underfinanced. When cash was needed at one end of the circuit there were no funds save ticket revenues. When, in spite of all expectations, the cotton crop was a failure, Laura had no backing to help her over the bad times.

Yet the idea worked for a time. The Southern Circuit opened with Laura and her own company in Norfolk on October 3. The second company opened on October 21. During November the circuit was operating so well that it appeared destined for success. The Ravel troupe was in Savannah, the Worrell sisters in Charleston, the Florences in Macon, Edwin Forrest with company number two was in Atlanta, and Laura with company number one was in Cuthbert, Georgia. The stars traveling through made money, but Laura was out of funds and couldn't continue the payrolls.

ii

At the same time, Colonel Brown's business was booming. It was so good that he moved uptown — to a large suite of offices attached to the Lina Edwin's Theatre. He took over the ownership of that theatre when he moved, and, having no tenant for the latter part of January and all of February, he offered it to Laura should she want to leave the road and act in New York again.

She moved into the Grand Central Hotel, that January of 1871, announced *Hunted Down* for her vehicle, and surrounded herself with the best company she could find. When she corresponded about her company for the South, she spoke of first and second ladies, singing chambermaids, and the whole dreary catalogue of lines of business. For her reappearance in New York she announced "each artist carefully selected for their fitness for the roles assigned." For the child's role, Willie Leigh, she selected young Minnie Maddern, at whose birth in New Orleans she had been an attendant. Years later, Minnie Maddern Fiske, the acknowledged American star, attempted an autobiography. She left a picture of Laura and her own appearance at Lina Edwin's Theatre.

"When I was six," the autobiography relates, "Mama and I came to New York; Laura Keene had asked me to play Willie Lee [*sic*] in her production of *Hunted Down*. I had reached a new height in my career; instead of seeking parts, managers came seeking me. My salary ranged from fifty to seventy-five dollars a week — a goodly sum for those days. I used to deposit most of it each week at the old Bowery Savings Bank. . .

"Miss Keene was very fond of me. Every day my nurse took me to her apartment at the Grand Central Hotel, where I would play for

A faded memento of Minnie Maddern's early career. She may have looked much like this when she played Willie Leigh with Laura Keene in Boucicualt's emotional drama, HUNTED DOWN. UNIVERSITY OF TULSA THEATRE COLLECTION.

an hour, and where frequently there was a new toy for me. When Miss Keene went upon a short tour she insisted that I accompany her, and, as it was impossible for my mother to leave the city, the great artist took me under her personal charge. She would not leave me out of her sight for a moment, insisting that I sleep beside her, not only at the hotels, but also in the sleepers of the railway trains when we traveled by night."

All newspapers agreed that Laura was welcomed back to New York by an audience "which must have been cheering and encouraging to the lady, and which furnished convincing proof that she had not been forgotten."

"Audiences have steadily increased," the *Clipper* reported on February 18, 1871. A week later, it noticed that "the character of the audiences has changed materially since Miss Keene's advent, and the prospect appears flattering for a permanent success. Many of the patrons and admirers of this artist in years that have passed are now nightly to be seen in the auditorium encouraging her by their presence."

The company was catching on, but unfortunately, the Lina Edwin's Theatre was rented to others beginning March 4. Laura's success had been a pleasant surprise for Colonel Brown. She had survived lukewarm notices and freezing weather. Wasn't there some way to keep her before the New York public? She would like nothing better. While she toured *Hunted Down* in nearby cities during the month of March, Brown and her lawyer, and the administrator of her trust worked out an arrangement for the Fourteenth Street Theatre. From Laura's trust funds, her representatives would lend $2,000 to Thomas A. Dow for him to open that theatre and employ "Miss Laura Keene as a Star Artiste . . . during the whole of his time of occupancy."

The sad history of this speculation can best be told in excerpts from four newspaper clippings.

"The intelligence that Miss Laura Keene will on Easter Monday [April 10] 1871, begin a dramatic season at the Fourteenth-Street Theatre calls for publication and notice. Miss Keene has secured the services of Mr. William Creswick, the distinguished English tragedian, who has awaited here for some months an opportunity to appeal to the judgement of American play-goers. The piece to be first acted is 'Nobody's Child.' "

"Laura Keene withdrew 'Nobody's Child' and Mr. Creswick as she was satisfied the public did not want either. The action on the part of this lady was a matter of business, and out of no disrespect to Mr. Creswick, and he should have so looked at it, and not have appealed to the public in a moment of temporary excitement, as he did on his closing night, April 15, when called before the curtain."

"The season at the Fourteenth Street Theatre terminated somewhat abruptly after the performance of Tuesday evening, April 18th. On Monday evening Miss Laura Keene appeared in 'Hunted Down' which had proved quite successful at a Broadway Theatre recently, and it was hoped that it might pull up the business, but the attendance was quite limited, and being still less so on the following evening, it was deemed prudent to terminate the season at once. . . Miss Laura Keene and the dramatic company which had been playing there, go upon a tour of neighboring cities."

"Laura Keene and her dramatic company performed in Bridgeport, Conn., April 24th and 25th; New Haven, 26th; and closed their performances on the 27th, and returned to New York, the speculation proving unremunerative."

Laura's response to fools and knaves was brutal in its incisiveness. Her experience with them had been a long one: Henry Wellington Taylor, Lester Wallack, William Burton, John Sleeper Clarke, and now William Creswick. Her grace was that she was equally brutal to herself.

She had made a botch of things. Again. Few things had gone as they should since that ill-fated Washington performance of *Our American Cousin* attended by Mr. Lincoln. When you thought about it, trying to hang on to that play as her exclusive property had started all her troubles.

Time to begin again. She authorized her lawyers to renew the rental agreement on her home at 34 Bond Street and to work out a rental agreement Sothern wanted for his exclusive use of *Our American Cousin*. The property produced $150 a month, the Sothern royalties produced $260. She was no pauper. She simply had no reserves. For that, Riverside Lawn was the answer. Let the income pile up while Jane and the girls and she lived frugally and quietly beside the Acushnet River. She should have felt chastened. She should have adopted sackcloth. Instead she had never been more creative. She was throwing off new ideas as if she were a St. Catherine's wheel and every spark a thought.

She invented a garbage box for which she sought a patent.

She initiated one of her most engaging gambits with a piano manufacturer, probably Chickering, the maker of her own instrument:

> I am about to visit some of the principal cities, and as I play to the very best people, the idea occurs to me, that it would be an excellent opportunity to introduce the upright piano, if it is, as I have always contended really the best for a lady's drawing room. Now pray do not mistake my object, I have nothing to gain, I have only a sincere wish to abolish the frightful "Square."
>
> If you think it worth the trouble, carry out the enclosed idea of an elegant circular, and it will reach the hands of many thousands whose attention will be called to its close inspection, between the acts.
>
> If this is not worth considering, pray throw it into the fire; and forget the suggestion of the sworn enemy of square pianos
> Laura Keene

The enclosed idea for "an elegant circular" was a fourfold dummy with penned instructions. The cover page had a note, "Leave this blank for the evening's entertainment." The centerfold, left, had for text, "How many elegant parlors & drawing rooms are spoiled by the dreadful coffin like piano, custom compels ladies to use. This struck me particularly after seeing the pretty instruments used in Europe," with a signature. Centerfold, right, had the suggestion, "There a pretty engraving of the piano."

The idea was not used.

iii

Sometime in this period of retreat out of the public eye, Laura conceived a magazine of the fine arts which became her next consuming passion. It was another beginning again.

Fine Arts was a family project. Both her girls worked at supplying copy and ideas. Eventually, through it, Emma met her husband-to-be, Albert Leighton Rawson, who became involved in providing illustrations, art scholarship, and hack services of all kinds. One of Laura's actress acquaintances, Emma Webb Wivert, was drawn in as a partner and then cast out when her nerve quailed. Madame Octavia LeVert, a friend from the world outside the theatre, brought her varied talents and prepossessing name to the project.

There was much to be done to send a magazine out into the world, much more than merely determining policy or writing articles or finding a motto. The ladies at Riverside Lawn learned this slowly and painfully. Also, they learned they could not retire totally from the world, as if to a cloister. The affairs of their friends intruded on their

FINE ARTS.

"Oh, had I but followed the Arts."—TWELFTH NIGHT.

Vol. I.—MARCH, 1872.—No. 1.

The Origin and Divisions of Art.

THERE are three general divisions of Arts, which are embraced under the names of *Mechanic Arts, Decorative Arts,* and *Polite Arts.*

I. The *Mechanic Arts* were born of the necessities of mankind.

Exposed to cold, hunger, and a thousand pressing and imperious wants, Nature ordains that the remedies shall be the price of man's own invention and industry. This department of Arts employs Nature solely for its use. Out of the materials of Nature it builds houses, bridges, wharves, ships, coaches, railroads, telegraphs, and constructs all the implements of printing, surgery, and ten thousand things, by which the convenience and happiness of man are subserved.

Without this department of Arts, mankind would be as stationary as the rocks or the forests. All, then, that has started and continued the human race on the path of progress, from savage to civilized life, came, in the first place, of the *Mechanic Arts.* In a certain sense they may be called the foundation of Arts.

II. *Decorative Arts* are those in which usefulness is combined with pleasure. Here is an element added to the mere usefulness of the purely *Mechanic Arts.* Pleasure is added to utility.

Architecture is the best illustration of *Decorative Art. Mechanic Arts* build the warm, safe, and commodious edifice, the convenient house, and the imposing temple. But *Decorative Arts* come forth and erect the glittering spire, the lofty turret, and the inspiring dome. *Necessity* first produced them; but *Taste* stepped in, and gave them their perfection and their beauty.

III. The *Polite Arts* have chiefly *pleasure* for their object. They seem to have been born more especially of the sweets of tranquillity and plenty. *Polite* comes from a verb which means *to polish.* And under this general head of *Polite Arts,* are included *painting, music, poetry, sculpture, dancing, dress, manners,* and the *drama.* Another, not inappropriate name, for all these would be *Beautiful Arts.* And this is the vast Art region to which this journal will be more especially devoted. It enters upon a field hitherto unoccupied by any single publication in this country, as has already been mentioned in our *Prospectus.* In attempting to supply this great demand upon all the resources of Taste and Beauty, we are not without many misgivings as to our ability to satisfy the expectations which may be awakened by such an enterprise. But we are consoled by the reflection that we enter upon the discharge of our duties with neither attachments nor prejudices which can warp the judgment or blunt the sense of justice. Art has neither *sex* nor *party* ; but it is as universal and impartial as the sunlight and the air. And in discussing all Art questions, we shall endeavor not to lose sight of the different objects and offices of the various kinds of Art.

For instance, no student must forget that the *Mechanic Arts* employ Nature, just as they find her, solely for *use* ; while the *Decorative Arts* employ and polish nature for *use* and *social pleasure* ; but the *Polite Arts* do not really *employ* Nature at all ; they only *imitate* her, and by bringing together in one piece, many distinct and separate charms, form, as it were, a new type of Nature. It is, therefore, the business of the artist to make choice of the most beautiful parts of Nature to form one exquisite whole, which shall be more perfect or more beautiful than mere Nature, without ceasing, however, to be natural. This is the principle upon which the fundamental plan of all Arts must necessarily have been built, and which all great artists have followed, in every age of the world. When the accomplished painter, *Zeuxis,* undertook the task of painting a perfect *Beauty,* he did not draw the picture of any particular woman, but he copied the separate features of several of the most distinguished *Beauties* then alive in Greece, and forming in his own mind an idea that resulted from all these charms combined, he created upon his canvas the form of a woman more beautiful than Nature, but which was nevertheless within the limits allowed to Art. His picture, which was probable and poetical in the whole, was true and historical only in its parts taken separately. And this is what every painter does when he represents the persons who sit to him, with more beauty and grace than they really possess.

And this license belongs to every department of Art, whose business it is to supply the deficiencies or correct the faults of Nature, in order to refine the taste and increase the happiness of man. When Moliere wanted to paint a man-hater, he did not search over the world for an original which he could simply copy. Had he done that, he would only have made a picture, a history, and he would have instructed by halves, but he collected every mark and every stroke of a gloomy temper that he had observed among men, and to these he added whatever his own imagination could supply; and from all these hints, well selected and well laid out, he drew a single character, which was not a representation of the *real,* but of the *probable.* His comedy was not the history of *Alceste,* but his picture of *Alcestes* was the history of man-hatred taken in general. And by this means he conveyed much more instruction than any historian could have done by relating the solitude. Six months' study and preparation were interrupted and the magazine's first issue delayed by the needs of Matilda Heron.

After an absence from the stage of two years, Miss Heron had accepted an engagement at DeBar's Opera House in St. Louis. Her opening night performance shocked and saddened her friends. Her articulation was slurred and her speech "almost unintelligible." She appeared nervous, stroking her hair, wiping her brow. Her comments at the fall of the curtain left no doubt that she was a very sick woman:

"I come not as I did many years ago, full of youth, hope and ambition, but rather as a pauper to strive to earn a little to support my gray hairs and to recover if possible, what I have been robbed of.

"I am now forty years of age and have ten years left me to achieve my lost laurels. I have genius and talent, that I know full well. My heart is in my soul, and my soul is with God. I don't care a fig for the world, and I am just as happy as a big sunflower."

The stage manager interrupted at this point, and the enthralled correspondent for the *Clipper* reported that Miss Heron "danced off stage, waving her arms in a wild manner."

The Keene establishment was shocked. They had known she was occasionally unbalanced. Investigation proved Miss Heron's financial affairs were as bad as she said they were.

The theatrical profession rallied round. A monster benefit for Matilda Heron's relief was organized. Edwin Booth, Lester Wallack, Emma Webb, Kate Reginolds, Emma Waller, and Laura were part of the committee on arrangements. The program that evolved for the afternoon of January 17, 1872, brought all the luminaries of the stage together. Edwin Booth and his company would present a brief version of *Katherine and Petruchio;* Wallack's company, with John Broughman, would present *His Last Legs;* Augustin Daly's Fifth Avenue Theatre

Company agreed to perform the third act of their current success, *Divorce;* and Laura, with John Jack, would present the first act of *School for Scandal.*

It was a stellar aggregation but unless the public thought so and bought tickets, poor Tilly would be no better off. One of the powers of the press at the time was William Winter, drama critic of the *Tribune.* Laura had known him since he came to New York from Boston in the early days of the Bohemians, toward whom he gravitated. Willy — as he was then — had married an aspirant to the theatrical profession from Laura's company. Winter adopted "the high aesthetic line" in his writing and could reel out memorial verses for any occasion. He had known Laura's sharpness only at second hand. "She impressed me as self-willed, volatile, capricious, and imperious," he later wrote. "The influence exerted upon her early in life by Madame Vestris fostered in her combative egotism and a cynical spirit." He was an admirer of all the men who worked with Laura; he named a son after Joe Jefferson and wrote laudatory books and poems about Edwin Booth. But Laura frightened him by her clear-eyed recognition of an unromantic world. Now she needed his help.

My dear Mr. Winter

Your kind and very just notice received by the ladies of M. Herons Committee with gratitude. We were certain sickness prevented an earlier response.

Convey our thanks to your lady. Our regrets at the cause of her absence on such an occasion.

You can indeed help us

May I suggest how?

Tell the public Matilde is penniless — starving
Public will shrug its shoulders
Very sorry!!
Tell them its going to be an ultra
fashionable Matinee
All the private boxes sold 25 and 50$ | *truth* |

    All the stalls going at high prices — then the generous public will want "standing room only" immediately

In great haste

William Winter (1836-1917) theatre critic for the New York TRIBUNE, *scarcely touched Laura's career while she lived. During his long life, his writing about Laura's associates — fulsome biographies of John Brougham, Edwin Booth and Joseph Jefferson, as well as frequent books of random reminiscences — left an impression of her as a virago and artistic failure. His obituary notice for her was typical of his later writings. "As an actress she was best in the utterances of what may be indicated as despairing delerium . . . She seldom presented a symmetrical work of art." John Crehan was moved to write Laura's first biography to refute Winter's account of her disagreements with Joe Jefferson.* UNIVERSITY OF TULSA THEATRE COLLECTION.

Faithfully yours
William Winter.

It was a standing room only affair. The income was $5,390. Matilda Heron could not be restrained from making a speech of thanks. The reporters said that "during the delivery of the address both Miss Heron and the audience were visibly affected." Laura thought it an unbecoming display. Where was her pride? How could she let herself say, "You have raised a woman out of the depths of misery and despair?"

Laura's performance was such that many present thought she would be the object of the next benefit. She struggled in the role of Lady Teazle. Laurence Hutton noted in his dramatic diary for January 17th, "Laura Keene is old, thin, haggard, scragged, horrid, her appearance is painful and made me think of some cartoon I've seen representing death in silks and satins dancing at a ball with youth and beauty. Never want to see Miss Keene in young parts again."

She was desperately ill. The time for Matilda's benefit had been given at the expense of her health and of her magazine. *Fine Arts* was to be, in her words, "high artistic literature." The first issue was delayed until late in February, 1872.

iv

Fine Arts could be described as a portrait of Laura Keene. It was impeccably styled and organized. It demonstrated breeding and taste. It was expensive. It was the Laura of the St. James Gallery, the lady of the theatre who longed for social acceptance, the lady of taste.

But the other Laura Keene was represented also. The bright learner who tried out a patent device to light simultaneously all the gas lights in her theatre, who informed herself on railroads and their time tables, who invented a garbage box — that self-same Laura ran a series of articles on the history of engraving. Her magazine would have been more successful had it been about mechanical arts rather than *Fine Arts*. There were those truly interested in the fine arts for whom Laura's magazine was too elementary. There were others who made pretensions but who would need someone to take the lead before they would dare to buy a magazine edited by an actress. Then there was a third audience who would have liked it and probably profited from it, finding it to be a means to refinement as the chromos in the lobbies of Laura's theatre had been an exposure to the beauties beyond drudgery, but that audience could not afford Laura's expensive magazine.

The articles have a faded charm. Although the editors claim there is no sex in the arts, their comments on manners are predicated on the idea that man is crude and rough without the softening influence of woman. Men are most frequently referred to as "bears." The magazine represented gentility devolving into sentimentality. The serialized novel reads like rejected copy for a Victorian valentine. The magazine comes alive in those articles signed with Laura's initials. Like her letters, they are written in a straightforward manner, free from the cant of the period.

The articles on the drama are a restatement of Laura's philosophy of the theatre. The playbills and daily advertisements of her theatre had given her scope to voice her theatrical ideals and ambitions. *Fine Arts* gave her space for second thoughts. She wrote about the ostracism of actors, which she felt hampered the development of the theatre as well as the actor. Her belief that the actor must have association with those in business, trade, and the professions, as well as the arts, came to be shared by Edwin Booth who a few years later founded The Players Club with provisions for a diversified male membership written into the charter. She wrote an appreciation of the actor Booth with insight and respect. The rancors of the post-assassination years were forgotten. In fact, in all Laura's writing in *Fine Arts,* there is a bittersweet quality of valedictory. Although her doctors had not yet pronounced her illness fatal, her articles read as if she were under death sentence. Her analysis of Booth as Mark Antony in his production of Julius Caesar shows the discerning eye that she brought to her own acting. "At his [Antony's] first entrance there is a cringing sycophancy in his demeanor toward Caesar which impresses the audience disagreeably. It is the slavish bearing of a Syrian freedman of the empire, rather than the self-respecting affection of a Roman, of a friend, and equal." She remarks on similar subtlety later in the play. "Then the great speech over the body, its art, its elocution, tact and subtle management of the crowd with the quicker and quicker delivery till it swells to a torrent of words; finally the leap from the tribune (a trick, but a very clever trick), and his thunderous denunciation of the traitors, were to us, we must confess, a marvel and a surprise. . . There was no room to doubt that we had seen and heard a great actor."

Nowhere in the Booth article does she trade upon her former association with him. Her self-confidence and pride of place are so innate she does not need to feed her ego by reminding readers "she knew him when."

Edwin Booth "was the gentlest and most considerate star I ever saw," said William A. Brady in SHOWMAN. *"His corrections and suggestions were made with courtesy and point — none of these bully-ragging, temperamental outbursts the smaller fry were so fond of."* UNIVERSITY OF TULSA THEATRE COLLECTION.

EDWIN BOOTH

INSIDE VIEW CIGARS.

" Unquestionably the Best 5 Cent Cigar Ever Made."

BARON & CO., Manufacturers,

1007-1009 East Pratt Street,   BALTIMORE, Md.

The Jefferson article is very different. It is a personal testament, but the thrust of its writing is, here is a man who has strayed from his true vocation; I knew him, and thus I can describe how far he has erred. Her sadness that Jefferson had deserted playing for starring, her descriptions of Booth's acting, and random lines from her other articles on the drama make up a handbook on acting. Her ideals of the theatre, as summarized in *Fine Arts,* placed next to the record of her actions as reported in the daily press, reveal a person who frequently caught herself up as she strayed from her ideal and who was constantly willing to start afresh. Her credo, the "disciples of every art should be worthy of that art's divine mission," is energizing but impossible. Her belief that "the actor's life is one of work — solid, anxious work" she demonstrated throughout her career. Despite the fact she had produced such fripperies as *Tib, The Cat* and *White Lies,* she continued to avouch "the theatre is a public school of virtue and refinement."

As with the theatre, so with her personal life. She printed an article on manners in which she incorporated her definition of a fine lady. It was a speech from a play she had never acted, Hannah Cowley's *Belle Stratagem.* She might have seen the play at one of its infrequent revivals in London. She might have read it among the books of her aunt's library. It spoke her ideal.

> She's a creature for whom nature has done much and education more; she has taste, elegance, spirit, understanding. In her manner she is free, her morals nice. Her behavior is undistinguishably polite to her husband and all mankind; her sentiments are for their hours of retirement. In a word, a fine lady is the life of conversation, the spirit of society, the joy of the public! Pleasure follows whenever she appears, and the kindest wishes attend her slumbers.

John Brougham (1810-1880), an Irish comedian, acted with Laura Keene when she first came to the United States. His first wife was her drama teacher. His writing provided Laura with roles. His career continued to touch hers until her untimely death.

Other articles in *Fine Arts* were not so autobiographical. The articles on ancient sculpture, Pompeii, the Academy of San Carlos, and art and architecture abroad are probably the work of Albert Rawson. Rawson lived at 4 Bond Street. The women of the Keene household passed his door every time they walked their street to Broadway. He was a personable widower, an artist, and an acknowledged authority on the Middle East. He tried for a state department appointment to that area, but lived out his life as a teacher and Chautauqua lecturer. His addresses were entitled, "Wandering of a Scribe in the East." His services to the magazine grew during its short history. By September of 1872, when he and Emma were married, his work ranged from the aesthetic, the drawing of a full-page frontispiece illustration for "Abou Ben Adhem," the compilation of an illustrated article on the temple of Chandravata, the writing of an article on the gift of art works from historically famous lovers to their *inamorati,* to the mundane, the application for the magazine's copyright as required by law. He was a balding forty-two when Emma accepted him. She was twenty-eight. The couple were married at the Nativity Roman Catholic Church on September 29.

Fine Arts would have been better served had the contributors been chosen for having something to say or for being recognized for ability to say it. The magazine suffered from a lack of direction. It is difficult to be editorially rigorous when your staff is made up of family and friends.

There is much not known about *Fine Arts:* what it cost the purchaser by the issue, what it cost the subscriber, what it cost to produce.

Laura's monetary involvement can be approximated. Her income from rentals and play royalties had met her debts by July 13, 1871.

The mortgages she then took on Riverside Lawn for four and, later, for three thousand dollars — both at eight percent interest — must have been to provide working capital for *Fine Arts.*

The publishing costs must have been frightening: oversize pages, slick paper, fancy press work, and no advertising. In the one place where she thought she could economize, she did. Her bill for thirteen weeks' food, breakfast and tea daily, came to $9.49 or 73 cents a week. With eggs selling at twenty-five cents a dozen and peaches at thirty cents a peck, the magnitude of a seven-thousand-dollar pre-publication cost comes into perspective.

v

Laura had an idea. What if . . . what if she were to go out on the lecture circuit to speak about the fine arts? A lecture might drum up subscribers for the magazine while at the same time producing income at the box office. She wrote to Colonel Brown, sending him copies of *Fine Arts* for his wife's parlor table. She signed up with the American Literary Bureau at 132 Nassau Street for guidance. She devised a costume recital in which she would speak about the drama, "illustrating certain scenes from standard plays by acting them upon the rostrum."

Laura's daughter Emma would not be able to help on the tour. She and Rawson were needed to keep up the editorial work from New York. Clara would help. She would act and Laura would play for her singing.

The last issue of *Fine Arts* came out in October of 1872 while Laura and Clara were trying to raise money to keep it alive. The lecture venture was now unnecessary: even if they interested thousands in the fine arts there was no magazine to sell. But Laura had committed them to a series of appearances under the American Literary Bureau's sponsorship, and the proceeds did help to pay off debt. Laura was impatient of the strictures of the bureau and wrote Colonel Brown she would be back acting for him "after this infernal bureau business is through." The lecture changed its character from town to town depending upon the equipment in the hall. Laura appeared with an

A Theatre Royal Haymarket of London playbill of OUR AMERICAN COUSIN *states that the "great originality and humour of Mr. Sothern's performance as Lord Dundreay being confirmed by the Public with Acclamations and Roars of Laughter; while his Reading of "Brother Sam's Letter having produced the unusual honor of an encore . . ."* UNIVERSITY OF TULSA THEATRE COLLECTION.

organist in some cities. She appeared with "Signor Morosini, pianist to the King of Italy" in others. Her inaugural recital was before a convention of ministers and teachers in Gloversville, New York, on September 3. The *Clipper* ran advertisements suggesting to persons responsible for the programs of literary societies or Young Men's Christian Associations, or Mercantile Libraries that Laura's costume recitals were just what they wanted. In a confidential burst of unexpected editorial candor, the *Clipper* avowed, "This is no clap-trap 'show' but a really artistic and cultivated entertainment."

The bookings were limited to neighboring cities, so that Laura and Clara could occasionally return to Bond Street, the fourth floor of which was now the address of Mr. and Mrs. Rawson, who kept a place for the ladies of the family until Emma could find a place of their own or Rawson took a post abroad.

To provide Emma with a dowry, Laura cut herself loose from a significant part of her past. She authorized her lawyers to negotiate the sale of *Our American Cousin* to E. A. Sothern, an action he had been soliciting for years. For a lump sum, $2,690, he bought her rights to the play in the United States and Canada, together with the original manuscript.

Lecturing gave time for singing lessons again for Clara and friends again for Laura. Agnes Robertson was in Laura's audience the first night the Fine Arts lecture was delivered in Philadelphia, December 12, 1872. The two had supper together. "Who was that young girl with the glorious voice who sang at the Academy tonight?" Miss Robertson asked of Laura. "There she is," replied Miss Keene, turning her eyes toward her daughter.

The next morning, John Creahan, who called, congratulated Clara on her performance.

"God alone knows how I managed to sing last night," she said. "I left my grandmother dead at home, and I have not the courage to tell aunt of grandma's death. Mr. Booth, our lawyer, is to meet us and will then break the news to my mother."

If Clara could sing under such circumstances, Laura could perform. Booth waited for them while they gave their final costume recital in Philadelphia.

The *Philadelphia Inquirer* reviewer reported, "Miss Keene addressed the audience in a defense of the arts of tragedy, comedy, and music, against all three of which, she said, unthoughtful persons rail. She reminded the audience that the stage, when properly used, and not abused, is a great moral teacher; adverted to the fact that the learned apostle, St. Paul, quoted from a dramatic poet." The reviewer enjoyed the performance of *Morning Call,* a one-act comedy, and scenes from *Much Ado About Nothing.* The one-act she had first played with Lester Wallack; she'd learned Beatrice for James Wallack. Dear God, what a happy time ago!

vi

It was another time for starting over. The lecture business was not her business. Colonel Brown announced that a strong dramatic company would begin a new tour with her in mid-April. Although small, the company was excellent, including Harry Hawk who had been with her that other April in 1865. Emma would accompany her mother, and Rawson agreed to act as advance man.

Business was good, the company compatible, the plays a pleasure to perform: *Our American Cousin, Hunted Down, Masks and Faces, She Stoops to Conquer.* They played hamlets hardly big enough to have a hall, but 750 people from a population of 7,000 was just as big an audience as 750 people from a population of 100,000, and a lot warmer to an actor. The people in the small towns thought the theatre was fairyland, "the young ladies are handsome and understand the bewitching art of dressing."

Colonel Brown booked the company into the Pennsylvania mountains during the hot days of summer. Laura relished the cool nights and good air, which was almost as good as the air of Paradise. That name Paradise, had always raised a laugh when the conductor called out the station, in the days when Laura and Lutz and Jane and the girls had summered there. She'd been the Peri of Paradise then.

Harry Hawk supervised all the company arrangements. Laura didn't need to do much. Emma took care of correspondence, bringing finished items to her only for her signature, but she did write the Wallack family at James Wallack's death in May. Everyone in the company was aware that the old order was passing. It seemed as if each issue of the *Clipper* told of the death of a contemporary and the destruction of another landmark. Fire had destroyed the old Winter

Garden, the New Bowery Theatre, the Music Hall at 444 Broadway, the Academy of Music, Niblo's Garden, Lina Edwin's, the Fifth Avenue Theatre, Barnum's Museum . . .

Laura had a massive hemorrhage while on stage in Tidioute, Pennsylvania, on Friday, July 4, 1873. The company marveled that she survived it. Emma took her home to Bond Street in Manhattan on Sunday, the first day she could be moved. Consultation with her doctor on Monday, July 7, was a formality. She was going to die.

It had been a short life. It was just twenty-two years since Mary Frances Taylor had decided to leave Henry Wellington Taylor's protection to achieve what she could as Laura Keene. No one would have guessed when she signed for lessons with Emma Brougham that she would play her last performance in Tidioute, Pennsylvania, population 4,000.

Chapter 13

Curtain

What is our life? a play of passion,
Our mirth the music of division.
Our mother's wombs the tiring houses be
Where we are dressed for this short comedy,
Heaven the judicious, sharp spectator is,
That sits and marks still who does act amiss,
Our graves that hid us from the searching sun,
Are like drawn curtains when the play is done,
Thus march we, playing, to our latest rest,
Only we die in earnest, that's no jest.
SIR WALTER RALEIGH

She was going to die.

But right now Laura Keene had a lot of arrangements to make. She didn't want people lamenting over her. She'd been an object of curiosity long enough. "We have had several persons call here today with faces long and grave for the occasion, and in search of excitement, ready to learn that Miss Keene was dying or dead," Clara said. Laura had Clara fob them off with the story that she had not returned to New York.

"She desires no one to know where she is, or she would be overrun with people of all sorts. Aunt did return to New York last Sunday in a very weak condition — emaciated and ill. . . Of course, we have not let her know how changed we find her."

Nor did Laura let them know she knew how changed she was. Her actions spoke her knowledge.

There would be no actor's benefit for her. Her lawyer William Booth was brought in to render an accounting.

Should she die immediately, her affairs were chaotic, was his report. Should she be spared, should the doctor's suggestion that she give herself a long, long rest . . . one can hear him "sloothering" like Boucicault.

He drew up the papers she asked for. On Wednesday, July 9, 1873, Laura transferred Riverside Lawn to Clara. Emma Rawson had her husband to take care of her. Both girls had rights in her plays, in the Bond Street house, and in her life insurance, but Clara would need supporting in her career in music. It wasn't the best Laura could do, but it was something she could do immediately. If she were granted time, she and Booth would work out something better.

William Booth brought in an accounting that could be read as a record of willfulness or, as Laura would prefer it, a record of challenges bravely dared: two thousand dollars to Dow to open the Fourteenth Street Theatre; seven, eight, nine thousand dollars to *Fine Arts*. There was no time to ponder whether the ventures could have been made to succeed. There would be time for thinking about them and all the other might-have-beens during the long sleepless nights. A deep breath. What were the facts? She owed what? In all, fifteen thousand dollars?

Not as bad as that. Call it $8,500. Less than that, really, because Jane Keene had forgiven Laura her debts.

Were there any lawsuits still unsettled?

Only a few. The Italian pianist, Morosini, claimed a breach of contract: one of the printers had a claim. Probably $150 would settle all the proceedings against her.

Pay them. Sell the farm and pay off everyone.

There would be no actor's benefit for Laura Keene. There were still the funeral arrangements to make. She told Booth what she wished. She wanted no open casket. She wanted no one to see her as she looked now. She wanted no visiting, no one dropping in at the house to harrow the girls. Could they keep the news of her death out of the papers until after the funeral? She reminded Booth that she had something due her from the American Dramatic Fund, a burial plot, if nothing else.

There were other story lines in the comedy which needed tying off. Sometime in August she wrote to Augustin Daly: "Permit me to introduce to you Miss Marie Livingstone who has been with me during the past season. I can conscientiously recommend her as one of the best Society Mothers on the Stage, and equally good in old comedies, and character parts. She has a fine stage appearance, and costumes with exquisite taste, and is willing to play any part for which she is cast. Miss Livingstone is in every way a lady worthy of a position in a first class theatre." Daly hired her.

That same month she wrote to Jamie Bullock about the "Lincoln dress." If he were to learn of her death and not know what she wanted done with the things of hers he had in storage, he might . . . no telling what he might do. He certainly didn't understand.

Dear Miss Keene
Your 11th received. You said in your letters that I did not understand. How could I not having opened the box until yesterday, then I found your note pined to the Dress which explain all your difficult and distress, it is two Bad after you workin hard as you have so many years.
But hope that you will in a few Days, Defy and Snap your Fingers at all your False Friends . . .
My wife say also it Could not have taken Place at a worse Time if it had only been three or four Month Later she would have camed.

The farm and all the personal property was advertised for sale by auction. It didn't bring what it should have brought, but it brought enough — $1,046.71, a balance left for Clara.

Where did she stand now? Actors from the last company taken care of. The dress to Emma. The debts paid off. The children would have income from royalties, house rent, the Sothern contract. . .

There were those who should have mementos and keepsakes. The girls were busied putting things aside for personal friends. The pictures of Madame Vestris and Edmund Kean which Joe Jefferson had always coveted were set aside for him, for example. Then, and only then, did she permit them to move her from the heat of the city. Laura Keene had completed her arrangements. It was up to another to ring the curtain down.

She died just after midnight, in the early morning of November 4. Her wishes were respected. There was a private funeral with only the girls in attendance at the solemn high mass. There were no newspaper notices in New York until the day of the funeral.

Emma and Clara finally had an opportunity to invoke the Victorian proprieties. The obituary material they provided called their mother Mrs. John Lutz; a marriage was claimed for 1857, place not specified. They did not speak of a previous marriage in England or of their relationship to her. They paid for her to be buried in the cemetery of The Holy Angels, Montclair, New Jersey, on November 7, 1873, as Frances Lutz.

Laura Keene wore that name as uneasily as she had worn the name Frances Taylor. In 1876, at the time of Clara's death, Laura's body was moved to the actor's section of Greenwood, where it was reinterred beside her mother and daughter under a monument whose simple inscription reads, "Laura Keene."

Acknowledgments

To record Laura Keene's career would have been impossible without the help and encouragement of others. Librarians, archivists, typists, have all done much.

Special assistance was given by Stanley Swift who made his library available, and John Brennan, who shared his indefatigable enthusiasm.

Assistance in England was given by Jack Reading, Secretary of The Society for Theatre Research; Frank Burrow, Assistant Secretary of the Licensed Victuallers Central Protection Society of London, Limited; Andrew Block, bookseller; and John Kennedy Melling, fellow theatre buff.

In Washington, D. C., I was first aided by Congressman Page Belcher and Ms. Freddie Lopp and Rosalie Sevier of his staff. At the National Archives I was aided by the Messrs. Edwin R. Flatequal, Tom Heenan, Albert Blair, George Chalou, and James D. Walker; at the Library of Congress by the Messrs. Bernard A. Bernier, Jr., Oliver Orr, Jim Gilreath, Ronald S. Wilkinson, and Charles Sens. At the National Gallery: Dr. Ellen Miles. At Ford's Theatre: Dr. Frank Hebblethwaite, historian.

In Georgetown, I was so fortunate as to have the wise help of Ms. Mathilde Williams, curator of the Peabody Room; Mother Mary Leonard Whipple, Georgetown Visitation Convent; Robert Truax, Librarian of the Columbia Historical Society; Jon Reynolds, University Archivist, Special Collections Division, Georgetown University Library; and George L. Kackley, Oak Hill Cemetery.

A miscellany of individuals answered specific needs. My thanks to Louis A. Rachow, Librarian, the Walter Hampden Memorial

Library, The Players, New York; D. J. Cross, Senior Archivist, the Archives Authority of New South Wales; E. F. Brooks, Jr., President of Chickering & Sons; John H. Ackerman, Editor, *The Sunday Standard-Times*, New Bedford, Massachusetts; Sister Grace Swift, New York City. For specialized help I am indebted to Evan Johnson, Jim Tripplehorn, Lewis Meyer, and Ken Jackson.

A work of this sort is done primarily among collections. Most gratefully I salute the Harvard theatre collection and its curator, Dr. Jeanne T. Newlin; New York Historical Society collection; and the Folger Shakespeare Library. At the University of Tulsa all librarians helped, particularly: Guy Logsdon, Sid Huttner, Hunter Miracle, Margaret Patty, Barbie Brown, Julie Mills, Doris Haynes, Beverly Callaway, June Stremme, Kathy Kane, Sandra Simpson, James McCue and Joel Burstein.

Academic colleagues such as Manly Johnson, Barney Hewitt, Tom Staley, and George and Portia Kernodle helped, as did the academic community through leave time and research grants.

The students who over the years have added typing information about Laura to their normal duties of grading papers are fondly and gratefully remembered: Ann Hiltz Spurgin, Kathy Hughes, Anne Williams, Joanna Van Der Tuin, Teri Bewley, Barbara Heinline Reiker, Barbara Nelson, Gail Hammersley, and last, but not least, Melissa Kirschke Stockdale.

And always, day after day, my enthusiasm and dejection were shared by Ellen Eaves Henneke, to whom this book is lovingly dedicated.

Notes

FOREWORD

Pg. X, ln. 17 *Dictionary of American Biography*. 20 vols. and 8 supplements to 1989. (New York: Charles Scribner's Sons).

Pg. X, ln. 24 Phyllis Hartnoll, ed., *The Oxford Companion to the Theatre*, 3rd ed. Oxford: (Oxford University Press, 1967).

Pg. XI, ln. 4 "Of all men, Wilson has lost most by this conflagration in the way of autograph letters, programs, and what not which I intended to send him." Francis Wilson, *Joseph Jefferson*, (London: Chapman and Hall, 1906) 282.

Pg. XI, ln. 5 *New Bedford Evening Standard*, 20 April 1897.

CHAPTER ONE

Pg. 1, ln. 2 Laura told the British census-taker on 30 March 1851 that she was 25. (H.O.107/1475; Parish of St. George, Hanover Square Westminster).

Pg. 1, ln. 5 In the block for the Rank or Profession of Father, Thomas King Moss's rank is given as Gentleman on Laura's certificate of marriage.

Pg. 1, ln. 7 The Moss family as I have been able to reconstruct it. Thomas King, father. Jane, mother, born 1797, died 11 December 1872, according to the *New York Herald* obituary of 16 December. First child, male, born 1817,

died in a shipwreck, 1874, according to John Creahan, *The Life of Laura Keene*, (Philadelphia; The Rodgers Publishing Company, 1887), 167. Second child, female, Hannah, born 1819, died 22 June 1878. Married to William Edward Stewart, *Herald* obituary, 24 June 1878. Third child, male, Thomas William, born 12 April 1824, (birth recorded in St. James Parish registry), died 1843? Laura Keene's daughter, Emma, told Creahan that her uncle had died before he was 21. Fourth child, female, Mary Frances.

Pg 2, ln. 4 Marriage certificate number 60.

Pg. 2, ln. 6 Creahan, 168.

Pg. 2, ln. 8 Genio C. Scott, "Sketches of the Actors," *Wilkes Spirit of the Times*, 1 March 1862.

Pg. 2, ln. 11 Letter William D. Booth to Laura, 24 November 1863. Speaking of her mother, he said, "she had pined for her absent pet Birdie." Keene folder, Manuscript Division, Library of Congress.

Pg. 2, ln. 13 *Montclair Herald*, December 1873.

Pg. 2, ln. 24 Scott.

Pg. 3, ln. 1 Birth certificates of Emma Eliza Taylor, 187, district of South Chelsea and Clara Stella, 448, District of Hanover Square, both Middlesex County.

Pg. 3, ln. 10 T. Allston Brown, *History of the American Stage*, (1870; reprint, New York: Benjamin Blom, 1969)202.

Pg. 4, ln. 19 *Era,* 12 October.

Pg. 5, ln. 2 Ibid.

Pg. 5, ln. 9 Fusion of *Era,* 26 October and 16 November.

Pg. 5, ln. 16 "Coming Events," *Era,* 24 December.

Pg. 5, ln. 21 Information on Madame Vestris: Leo Waitzkin, *The Witch of Wych Street,* (Cambridge, Mass.: Harvard University Press, 1933).

Pg. 8, ln. 5 Orville A. Roorbach, "Laura Keene," *Actors as They Are,* (New York 1856) 41.

Pg. 8, ln. 12 George Vandenhoff, *Leaves from an Actor's Notebook* (New York: D. Appleton and Company, 1859) 72.

Pg. 8, ln. 19 William W. Appleton, *Madame Vestris and the London Stage* (New York: Columbia University Press, 1974)183 ff.

Pg. 8, ln. 26 *Spirit of the Times,* 8 May 1852.

Pg. 8, ln. 28 Information on the stock company, lines of business, the green room, benefits, etc. of the Nineteenth Century theatre is in Otis Skinner, *Footlights and Spotlights,* (Indianapolis: Bobbs-Merrill Co., 1923); Edward William Mammen, *The Old Stock Company School of Acting,* (Boston: Published by the Trustees of the Public Library, 1945).

Pg. 11, ln. 23 *Clipper,* 20 December 1856.

Pg. 12, ln. 6 *Era,* 28 October 1855. Mr. Wilton "has great satisfaction in quoting the undermentioned parties of celebrity to whom he has had the honour of being most successfully associated; Mdlle. Jenny Lind Goldschmidt. . . J. W. Wallack, esq. . . Miss Laura Keene."

Pg. 12, ln. 17 Passenger index, Consular Correspondence, Liverpool, August 1852. National Archives.

Pg. 12, ln. 21 George C. D. Odell, *Annals of the New York Stage,* (New York: Columbia University Press, 1927) 7:191.

Pg. 13, ln. 10 Keene, "The Drama," *Fine Arts,* 7.

Pg. 13, ln. 14 F.G. DeFontaine, ed. *Birds of a Feather Flock Together: Or Talks with Sothern,* (New York: G.W. Carleton & Co., Publishers, 1878)57.

Pg. 13, ln. 16 W. J. Florence, "Lester Wallack," *North American Review,* 147 (October, 1888)453.

Pg. 13, ln. 21 Roorbach, 21.

Pg. 16, ln. 4 Fred Belton, *Random Recollections of an Old Actor,* (London: Tinsley Brothers, 1880)116.

Pg, 16, ln. 7 *Times,* 21 September 1852.

Pg. 16, ln. 12 Henry James, *A Small Boy and Others,* (New York: Charles Scribner's Sons, 1913)110.

Pg. 16, ln. 16 *Spirit of the Times,* 13 November 1852.

Pg. 16, ln. 26 James.

Pg. 17, ln. 10 Brander Matthews and Laurence Hutton, *Actors and Actresses of Great Britain and the United States,* (New York: Cassell & Company, 1886) 5:293.

Pg. 18, ln. 10 Ibid.

Pg. 18, ln. 16 *Times,* 6 March 1853.

Pg. 18, ln. 21 "Pauline as Seen by Diogenes," *Lantern,* 19 March 1853.

Pg. 19, ln. 12 *Lantern,* 2 October 1852.

Pg. 19, ln. 18 *Times,* 14 June 1853.

CHAPTER TWO

Pg. 21, ln. 1 *Era.* Letter, 27 June reports her re-engagement; 3 July that Wallack's leading lady received nine pounds per week.

Pg. 21, ln. 5 *Times,* 8 November 1853.

Pg. 22, ln. 4 *City of Glasgow,* 27 June 1853. Passenger index, National Archives.

Pg. 22, ln. 13 Obituary of Patrick Hearn(sic). *Herald,* 6 July 1859.

Pg. 22, ln. 15 Laura Keene to unnamed correspondent, 17 July 1856, "a Mr. Hearne Lawyer Wall Street. . . he is the great theatrical lawyer." Harvard Theatre Collection.

Pg. 22, ln. 21 Lutz House, Georgetown, is described in "Historic American Building Survey," HABS, No. DC-105. It is now *The Aged Woman's Home of Georgetown.* A letter from Martha Parke Custis to the revolutionary war veteran hangs on a wall of the home.

Pg. 22, ln. 23 1850 census shows John having no employment. He was excluded from the will made by his father in 1841. Francis is named executor. Will book 5/203, Maryland.

Pg. 22, ln. 26 Deed 31 May 1851, John Lutz to Adelaide M. Lutz.

Pg. 23, ln. 4 Quoted in Paxton Hibben, *Henry Ward Beecher,* (1927; reprint, New York: The Readers Club, 1942) 203.

Pg. 23, legend William Winter, *Vagrant Memories,* (New York: George H. Doran Company, 1915)114.

Pg. 24, ln. 3 *Times,* 14 October 1853.

Pg. 24, ln. 4 *Herald,* 12 October 1853.

Pg. 24, ln. 13 Lester's letter, *New York Weekly Herald,* 29 November 1853.

Pg. 24, ln. 14 Laura's letter, *Herald,* 29 November 1853.

Pg. 24, ln. 25 Roorbach, 23.

Pg. 25, ln. 9 *National Intelligencer,* 12 April 1865.

Pg. 25, ln. 26 "Matters and Things in Baltimore," *Spirit of the Times,* 11 February 1854.

Pg. 26, ln. 6 *Alta,* 29 June 1854.

Pg. 26, ln. 18 Molyneux St. John, "New York Theatres," *The Broadway,* (February, 1868)473.

Pg. 27, ln. 9 *Spirit of the Times,* 10 June 1876.

Pg. 28, ln. 21 Compilation made from playbills and newspaper advertisements.

Pg. 29, ln. 2 Baltimore correspondent, *Porter's Spirit of the Times,* 3 October 1856.

Pg. 29, ln. 8 *Spirit of the Times,* 18 February 1854.

Pg. 29, ln. 12 Advertisement for the U.S. Mail Line steamship, *Ohio, Herald,* 23 February 1854.

Pg. 29, ln. 18 Constance Rourke, *Troupers of the Gold Coast*. (New York: Harcourt, Brace and Company, 1928)51.

Pg. 29, ln. 21 C. A. MacMinn, *The Theatre of the Golden Era*. (Caldwell, Idaho: Caxton Printers, 1941) 133.

Pg. 30, ln. 3 Passenger list, *Alta*, 3 April 1854.

Pg. 30, ln. 9 Advertisement, *Alta*, 10 April 1854, says only 18 miles of mule travel, with the total time across the Isthmus, now nine hours.

Pg. 31, ln. 10 The passenger lists printed in the New York *Commercial Advertiser* for 1854 show an F. Lutz sailing on the *Georgia*. Since John's brother Francis was always helping out, it is logical to suppose the ticket purchase was made in his name. Accounts of the *Georgia*, daily in the *Commercial Advertiser* for February 1854.

Pg. 31, ln. 26 "Editor's table," *Pioneer Magazine*, 249.

Pg. 32, ln. 2 Eleanor Ruggles, *Prince of Players*, (New York: W. W. Norton & Company, Inc., 1953)69.

Pg. 32, ln. 17 The Stockton experience is based on descriptions of the theatre of 1854 in Benjamin Maunard Noid, "History of the Theatre in Stockton, California 1850-1892," Ph.D. Diss. University of Utah, 1968.

Pg. 33, ln. 2 *Lantern*, 81.

Pg. 33, ln. 12 *Alta*, 1 July 1854.

Pg. 33, ln. 25 *Alta*, 13 May 1854.

Pg. 34, ln. 5 Passenger Manifest, Archive Authority, New South Wales.

Pg. 34, ln. 10 *Alta* letter from "Our Lady Correspondent," New York 20 September 1854.

Pg. 34, ln. 12 Creahan, 168.

Pg. 34, ln. 14 Deposition of John S. Lutz, 23 May 1859, Cadwalader Case File in Equity, No. 28, United States Circuit Court for the Eastern District of Pennsylvania, 1858, Laura Keene vs. William Wheatley and John S. Clarke, National Archives Record Group 21.

Pg. 34 ln.16 Jeems Pipes was Stephen C. Massett, who shared a dwelling with Edwin Booth in California, McMinn, *The Theatre of the Golden Era in California*, 368ff.

Pg. 34, ln. 24 *Spirit of the Times*, 20 January 1855, printed Pipes letter dated 16 December 1854.

Pg. 36, ln. 8 *Alta*, 30 May 1855.

Pg. 36, ln. 10 "California Theatricals," *Spirit of the Times*, 30 June 1855.

Pg. 36, ln. 15 Malvina S. Lutz, age 43, was interred in lot 84 Oak Hill Cemetery, Georgetown, on June 24, 1855. Records of the cemetery.

Pg. 36, ln. 19 Passenger index, National Archives.

Pg. 36, ln. 23 *Alta*, 4 October 1855.

Pg. 37, ln. 20 *Chronicle of California*, 5 October 1855, quoted in *Spirit of the Times*, 15 December 1855.

CHAPTER THREE

Pg. 39, ln. 6 Compilation of notices in *Herald, Times* and *Spirit of the Times* for August through November 1855.

Pg. 39, legend The *Albion*, 25 September 1852.

Pg. 40, ln. 12 Charles Dickens, ed., *The Life of Charles James Mathews*, (London: Macmillan and Co., 1879)2:262.

Pg. 41, ln. 14 LaFarge contract information is from Hearne vs Keene, Cases in the Superior Court, New York, December, 1859, 579ff; reports of the breach of contract carried in the press: *Herald*, 12 June 1856; *Spirit of the Times*, 14 June 1856; *Era*, 6 July 1856.

Pg. 42, ln. 4 Salary list for Wallack's, 1857-58. Odell, 2:19.

Pg. 42, ln. 15 *Herald*, 28 August 1854.

Pg. 42, ln. 21 "The Public Amusements of New York from a Business Point of View," *Herald*, 9 December 1856.

Pg. 42, ln. 24 *Herald*, 24 November 1855.

Pg. 43, ln. 6 *Wilkes Spirit of the Times*, 26 March 1864.

Pg. 43, ln. 21 Catherine Reignolds-Winslow, *Yesterday With Actors*, (New York: 1887), 63.

Pg. 45, ln. 7 Roorbach, 15; William L. Keese, *William E. Burton*, (New York: The Dunlap Society, 1891); Joseph Jefferson, *Autobiography*, (New York: The Century Co., 1889)101.

Pg. 45, ln. 10 James Murdoch, *The Stage*, (Philadelphia: J. M. Stoddard & Co., 1880)224.

Pg. 45, ln. 16 *Times*, 24 December 1855.

Pg. 45, ln. 30 *Herald*, 28 August 1854, described the opening of The Metropolitan.

Pg. 46, ln. 6 *Times*, 24 December.

Pg. 46, ln. 13 *Spirit of the Times*, 29 December.

Pg. 46, ln. 18 *Times*, 27 December.

Pg. 46, ln. 19 *Herald*, 26 December.

Pg. 46, ln. 21 Rue Corbett Johnson, "The Theatrical Career of William E. Burton," 434. Ph.D.Diss., Indiana University 1966.

Pg. 47, ln. 6 Mortgage on Acushnet property for $3,000 given by Laura Keene to Jane Keene. 25 October 1871. Keene Folder.

Pg. 47, ln. 15 *Times*, 28 December 1855.

Pg. 47, ln. 24 *The Diary of George Templeton Strong*, (New York: The Macmillan Company, 1952), 2:250.

Pg. 48, ln. 3 Ibid.

Pg. 48, ln. 7 Brown, *History of the American Stage*, 468.

Pg. 48, ln. 12 *Times*, 8 January 1856.

Pg. 48, ln. 13 *Herald*, 4 March.

Pg. 48, ln. 15 *Times*, 7 March.

Pg. 48, ln. 25 Reignolds-Winslow, 72.

Pg. 49, ln. 1 *Sunday Herald*, 20 April, 1856.

Pg. 49, ln. 1 *Herald*, 24 February.

Pg. 49, ln. 6 Unidentified Clipping, Harvard Theatre Collection.

Pg. 49, ln. 7 *New York Illustrated News*, 25 October 1862.

Pg. 49, ln. 17 *Spirit of the Times*, 1 March 1856.

Pg. 49, ln. 19 *Herald*, 28 February.

Pg. 49, ln. 19 Metropolitan Theatre, San Francisco, 19 September 1855.

Pg. 50, ln. 2 *Times*, 29 March.

Pg. 50, ln. 6 *Herald*, 21 April.

Pg. 50, ln. 9 Letter to Mr. Smith, 14 June. Simon Gratz Collection, Historical Society of Pennsylvania.

Pg. 50, ln. 14 Laura's letter about the Hawthornes 23 May. Passage payment is proposed 17 July. Harvard Theatre Collection.

Pg. 50, ln. 26 Letter to English agent for copy of *Agnes*, 17 July 1856. Harvard Theatre Collection.

Pg. 52, ln. 17 "Drama," *Round Table*, 2 January 1864.

Pg. 52, ln. 18 Francis Wolle, *Fritz-James O'Brien*, 1944; 131.

Pg. 52, ln. 23 *Times*, 28 December 1855.

Pg. 53, ln. 2 *Times*, 9 April 1856.

Pg. 53, ln. 9 Creahan, 163.

Pg. 53, ln. 15 *Picayune*, 29 November 1856.

Pg. 53, ln. 23 *Times*, 9 September 1856.

Pg. 54, ln. 2 Unidentified clipping, Harvard Theatre Collection.

Pg. 54, ln. 11 *Herald*, 12 June.

Pg. 54, ln. 19 *Times*, 9 June.

Pg. 54, ln. 24 *Times*, 10 June.

Pg. 54, ln. 27 *Herald*, 10 June.

Pg. 55, ln. 4 *Herald*, 12 June.

Pg. 55, ln. 7 *Times*, 9 June.

Pg. 55, legend *Era*, 1 January 1852.

Pg. 56, ln. 15 *Times*, 21 June.

Pg. 57, ln. 2 *Times*, 23 June.

Pg. 57, ln. 5 *Herald*, 22 June.

Pg. 57, ln. 8 *Era*, 20 July.

Pg. 57, ln. 14 *Herald*, 23 June.

CHAPTER FOUR

Pg. 59, ln. 3 Opening address, *Herald*, 19 November 1856.

Pg. 59, ln. 9 Obituary, *Wilkes Spirit of the Times*, 15 June 1867.

Pg. 60, ln. 2 T. Allston Brown, *A History of the New York Stage*, (New York: 1903)2:164.

Pg. 60, ln. 6 *Herald*, 2 September 1856.

Pg. 60, ln. 9 *Times*, 29 April 1859.

Pg. 60, ln. 15 *Herald*, 19 July 1856.

Pg. 60, ln. 20 *Herald*, 21 July 1856.

Pg. 61, ln. 1 Testimony, *Times*.

Pg. 61, ln. 4 Brown, *New York Stage*, 2:123.

Pg. 61, ln. 7 Testimony, *Times*.

Pg. 61, ln. 26 *Spirit of the Times*, 2 August 1856.

Pg. 62, ln. 8 *Herald,* 2 September 1856.

Pg. 62, ln. 10 *Herald,* 9 September 1856.

Pg. 62, ln. 14 *Herald,* 13 October; 27 October 1856.

Pg. 62, ln. 16 *Baltimore Sun,* 14 October.

Pg. 62, ln. 19 *Herald,* 1 November.

Pg. 63, ln. 5 *Clipper,* 20 September.

Pg. 63, ln. 6 *Washington Evening Star,* 6 September.

Pg. 63, ln. 14 Playbill, John T. Ford Collection, Manuscript Division, Library of Congress.

Pg. 63, ln. 19 *Clipper,* 8 November 1856.

Pg. 63, ln. 24 Reported in Creahan, 164.

Pg. 64, ln. 1 Edward P. Mitchell, *Memories of Editor,* (New York: Charles Scribner's Sons, 1924)19.

Pg. 64, ln. 5 Description of the theatre in *Spirit of the Times,* 22 November 1856; *Frank Leslie's Illustrated Newspaper,* 13 December 1856; *Wilkes Spirit of the Times,* 26 March 1863.

Pg. 64, ln. 25 *Spirit of the Times,* 22 November 1856.

Pg. 65, ln. 20 *Clipper,* 15 April 1865 specifies the seating.

Pg. 66, ln. 1 *Spirit of the Times,* 22 November 1856.

Pg. 66, ln. 2 *Clipper,* 4 November 1863.

Pg. 66, ln. 9 *Herald,* 19 November 1856.

Pg. 66, ln. 15 Opening Address, ibid.

Pg. 67, ln. 27 *Spirit of the Times,* 11 April 1857.

Pg. 68, ln. 3 Roorbach, 43.

Pg. 68, legend Brander Matthews and Laurence Hutton, eds. *Actors and Actresses of Great Britain and the United States,* (New York: Cassell and Company, 1886)5:154.

Pg. 69, ln. 3 Jefferson, *Autobiography,* 206.

Pg. 69, ln. 8 *New York Sunday Times,* 8 May 1859.

Pg. 69, ln. 19 *Philadelphia Inquirer,* 11 October 1869.

Pg. 69, ln. 23 *Fine Arts,* 55.

Pg. 69, ln. 29 *Times,* 17 September 1857.

Pg. 70, ln. 6 Letter to R. M. Field, Boston Museum, 24 September 1872, Harvard Theatre Collection.

Pg. 70, ln. 14 *Spirit of the Times,* 15 November 1873.

Pg. 70, ln. 24 Asia Booth Clarke, *The Elder and the Younger Booth,* (Boston: James R. Osgood and Company, 1882)147.

Pg. 71, ln. 7 *Clipper,* 13 December 1856.

Pg. 71, ln. 15 Reignolds-Winslow, 69.

Pg. 71, ln. 23 *Tribune,* 2 September 1857.

Pg. 71, ln. 25 Francis Wilson, *Joseph Jefferson,* (New York: Charles Scribner's Sons, 1906)100.

Pg. 71, ln. 29 *Tribune,* 13 August 1860.

Pg. 72, ln. 11 Creahan, 138.

Pg. 72, ln. 19 Printed Rules Laura Keene's Varieties. Keene Folder.

Pg. 72, ln. 20 Creahan, 138.

Pg. 72, ln. 23 *Spirit of the Times,* 29 November 1856.

Pg. 73, ln. 6 Jefferson, *Autobiography,* 190-192.

Pg. 74, ln. 18 *Fine Arts,* 7.

Pg. 74, ln. 22 *Spirit of the Times,* 14 March 1857.

Pg. 75, ln. 5 *Herald,* 15 October 1857.

Pg. 76, ln. 3 *Herald,* 16 October 1857.

Pg. 76, ln. 12 Jefferson, *Autobiography,* 187.

Pg. 76, ln. 25 *Clipper,* 1 October 1857.

Pg. 77, ln. 5 Reignolds-Winslow, 31.

Pg. 77, ln. 10 Joseph Francis Daly, *The Life of Augustin Daly,* (New York: The Macmillan Company, 1917)47.

Pg. 77, ln. 13 *Times,* 15 May 1858.

Pg. 77, ln. 22 *Times,* 4 February 1857.

Pg. 77, ln. 26 Laurence Hutton, *Curiosities of the American Stage,* (New York: Harper & Brothers, 1891) 23.

Pg. 77, ln. 27 *Times,* 29 August 1857.

Pg. 78, ln. 7 25 January 1858, Harvard Theatre Collection.

Pg. 78, ln. 16 *Herald,* 31 January 1858.

Pg. 78, ln. 17 Jefferson, *Autobiography,* 184.

Pg. 78, ln. 23 *Times,* 3 February 1857.

Pg. 79, ln. 10 Playbill in the author's collection.

Pg. 79, ln. 22 Letter dated 23, 1857, Harvard Theatre Collection.

Pg. 79, ln. 24 *Spirit of the Times,* 2 January 1858.

Pg. 80, ln. 2 *Times,* 27 February 1857.

Pg. 80, ln. 11 *Herald,* 11 March 1858.

Pg. 80, ln. 17 *Frank Leslie's Illustrated Newspaper,* 19 September 1857.

Pg. 80, ln. 18 *Spirit of the Times,* 12 September 1857.

Pg. 80, ln. 23 *Times,* 4 July 1857.

Pg. 81, ln. 2 *Spirit of the Times,* 17 October 1857.

Pg. 81, ln. 10 *Era,* 7 March 1858.

Pg. 81, ln. 20 *Spirit of the Times,* 6 February 1858.

CHAPTER FIVE

Pg. 84, ln. 2 Pierre M. Irving, *The Life and Letters of Washington Irving,* (New York: G.P. Putnam, 1864) 4:253.

Pg. 84, ln. 7 *Clipper,* 1 August 1857.

Pg. 84, ln. 10 *Clipper,* 27 November 1858.

Pg. 85, ln. 8 *Herald,* 23 January 1857.

Pg. 85, ln. 13 *Herald,* 11 July 1858.

Pg. 86, ln. 13 Laura told Mrs. Vincent of the confrontation, Creahan, 71. Sothern's version is in *Birds of a Feather,* 185.

Pg. 86, ln. 19 Opening of season playbill, Theatre Collection, New York Public Library.

Pg. 86, ln. 21 *Herald,* 4 October 1858.

Pg. 86, ln. 26 Jefferson, *Autobiography,* 193.

Pg. 87, ln. 13 Reignolds-Winslow, 86.

Pg. 87, ln. 24 Eugenia Paul Jefferson, *Intimate Recollections of Joseph Jefferson,* (New York: Dodd, Mead and Company, 1909)163.

Pg. 87, ln. 25 Laurence Hutton, *Plays and Players,* (New York: Hurd and Houghton, 1875)47.

Pg. 88, legend *Wilkes Spirit,* 18 August 1860.

Pg. 89, ln. 6 *Birds of a Feather,* 46.

Pg. 89, ln. 20 *Our American Cousin,* Act I, scene 1.

Pg. 89, ln. 25 Fish and Wharton, eds., *American Law Register,* (Philadelphia: 1861)9:36. Hereinafter: 9 Am L. Reg. 33, and the appropriate page number.

Pg. 90, ln. 3 *Clipper,* 18 January 1862.

Pg. 90, ln. 6 "Weeping-Willow Whiskers," was a reporter's phrase, *Commercial Times* 30 October 1858, reprinted in an advertisement, *Herald,* 2 November 1858.

Pg. 90, ln. 13 *Birds of a Feather,* 24.

Pg. 91, ln. 1 Information about the manuscript which can be found nowhere else is from Cadwalader opinions, Laura Keene vs Wheatley & Clarke, 9 Am. L. Reg. 33.

Pf.91, ln. 3 Letter Laura to Wm D. Booth, 25 December 1865. Harvard Theatre Collection.

Pg. 91, ln. 6 Testimony, Keene vs. Wheatley.

Pg. 91, ln. 8 Copyright title page, Keene Folder.

Pg. 92, ln. 3 Emma Taylor letter to the *New York Sun,* 2 September 1877, "Mr. John Lutz . . . named Our American Cousin." Keene Folder.

Pg. 92, ln. 11 Odell, 7:126.

Pg. 92, ln. 16 *Era,* 19 December 1858.

Pg. 92, ln. 20 Jefferson, *Autobiography,*194.

Pg. 93, legend Quoted in the introduction, Dion Boucicault, *The Art of Acting,* (New York: Columbia University Press, 1926)12.

Pg. 94, ln. 7 Jefferson, *Autobiography,* 196.

Pg. 94, ln. 21 Jefferson, *Intimate Recollections,* 164.

Pg. 94, ln. 23 *Times,* 22 December 1858.

Pg. 95, ln. 3 *Sunday Times,* 23 January 1859.

Pg. 95, ln. 9 *The Education of Henry Adams,* (1918) 1942, 169.

Pg. 95, ln. 20 *Porter's Spirit of the Times,* 16 January 1859.

Pg. 95, ln. 29 George Henry Lewes, *On Actors and the Art of Acting,* 2nd ed., (London: Smith, Elder & Co., 1875) 129.

Pg. 96, ln. 11 Lutz deposition, Keene vs. Wheatley & Clarke.

Pg. 96, ln. 26 *Herald,* 18 Februrary 1859.

Pg. 97, ln. 16 Ticket information from a playbill of the fourth week of the run. Harvard Theatre Collection.

Pg. 97, ln. 25 Daly, 29.

Pg. 97, ln. 28 *Clipper,* 15 January 1859.

Pg. 98, ln. 14 Letter to the Managers of the Mount Vernon Association, 14 December 1858. Advertisement *Herald,* 29 December 1858.

Pg. 98, ln. 16 Information leaflet, The National Trust for Historic Preservation, 1975.

Pg. 98, ln. 17 Response to Laura in the advertisement *sup.*

Pg. 98, ln. 18 *Times,* 19 January 1859.

Pg. 100, ln. 5 *Porter's Spirit of the Times,* 12 February 1859.

Pg. 100, ln. 6 *Times,* 7 February 1859.

Pg. 100, ln. 20 *Spirit of the Times,* 14 September 1861.

Pg. 100, ln. 24 Letter 21 January 1859, quoted in Thomas Edgar Pemberton, *A Memoir of Edward Askew Sothern,* (London: Richard Bentley and Son, 1890),162.

Pg. 100, ln. 25 Ibid, 161.

Pg. 101, ln. 27 Jefferson, *Autobiography,* 204.

Pg. 102, ln. 9 Ibid.,203.

Pg. 102, ln. 16 Letter from Joseph Crosby to Joseph Parker Norris, Folger Shakespeare Library.

Pg. 102, ln. 23 *Spirit of the Times,* 8 January 1859.

Pg. 103, ln. 2 Ibid., 30 April 1859.

Pg. 103, ln. 6 Advertisement, *Herald,* 19 April 1859.

Pg. 103, ln. 9 Playbill of April 19, Harvard Theatre Collection.

Pg. 103, ln. 22 Preface to the production reproduced in Creahan, 143. Those who assisted Laura are represented by initials, H - and W - . William Winter identifies W - as White, a friend of Burton's. Hallack was at Harvard, also a friend of Burton's. That he is the H - mentioned by Laura is conjecture.

Pg. 104, ln. 4 Obituary, *Times,* 20 December 1879.

Pg. 104, ln. 9 *Era,* 26 June 1859.

Pg. 106, ln. 2 Cadwalader opinion, 9 Am. L. Reg. 33, p52.

Pg. 106, ln. 20 *Fine Arts, 71.*

CHAPTER SIX

Pg. 108, ln. 1 To a Miss Attwood, 16 June 1859. Harvard Theatre Collection.

Pg. 108, ln. 2 *Times,* 3 September 1860.

Pg. 108, ln. 7 *Herald,* 27 July 1859.

Pg. 108, ln. 11 Undated letter, Harvard Theatre Collection.

Pg. 109, ln. 7 "Drama," *Frank Leslie's Illustrated Newspaper,* 10 September 1859.

Pg. 109, ln. 22 *Wilkes Spirit of the Times,* 10 September 1859.

Pg. 110, legend Sothern's son quoted in George Middleton, *These Things Are Mine,* (New York: MacMillan Company, 147) 390.

Pg. 111, ln. 1 *Times,* 16 September 1859.

Pg. 111, ln. 13 The need for citizenship stated 9 Am. L. Reg. 33; 46.

Pg. 111, ln. 27 Brougham quip quoted Wallack, 198.

Pg. 111, ln. 29 *Herald,* 26 November 1859.

Pg. 112, ln. 2 *Times,* 17 October 1859.

Pg. 112, ln. 5 *Times,* 28 December 1859.

Pg. 112, ln. 12 *Herald,* 1 January 1860.

Pg. 112, ln. 15 *Herald,* 2 January 1860.

Pg. 112, ln. 15 *Times,* 7 January 1859.

Pg. 113, ln. 2 Odell, 7:218.

Pg. 114, ln. 3 *Times,* 22 November 1859.

Pg. 115, ln. 13 *Wilkes Spirit of the Times,* 4 May 1861.

Pg. 115, ln. 23 *Times,* 6 January 1860.

Pg. 116, ln. 3 *Saturday Press,* 28 May 1859.

Pg. 116, ln. 6 *Clipper,* 19 March 1859.

Pg. 116, ln. 14 *San Joaquin Republic,* 16 March 1862, quoted in Noid, "History of the Theatre in Stockton, California, 1850-1892," 74.

Pg. 117, legend Matthews and Hutton, 5:84.

Pg. 117, ln. 2 *Herald,* 16 January 1860.

Pg. 117, ln. 4 Advertisement, *Times,* 9 January 1860.

Pg. 117, ln. 7 Advertisement, *Times,* 16 January 1860.

Pg. 118, ln. 5 Boucicault's pride in this exchange is inferred from his singling it out as an example of good theatre which could not be "found in Scott's novel or Dibdin's play or any other work whatever," MSS signed by D. Boucicault written to the editor of an unnamed newspaper concerning Jean Davenport's pirating of his play. Harvard Theatre Collection.

Pg. 118, ln. 14 Letter to Augustin Daly, endorsed August, 1868, Daly collection, Folger Shakespeare Library.

Pg. 119, ln. 3 *Wilkes Spirit of the Times,* 21 January 1860.

Pg. 119, ln. 18 Edward Krause, ed., *Dolmen Boucicault* (Chester Springs, Pennsylvania: Dufour Editions, 1965) 47.

Pg. 120, ln. 6 Odell, 7:213.

Pg. 120, ln. 23 Playbill, Harvard Theatre Collection.

Pg. 122, ln. 3 "Leaves from a Dramatist's Diary," *North American Review,* August 1889, 231.

Pg. 122, ln. 31 Townsend Walsh, "A Chat with Mrs. Barney Williams," quoted in Townsend Walsh, *The Career of Dion Boucicault,* n72.

Pg. 123, ln. 5 Clement Scott, *The Drama of Yesterday and Today,* (London: Macmillan and Co., Limited, 1899), 1:100.

Pg. 123, ln. 16 The book for the first performance was three copy books, one for each act. Harvard Theatre Collection.

Pg. 123, ln. 17 Walsh, 81.

Pg. 124, ln. 18 Adapted from Harvard Promptbook.

Pg. 124, ln. 25 Krause, 42.

Pg. 126, ln. 10 Roorbach, 26.

Pg. 126, ln. 12 Reignolds-Winslow, 65.

Pg. 126, ln. 22 Dion Boucicault, "The Debut of a Dramatist," *The North American Review*, April 1889, 461.

Pg. 126, ln. 26 Unidentified clipping, *Dion Boucicault Scrapbook,* Theatre Collection, New York Public Library.

Pg. 127, ln. 8 Kate Ryan, *Old Boston Museum Days*, (Boston: Little Brown, and Company, 1915) 185.

Pg. 127, ln. 19 *Tribune*, 14 May 1860.

CHAPTER SEVEN

Pg. 131, ln. 10 *Herald*, 24 December 1858.

Pg. 132, ln. 7 Lutz deposition.

Pg. 132, ln. 17 *Clipper*, 18 August 1860.

Pg. 132, ln. 25 Cadwaladar's opinion, 9 Am. L. Reg. 33; p34.

Pg. 132, ln. 29 Ibid., 51.

Pg. 133, ln. 7 Report of Laura Keene vs. Moses Kimball, 16 Gray (Mass.) Boston: Little, Brown & Co., 1871, 548.

Pg. 133, ln. 18 *Times*, 4 March 1868.

Pg. 134, ln. 9 9 Am. L. Reg. 33, pp. 100-101.

Pg. 134, ln. 24 Ibid, 60.

Pg. 141, ln. 2 Lutz deposition.

Pg. 141, ln. 24 Thomas Hailes Lacy, "Acting Edition," *Colleen Bawn*.

Pg. 141, ln. 26 Daly vs. Palmer et. al. Case No. 3,522, 6 Fed. Case., pp 1132-1139.

Pg. 142, ln. 9 Ibid., 1136.

Pg. 142, ln. 11 Ibid., 1137.

Pg. 143, ln. 4 Samuel Henry Wandell, *The Law of the Theatre*, (Albany: J.B. Lyon, 1891), 483.

CHAPTER EIGHT

Pg. 145, ln. 11 Statement of C. Young, Treasurer of Laura Keene's Theatre, 11 March 1862. Keene Folder.

Pg. 145, ln. 16 *Herald*, 6 September 1860.

Pg. 146, ln. 20 *Wilkes Spirit of the Times,* 27 April 1861.

Pg. 147, ln. 2 *Herald*, 13 May 1861.

Pg. 147, ln. 8 Young's statement, ibid.

Pg. 147, ln. 25 Copyright page, Keene Folder.

Pg. 148, ln. 3 Advertisement, *Herald*, 26 November 1860.

Pg. 148, ln. 28 *Times*, 29 September 1859.

Pg. 149, ln. 9 *Times*, 26 November 1860.

Pg. 149, ln. 14 *Herald*, 26 November 1860.

Pg. 149, ln. 19 *Clipper*, 1 December 1860.

Pg. 149, ln. 23 *Wilkes Spirit of the Times,* 5 October 1860.

Pg. 149, ln. 24 Note in *The Programme*.

Pg. 150, ln. 7 *Wilkes Spirit of the Times,* 21 June 1862.

Pg. 150, ln. 14 *Times*, 30 August 1859.

Pg. 150, ln. 15 *Clipper*, 9 February 1861.

Pg. 150, ln. 19 *Clipper*, 4 October 1862.

Pg. 151, ln. 3 Baker Music Collection, Library of Congress.

Notes 289

Pg. 151, legend *Mirror,* 14 January 1887.

Pg. 152, ln. 13 Advertisement, *Herald,* 11 April 1859.

Pg. 152, ln. 18 *Times,* 30 August 1859.

Pg. 153, ln. 9 Wilson A. Disher, *The Cowells in America,* (London: Oxford University Press, 1934)247.

Pg. 153, ln. 21 Skinner, 58.

Pg. 153, ln. 25 *Era,* 23 December 1861.

Pg. 154, ln. 2 *Spirit of the Times,* 5 January 1861.

Pg. 154, ln. 6 *Clipper,* 9 February 1861.

Pg. 154, ln. 8 *Wilkes Spirit of the Times,* 11 May 1861.

Pg. 154, ln. 12 *Herald,* 29 July 1861.

Pg. 154, ln. 20 Advertisement, *Herald,* 2 December 1860.

Pg. 154, ln. 25 *Wilkes Spirit of the Times,* 8 December 1860.

Pg. 154, ln. 26 *Clipper,* 8 December 1860.

Pg. 155, ln. 9 Advertisement, *Herald,* 8 December 1860.

Pg. 156, ln. 17 *Wilkes Spirit of the Times,* 14 September 1861.

Pg. 156, ln. 19 *Sunday Times,* 2 December 1860.

Pg. 156, ln. 20 *Wilkes Spirit of the Times,* 14 September 1861.

Pg. 156, ln. 24 *Wilkes Spirit of the Times,* 26 March 1864.

Pg. 156, ln. 29 Brown, *History of the American Stage,* 236.

Pg. 157, ln. 4 Disher, 247-248.

Pg. 157, ln. 7 *Wilkes Spirit of the Times,* 26 October 1861.

Pg. 157, ln. 8 *Clipper,* 29 June 1861; 8 December 1860.

Pg. 157, ln. 14 *Clipper,* 24 August 1861.

Pg. 157, ln. 19 *Herald,* 26 November 1860.

Pg. 157, ln. 25 Advertisement, *Herald,* 10 February 1861.

Pg. 158, ln. 3 He left the company May 20. He died 27 May 1861.

Pg. 158, ln. 20 There is no known script of *The Seven Sisters.* All lines are from advertisements or reviews. Advertisement, *Herald,* 10 February 1861.

Pg. 159, ln. 10 *Clipper,* 23 March 1861.

Pg. 159, ln. 26 *Clipper,* 20 April 1861.

Pg. 160, ln. 19 *Herald* reported $310. *Wilkes Spirit of the Times* reported $810.

Pg. 161, ln. 6 Advertisement, *Herald,* 27 September 1861.

Pg. 161, ln. 24 *Wilkes Spirit of the Times,* 5 October 1861.

Pg. 162, ln. 5 *Herald,* 27 September 1861.

Pg. 162, ln. 25 *Clipper,* 8 March 1862.

Pg. 163, ln. 27 Advertisement, *Herald,* 8 October 1862.

Pg. 164, ln. 4 *Wilkes Spirit of the Times,* 13 September 1862.

Pg. 164, ln. 9 *Herald,* 1 December 1862.

Pg. 164, ln. 16 *Herald,* 26 November 1862.

Pg. 165, ln. 3 *Clipper,* 1 November 1862.

Pg. 165, ln. 15 *Clipper,* 16 May 1857.

Pg. 165, ln. 26 Card of Lennox and Raymond, *Herald,* 7 March 1863.

Pg. 165, ln. 26 *Herald,* 8 March 1863.

Pg. 167, ln. 5 Lennox & Raymond, ibid.

Pg. 167, ln. 9 Advertisement, *Herald,* 17 April 1863.

Pg. 167, ln. 13 *The Programme,* 4 May 1863.

Pg. 167, ln. 17 *Clipper,* 16 May 1863.

Pg. 168, ln. 8 *The Programme,* ibid.

Pg. 168, ln. 15 Odell, 7:47.

Pg. 168, ln. 23 *Wilkes Spirit of the Times,* 28 January 1862.

Pg. 169, ln. 1 Ibid.

Pg. 169, ln. 9 Documents of Rawdon Pullam, Keene Folder.

Pg. 169, ln. 16 Frank P. Morse, *Backstage with Henry Miller,* (New York: E.P. Dutton & Co., 1938) 68.

Pg. 170, ln. 7 Creahan, 175.

Pg. 170, ln. 27 Keene Folder.

Pg. 171, ln. 6 Creahan, 23; William Winter, *Vagrant Memories,* (New York: George H. Doran Company, 1915) 54.

Pg. 172, ln. 3 *Wilkes Spirit of the Times,* 26 March 1864.

Pg. 172, ln. 7 Lloyd Morris, *Curtain Time,* (New York: Random House, 1953) 193.

Pg. 172, ln. 9 Duff statement, *Clipper,* 3 August 1867.

Pg. 172, ln. 14 25 December 1865. Harvard Theatre Collection.

CHAPTER NINE

Pg. 176, ln. 15 Sol Smith, *Theatrical Management in the West and South* (New York: Harper & Brothers, 1868) 79.

Pg. 177, ln. 26 13 January 1863. Harvard Theatre Collection.

Pg. 178, ln. 6 Contract between Richmond Theatre and Col. T. Allston Brown's Agency, 18 August 1870. Keene Folder.

Pg. 178, ln. 11 Undated letter to John Dyott. Probably February 1865. Harvard Theatre Collection.

Pg. 178, ln. 24 *Clipper,* June 27.

Pg. 179, ln. 12 Edwin A. Field, *Through the Stage-Door: A Complete Handbook of the Theatre* (Boston: 1896) 8.

Pg. 180, ln. 2 Cards with drawings of floor plans, along with property list for manager of Springfield, Mass. Theatre. No date. Harvard Theatre Collection.

Pg. 181, ln. 2 *Washington City Directory,* 1855-56.

Pg. 181, ln. 13 The grill existed well into the second half of this century, according to Mother Leonard Whipple.

Pg. 182, ln. 3 Clara Louise Kellogg, *Memoirs of an American Prima Donna,* (New York: G.P. Putnam's Sons, 1913) 11.

Pg. 183, ln. 6 Alfred Bunn, *Old England and New England* (London: Richard Bentley, 1863) 1:280.

Pg. 183, ln. 29 Olive Logan, *The Mimic World* (Philadelphia: New World Publishing Company, 1871)241 ff.

Pg. 184, ln. 12 Mitchell, *Memoirs of an Editor*, 20.

Pg. 184, ln. 28 Charles H. Day, "An Early Combination," *New York Dramatic Mirror*, 3 August 1901.

Pg. 185, ln. 3 An example of Lutz leather work for ladies in the Peabody Room, Georgetown, Washington Public Library.

Pg. 185, ln. 4 Logan, 194.

Pg. 185, legend Correspondence with E.F. Brooks, Jr., President of Chickering & Sons, 1972-1973.

Pg. 185, ln. 9 Laura, 11 April 1869 to an unnamed piano manufacturer, said she traveled with her piano.

Pg. 186, ln. 5 J.M.D. Hardwick, *Emigrant in Motley* (London, 1954) 228.

Pg. 186, ln. 6 Described in Dorothy Jean Taylor, "Laura Keene in America, 1852-1873," 317. Ph.D. Diss., Tulane University, 1966.

Pg. 186, ln. 7 Disher, 48.

Pg. 186, ln. 11 *Clipper*, 19 March 1870.

Pg. 186, ln. 21 Letter, 25 December 1865. Harvard Theatre Collection.

Pg. 186, ln. 25 *Memories of the Professional and Social Life of John Owens by His Wife*. (Baltimore: John Murphy and Company, 1892) 165.

Pg. 187, ln. 27 *Wilkes Spirit of the Times*, 14 June 1862.

Pg. 188, ln. 6 Letter to Field 9 February and 16 March 1873. Harvard Theatre Collection.

Pg. 188, ln. 16 Copyrights granted to Laura Keene, 21, 25, 26, January 1865. Keene Folder.

Pg. 190, ln. 14 Endorsed 27 January 1865, Harvard Theatre Collection.

Pg. 190, ln. 21 Memorandum 3 February 1865. Keene Folder.

Pg. 190, ln. 24 Letter 8 February 1865. Harvard Theatre Collection.

Pg. 190, ln. 27 *Baltimore Sun*, 20 February 1865.

Pg. 191, ln. 1 Advertisement, *Sun*, 25 February 1865.

Pg. 191, ln. 17 Advertisement, *Washington Star*, 6 April 1865.

Pg. 191, ln. 23 Undated letter, John Ford to J.B. Wright, Harvard Theatre Collection.

CHAPTER TEN

Pg. 193, ln. 17 W.J. Ferguson, "Lincoln's Death," *The Saturday Evening Post*, 12 February 1927, 40.

Pg. 194, ln. 7 Testimony, Benn Pitman comp. *Assassination of President Lincoln and the Trial of the Conspirators*, (New York: Moore, Wilstach & Baldwin, 1865) 76.

Pg. 195, ln. 3 George J. Olszewski, *Restoration of Ford's Theatre*, (Historic Structures Report, 1963) 45n. 163.

Pg. 195, ln. 9 George D. Ford, *Those Were Actors,* (New York: Library Publishers, 1955) 302.

Pg. 195, ln. 12 Pitman, 99.

Pg. 195, ln. 14 Pitman, 100-101.

Pg. 195, ln. 24 *Star,* 14 April 1865.

Pg. 197, ln. 2 Pitman, 99.

Pg. 197, ln. 16 Ferguson, 44.

Pg. 198, ln. 9 Carl Sandburg, *Abraham Lincoln, The War Years,* (New York: Harcourt Brace & Company, 1939) 4:269.

Pg. 198, ln. 20 Pitman, 102.

Pg. 199, ln. 3 Pitman, 104.

Pg. 199, ln. 8 Withers Testimony, Osborn H. Oldroyd, *The Assassination of Abraham Lincoln* (Washington, 1901) 21.

Pg. 199, ln. 13 Ford, 306.

Pg. 199, ln. 26 Ferguson, 40.

Pg. 200, ln. 19 Oldroyd, 20.

Pg. 200, ln. 25 Ferguson, 39.

Pg. 201, ln. 6 *Boston Sunday Herald,* 11 April 1897.

Pg. 201, ln. 17 Ferguson, 40.

Pg. 203, legend Stephen Vincent Benét, *John Brown's Body* (New York: Heritage Press, 1948) 447.

Pg. 203, ln. 11 Fusion of testimony, Pitman, 74, 105, 7, 76.

Pg. 204, ln. 14 Hawk, *Sunday Herald.*

Pg. 204, ln. 17 Pitman, 78.

Pg. 204, ln. 26 Pitman, 79.

Pg. 205, ln. 21 *New York Herald,* 17 April 1865.

Pg. 205, ln. 26 Charles A. Leale, *Lincoln's Last Hours* (N.P., 1909) 4.

Pg. 206, ln. 3 *Herald,* 17 April 1865.

Pg. 206, ln. 10 Ferguson, 44.

Pg. 206, ln. 28 Leale, 5, 6.

Pg. 207, ln. 5 Leale, 7.

Pg. 207, ln. 15 Pitman, 79.

Pg. 207, ln. 26 "Recollections of Lincoln's Assassination," *North American Review,* April 1896, 425.

Pg. 208, ln. 6 Hawk, *Sunday Herald.*

Pg. 208, ln. 7 Ferguson, 48.

Pg. 208, ln. 9 Pitman, 108.

Pg. 209, ln. 6 John T. Ford, "Behind the Curtain of Conspiracy," *North American Review,* April 1889. 486.

Pg. 209, ln. 24 Hawk, *Sunday Herald.*

Pg. 209, ln. 28 The editor of the facsimile reproductions of Tanner's holograph records of Lincoln testimony published by Union League Club of Philadelphia, 1968, *While Lincoln Lay Dying,* says "Many years later Tanner stated that Laura Keene also appeared to give testimony, but if her statement was recorded it has not survived in the Tanner papers." 5.

Pg. 210, ln. 1 The card printed in the Mobile Newspaper was quoted *Clipper,* 2 March 1867.

Pg. 210, ln. 10 Pitman, 110.

Pg. 211, ln. 3 Emma Taylor said, "If they have no relative in the box office, they are both mismanaged and robbed. . . . "Tips of five dollars are thought little of. Creahan, 250.

Pg. 212, ln. 15 Description of the dress, *Baltimore Sun*, 18 August of an unspecified year, in the Hoblitzelle Theatre Arts Library, University of Texas.

Pg. 212, ln. 15 The Smithsonian has an envelope containing Laura Keene's "bloody cuff." According to M.J. Adler, nephew of John Lutz, "she gave me this cuff the next morning at the Metropolitan Hotel." I am indebted to John Brennan for locating and photographing it.

Pg. 213, ln. 4 *Baltimore Sun*, 19 April 1865.

Pg. 213, ln. 14 Letter received by Col. H.L. Burnett, File no. 28, Investigation and Trial Papers Relating to the Assassination of President Lincoln, National Archives, Washington, D.C. Microcopy 599, reel 2, frames 0052, 0053, 0050, 0054.

Pg. 213, ln. 20 The political power of F.A. Lutz is borne out in a small incident. The only exhibit in the Laura Keene passport file in Department of State archival documents is a letter from W.D. Booth, Laura's lawyer to F.A. Lutz asking, "If you will get the passport and send it to me, I will see that it is forwarded to her at London."

Pg. 214, ln. 14 Undated clipping from *Philadelphia Weekly Times* containing a letter from Emma Rawson. Keene Folder.

Pg. 214, ln. 18 Creahan, 25.

CHAPTER ELEVEN

Pg. 215, ln. 14 *Clipper*, 20 May 1865.

Pg. 216, ln. 10 Phineas D. Gurley, *The Voice of the Rod*, (Washington, D.C., 1865) 14-15.

Pg. 216, ln. 22 Richard Lockridge, *Darling of Misfortune*, (New York: The Century Co., 1932) 160.

Pg. 217, ln. 7 *Herald*, 16 April 1865.

Pg. 217, ln. 11 Quoted, *Herald*, 24 February 1867.

Pg. 217, ln. 16 Quoted, *Clipper*, 2 March 1867.

Pg. 217, ln. 27 Mrs. Eldridge said that Laura showed her the gown in Cincinnati. Creahan, 135.

Pg. 218, ln. 6 *Cincinnati Enquirer*, 22 April 1865.

Pg. 218, legend Creahan, 176.

Pg. 219, ln. 7 Samuel Clemens, *Mark Twain's Autobiography*, (New York: Harper & Brothers Publishers, 1924) 2:313.

Pg. 219, ln. 13 Keene Folder.

Pg. 219, ln. 16 Will of Emma Rawson, *Liber* 304 of wills, 345, Surrogate court, county and state of New York.

Pg. 219, ln. 19 Clipping from the *Baltimore Sun*, August 18 of an unspecified year, probably 1896, in the Hoblitzelle Theatre Arts Library, University of Texas.

Pg. 219, ln. 23 A mozaic of data from the Advertisement of George F. Bourne, 31 July 1873, *Evening Standard*, New

Bedford, Auctioning off Laura's farm; Franklyn Howland, *A History of the Town of Acushnet,* Published by the Author, New Bedford, Mass. 1907; article about Laura Keene, 10 July 1949, *New Bedford Standard Times.*

Pg. 220, ln. 29 Arthur Shorman Phillips, *The Phillips History of Fall River,* Dover Press, 1945.

Pg. 223, ln. 9 Letter 29 September 1865, *Herald,* 2 October 1865.

Pg. 224, ln. 16 To Augustin Daly. Daly Collection, Folger Shakespeare Library.

Pg. 226, ln. 22 Notice, *Clipper,* 6 January 1869.

Pg. 226, ln. 28 *Buffalo Express,* 5 June 1867.

Pg. 227, ln. 13 *Clipper,* 8 May 1869.

Pg. 227, ln. 18 *Washington Star,* 19 April 1869.

Pg. 227, ln. 28 Malvina S. Lutz, who had been interred in lot 84 Oak Hill Cemetery, was moved to lot 565 29 May 1865. John S. Lutz was buried in the same grave on 20 April 1869. Records of Oak Hill.

Pg. 228, ln. 20 Advertisement, *Public Ledger,* 17 September 1869.

Pg. 229, ln. 7 Copy-right pages, Keene Folder.

Pg. 229, ln. 12 Letter dated Saturday, Daly Collection, Folger Shakespeare Library.

Pg. 229, ln. 24 Back dated 1870. Daly Collection.

Pg. 229, ln. 27 Letter dated Tuesday. Daly Collection.

Pg. 230, ln. 7 Marvin Felheim, *The Theatre of Augustin Daly,* (Cambridge: Harvard University Press, 1956) 200.

Pg. 230, ln. 20 Creahan, 193.

Pg. 231, ln. 11 *Philadelphia Inquirer,* 27 November 1869.

Pg. 231, ln. 15 *Philadelphia Press,* 13 October 1869.

Pg. 231, ln. 23 Certified copy of decree in the matter of a trust created for the benefit of Laura Keene and others, entered 10 May 1870. Keene Folder.

Pg. 231, ln. 25 Margaret Morris rental, 5 March 1870, Keene Folder.

Pg. 234, ln. 2 *Washington Star,* 15 February 1870.

Pg. 234, ln. 13 Creahan, 140.

Pg. 234, ln. 16 Mortgage of personal wardrobe and properties to Charles H. Day, 25 October 1870. Keene Folder.

Pg. 235, ln. 2 Creahan, 235.

Pg. 235, ln. 17 Robert Somers, *The Southern States Since the War 1870-71,* rpt, (University of Alabama Press, 1965), 38-39.

Pg. 235, ln. 24 Somers, 99.

Pg. 235, ln. 27 Jefferson, *Autobiography,* 132.

Pg. 236, ln. 1 Somers, 82.

Pg. 236, ln. 5 Somers, 67.

Pg. 237, ln. 5 Remainder of chapter based on Charles Day, "An Early Combination,"

New York Dramatic Mirror, 31 August 1901.

CHAPTER TWELVE

Pg. 239, ln. 8 Brown's first clients are listed in his advertisement, *Clipper* 1 June 1870.

Pg. 241, ln. 12 Laura to Colonel Brown, 30 July, no year. Of Mr. Tyler, she said, "I wished him to act as my agent in connexion with you." Harvard Theatre Collection.

Pg. 242, ln. 28 Advertisement, *Clipper,* 10 September 1870.

Pg. 243, ln. 4 Advertisement, *Clipper,* 8 October 1870.

Pg. 243, ln. 10 Advertisement, *Clipper, 15 October 1870.*

Pg. 244, ln. 10 Undated letter. Harvard Theatre Collection.

Pg. 245, ln. 3 *Clipper,* 21 January 1871.

Pg. 245, ln. 13 Advertisement, *Times* (New York), 22 January 1871.

Pg. 246, ln. 7 Archie Binns, *Mrs. Fiske and the American Theatre,* (New York: Crown Publishers, 1955) 17.

Pg. 247, ln. 4 *Clipper,* 4 February 1871.

Pg. 247, ln. 10 25 February 1871.

Pg. 247, ln. 21 Memorandum of Agreement. Keene Folder.

Pg. 248, ln. 2 *Times* (New York), 30 March 1871.

Pg. 248, ln. 8 Brown, *A History of the New York Stage,* 2:460.

Pg. 248, ln. 17 *Clipper,* 29 April 1871.

Pg. 248, ln. 21 *Clipper,* 6 May 1871.

Pg. 249, ln. 7 Daniel Berrien's recapitulation of Laura Keene's funds for July through December 1871 and January through February 1872. Keene Folder.

Pg. 249, ln. 14 Receipt for fees on application for patent, 25 May 1872. Keene Folder.

Pg. 250, ln. 8 Letter with enclosure, 11 April 1869. Harvard Theatre Collection.

Pg. 250, ln. 18 Legal document dissolving the partnership, 22 June 1872. Keene Folder.

Pg. 250, ln. 20 Mrs. Thaddeus Horton, "Madame Le Vert and Her Friends," *Uncle Remus Magazine,* August 1907.

Pg. 252, ln. 18 *Clipper,* 2 December 1871.

Pg. 253, ln. 15 Winter, *Vagrant Memories,* 58.

Pg. 254, ln. 17 Dated, 11 January 1872. Folger Shakespeare Library.

Pg. 254, legend *Tribune,* 7 November 1873.

Pg. 256, ln. 7 *Clipper,* 27 January 1872.

Pg. 256, ln. 14 Manuscript Dramatic Diary, 3.

Pg. 256, ln. 17 Creahan, 78.

Pg. 256, ln. 19 Only copy of *Fine Arts,* New York Public Library.

Pg. 258, ln. 17 *Fine Arts,* 30.

Pg. 258, legend Brady, 66.

Pg. 260, ln. 4 *Fine Arts,* 70-71.

Pg. 260, ln. 13 Ibid., 42.

Pg. 260, ln. 16 Ibid., 29.

Pg. 260, ln. 29 Act II, scene 1.

Pg. 262, ln. 3 "Rawson Lectures"
envelope, Keene Folder.

Pg. 262, ln. 11 Rawson passport
application 24 March 1874, number 3754,
vol 433, Archives of the Department of
State.

Pg. 262, ln. 13 Marriage license,
Department of Records, City of New
York.

Pg. 262, ln. 25 Keene Folder.

Pg. 263, ln. 1 Receipted bill, Keene Folder.

Pg. 263, ln. 9 Letter 13 May 1872.
Harvard Theatre Collection.

Pg. 263, ln. 12 *Clipper*, 7 September 1872.

Pg. 263, ln. 25 Undated letter, Harvard
Theatre Collection.

Pg. 265, legend Playbill, Theatre Royal
Haymarket, 18 November 1861,
University of Tulsa Theatre Collection.

Pg. 265, ln. 2 All information in this
paragraph from, *Clipper*, 12 October 1872.

Pg. 265, ln. 9 *Clipper*, ibid.

Pg. 265, ln. 20 Assignment Laura Keene
to Edward A. Sothern, 1 September 1872.
Keene Folder.

Pg. 266, ln. 13 Creahan, 93.

Pg. 266, ln. 22 *Inquirer*, 14, 1872. Jane
Keene died 11 December, 1872, Death
certificate, Department of Records, New
York City.

CHAPTER THIRTEEN

Pg. 269, ln. 12 Letter from Clara Taylor
to John Creahan, 14 July 1873. Creahan,
96.

Pg. 270, ln. 8 Keene Folder.

Pg. 271, ln. 7 This recapitulation is drawn
from deeds, account sheets and letters,
Keene Folder.

Pg. 271, ln. 16 Augustin Daly file, Folger
Shakespeare Library.

Pg. 271, ln. 29 16 August 1873, Keene
Folder.

Pg. 272, ln. 3 The accounting, with a bill
to Rachel, as well as the letter of 25 April
1870 from Clarke to Booth in which he
says, "I charge her no fees." Keene Folder.

Pg. 272, ln. 10 Jefferson, *Autobiography*,
205.

Pg. 272, ln. 15 Obituary, "The Days
Doing", 21 November 1873, an
unidentified clipping, Harvard Theatre
Collection.

Pg. 272, ln. 24 A receipt made out to
Clara for grave number 223. Keene Folder.

Pg. 272, ln. 29 An order to Mr.
McGovern, Green-Wood Cemetery,
Brooklyn, 19 April 1876 to remove the
remains of "Frances Lutz" to lot 21444.
The name of Laura Keene is written in
above that of Frances. Keene Folder.

List of Works Cited

The following is by no means a complete record of all the sources I have consulted, but it is a record of the sources used. Microfilm, microdot, microfiche have brought the newspapers of three continents where Laura acted into my carrel. The wonders of the archival systems of Great Britain and the United States have made it possible to follow the most tenuous clues.

Adams, Henry. *The Education of Henry Adams*. 1918. Reprint. New York: Heritage Press, 1942

Appleton, William M. *Madame Vestris and the London Stage*. New York: Columbia University Press, 1974.

Belton, Fred. *Random Collections of an Old Actor*. London: Tinsley Brothers, 1880.

Benét, Stephen Vincent. *John Brown's Body: A poem*. 1927. Reprint. New York: Heritage Press, 1948.

Binns, Archie. *Mrs. Fiske and the American Theatre*. New York: Crown Publishers, 1955.

Boucicault, Dion. *Colleen Bawn*. Acting Edition. London: Thomas Hailes Lacy, ND.

——— , *The Art of Acting*. New York: Columbia University Press, 1926.

Brady, William A. *Showman*. New York: E. P. Dutton & Co., 1937.

Brown, T. Allston. *History of the American Stage: Containing Biographical Sketches of Nearly Every Member of the Profession that has Appeared on the American Stage, From 1733 to 1870*. 2nd ed., 1870. Reprint. New York: Benjamin Blom, 1969.

——— , *A History of the New York Stage: From the First Performance in 1732 to 1901*. 3 vols. 2nd ed., 1903. Reprint. New York: Benjamin Blom, 1964.

Bunn, Alfred. *Old England and New England: In a series of Views Taken on the Spot*. 2 vols. London: Richard Bentley, 1853.

Clarke, Asia Booth. *The Elder and the Younger Booth*. Boston: James R. Osgood and Company, 1882.

Clemens, Samuel. *Mark Twain's Autobiography*. 2 vols. New York: Harper & Brothers Publishers, 1924.

Creahan, John. *The Life of Laura Keene: Actress, Artist, Manager and Scholar, Together with Some Interesting Reminiscences of Her Daughters*. Philadelphia: Rodgers Publishing Company, 1897.

Daly, Joseph Francis. *The Life of Augustin Daly*. New York: The Macmillan Company, 1917.

DeFontaine, F. G. ed. *Birds of a Feather Flock Together: or Talks with Sothern*. New York: G. W. Carleton, 1878.

Dictionary of American Biography. 20 vols. and 8 supplements. New York: Charles Scribner's Sons, 1989.

Disher, M. Willson, ed. *The Cowells in America: Being the Diary of Mrs. Sam Cowell During Her Husband's Concert Tour in the Years 1860-1861*. London: Oxford University Press, 1934.

Federal Cases, vol. 6. St. Paul, Minn.: West Publishing Co., 1894.

Felheim, Marvin. *The Theatre of Augustin Daly: An Account of the Late Nineteenth Century American Stage*. Cambridge: Harvard University Press, 1956.

Field, Edwin A. *Through The Stage-Door: A Complete Hand-book of the Theatre*. Boston Engraving & McIndoe Printing, 1896.

Fisk, Asa I. and Wharton, Henry, eds. *The American Law Register*, vol. 9. Philadelphia: D. B. Canfield and Co., 1861.

Ford, George D. *Those Were Actors: A Story of the Chapmans and the Drakes*. New York: Library Publishers, 1955.

Gray, Horace Jr. *Reports of Cases Argued and Determined in the Supreme Judicial Court of Massachusetts*, vol 16. Boston: Little, Brown & Co., 1871.

Gurley, Phineas D. *The Voice of The Rod: A Sermon Preached on Thursday, June 1, 1865 in the New York Avenue Presbyterian Church*, Washington D. C. Washington: William Ballentyne Bookseller, 1865.

Hardwick, J. M. D. *Emigrant in Motley*. London: Rockcliff, 1954.

Hartnoll, Phyllis, ed. *The Oxford Companion to the Theatre*. 3rd ed. London: Oxford University Press, 1967.

Hibben, Paxton. *Henry Ward Beecher: An American Portrait*. 1927. Reprint. New York: Press of the Reader's Club, 1942.

Howland, Franklyn. *A History of the Town of Acushnet*. Published by the Author, New Bedford, Massachusetts, 1907.

Hutton, Laurence. *Curiosities of the American Stage*. New York; Harper & Brothers, 1891.

——, *Plays and Players*. New York: Hurd and Houghton, 1875.

——, *Manuscript Dramatic Diary*. 6 vols. Ann Arbor, Mich. University Microfilms, 1956. (Source materials in the field of theatre; reel 12).

Irving, Pierre M. *The Life and Letters of Washington Irving*. 4 vols. New York: G. P. Putnam, 1864.

James, Henry. *A Small Boy and Others*. New York: Charles Scribner's Sons, 1913.

Jefferson, Eugenie Paul. *Intimate Recollections of Joseph Jefferson*. New York: Dodd, Mead and Company, 1909.

The Autobiography of Joseph Jefferson. New York: Century Co., 1889.

Keese, William L. *William E. Burton: Actor, Author, and Manager — A Sketch of His Career Other Than That of Actor, with Glimpses of His Home Life, and Extracts from His Theatrical Journal*. New York: Dunlap Society, 1891.

Kellogg, Clara Louise. *Memoirs of an American Prima Donna*. New York: G. P. Putnam's Sons, 1913.

Krause, David, ed. *The Dolmen Boucicault*. With an Essay By The Editor on The Theatre of Dion Boucicault. Chester Springs, Pennsylvania: Dufour Editions, 1965.

Leale, Charles A. *Lincoln's Last Hours*. N. P., 1902.

Lewes, George Henry. *On Actors and the Art of Acting*. 2nd ed., London: Smith, Elder & Co., 1875.

Lockridge, Richard. *Darling of Misfortune*. New York: Century Co., 1932.

Logan, Olive. *The Mimic World, and Public Exhibitions*. Philadelphia: New World Publishing Company, 1871.

Lytton, Edward Bulwer. *The Dramatic Works*. Vol. 9. New York: P. F. Collier, Publisher, ND.

MacMinn, George R. *The Theatre of the Golden Era in California*. Caldwell, Idaho: The Caxton Printers, 1914.

Mammen, Edward William. *The Old Stock Company School of Acting: a Study of the Boston Museum*. Boston: Published by the Trustees of the Public Library, 1945.

The Life of Charles James Mathews: Chiefly Autobiographical with Selections from His Correspondence and Speeches. ed. Charles Dickens. 2 vols. London: Macmillan and Co., 1879.

Matthews, Brander and Hutton, Laurence, eds. *Actors and Actresses of Great Britain and the United States: from the Days of David Garrick to the Present Time*. 5 vols. New York: Cassell and Company, Limited, 1886.

Middleton, George. *These Things Are Mine*. New York: Macmillan Company, 1947.

Mitchell, Edward P. *Memoirs of an Editor: Fifty Years of American Journalism*. New York: Charles Scribner's Sons, 1924.

Morris, Lloyd. *Curtain Time: The Story of The American Theater*. New York: Random House, 1953.

Morse, Frank P. *Backstage with Henry Miller*. New York: E. P. Dutton & Co., 1938.

Murdock, James E. *The Stage: or Recollections of Actors and Acting From An Experience of Fifty Years*. Philadelphia: J. M. Stoddard & Co., 1860.

Odell, George C. D. *Annals of the New York Stage*. 15 vols. New York: Columbia University Press, 1931.

Oldroyd, Osborn H. *Assassination of Abraham Lincoln*. Washington D. C.: O. H. Oldroyd, 1901.

Olszewski, George J. *Restoration of Ford's Theatre, Washington, D. C.* Historic Structures Report, Department of the Interior, National Park Service. Washington: U. S. Government Printing Office, 1963.

Memories of the Professional and Social Life of John Owens by His Wife. Baltimore: John Murphy and Company, 1892.

Pemberton, Thomas Edgar. *A Memoir of Edward Askew Sothern.* 4th ed., London: Richard Bentley and Son, 1890.

Pitman, Benn. Comp. *The Assassination of President Lincoln and the Trial of the Conspirators.* Cincinnati: Moore, Wilstach & Baldwin, 1865.

Phillips, Arthur Sherman. *The Phillips History of Fall River.* Fall River, Massachusetts: Dover Press, 1945.

Reignolds-Winslow , Catherine Mary. *Yesterdays with Actors.* 1887. Reprint. Freeport, New York: Books for Libraries Press, 1972.

Roorbach, Orville Augustus. *Actors As They Are: A Series of Sketches of the Most Eminent Performers Now on the Stage.* New York: O. A. Roorbach, Jr., 1856.

Rourke, Constance. *Troupers of the Gold Coast; or The Rise of Lotta Crabtree.* New York: Harcourt, Brace and Company, 1928.

Ruggles, Eleanor. *Prince of Players: Edwin Booth.* New York: W. W. Norton & Company, 1953.

Ryan, Kate. *Old Boston Museum Days.* Boston: Little, Brown, and Company, 1915.

Sandberg, Carl. *Abraham Lincoln: The War Years.* 4 vols. New York: Harcourt, Brace & Company, 1939.

Scott, Clement. *The Drama of Yesterday & To-Day.* 2 vols. London: Macmillan and Co., Limited, 1899.

Skinner, Otis. *Footlights and Spotlights: Recollections of My Life on the Stage.* Indianapolis: The Bobbs-Merrill Co., 1923.

Smith, Sol. *Theatrical Management in the West and South for Thirty Years: Interspersed with Anecdotal Sketches.* New York: Harper & Brothers, Publishers, 1868.

Somers, Robert. *The Southern States Since The War 1870-1871.* Reprint. University, Alabama: University of Alabama Press, 1965.

The Diary of George Templeton Strong. Allan Nevins and Milton Halsey Thomas, ed. 4 vols. New York: Macmillan Company, 1952.

Vandenhoff, George. *Leaves From An Actor's Note Book.* New York: D. Appleton and Company, 1859.

Waitzkin, Leo. *The Witch of Wych Street: A Study of the Theatrical Reforms of Madame Vestris.* Cambridge, Mass.: Harvard University Press, 1933.

Wallack, Lester. *Memories of Fifty Years.* New York: Charles Scribner's Sons, 1889.

Walsh, Townsend. *The Career of Dion Boucicault.* New York: Dunlap Society, 1915.

Wandell, Samuel Henry. *The Law of the Theatre.* Albany: J.B. Lyon, 1891.

Washington City Directory, 1855-56.

While Lincoln Lay Dying. A Facsimile Reproduction of the First Testimony Taken in Connection with the Assassination of Abraham Lincoln as Recorded by Corporal James Tanner. With a Biographical Introduction by Maxwell Whiteman. Philadelphia: The Union League of Philadelphia, 1968.

Wilson, Francis. *Joseph Jefferson: Reminiscences of a Fellow Player.* London: Chapman and Hall, 1906.

Winter, William. *Vagrant Memories: Being Further Recollections of Other Days.* New York: George H. Doran Company, 1915.

Wolle, Francis. *Fitz-James O'Brien: A Literary Bohemian of the Eighteen-Fifties.* Boulder: University of Colorado Studies Series B, Studies in the Humanities, vol. 2, no. 2., 1944.

Articles

Brougham, John. "Pauline as seen by Diogenes." *The Lantern,* 19 March, 1853.

"Drama." *The Round Table,* 2 January 1864.

"Editor's Table," *The Pioneer Magazine,* April 1854.

Ferguson, William J. "Lincoln's Death." *The Saturday Evening Post,* February 12, 1927.

Florence, W. J., "Lester Wallack." *North American Review,* October 1888.

Ford, John T. "Behind the Curtain of Conspiracy." *North American Review,* April 1889.

Horton, Mrs. Thaddeus. "Madame Le Vert and her Friends." *Uncle Remus Magazine,* August 1907.

Keene, Laura. "Drama." *Fine Arts.* March 1872.

—— "Drama — Ostracism of Actors." April 1872.

—— "Edwin Booth." April 1872.

—— "Joseph Jefferson." June 1872.

—— "Manners." May 1872.

Munroe, Seaton, "Recollections of Lincoln's Assassination." *North American Review,* April 1896.

Scott, Genio C. "Sketches of The Actors, No. VIII: Miss Laura Keene." *The Spirit of the Times,* March 1, 1862.

St. John, Molyneaux. "New York Theatres, Part I." *The Broadway,* February 1868.

Newspapers

Albion (London)

Alta California (San Francisco).

Baltimore Sun.

Boston Sunday Herald.

Buffalo Morning Express.

Era (London).

*Frank Leslie's Illustrated
    Newspaper* (New York).

Louisville Courier Journal.

Montclair Herald.

New Bedford Evening Standard.

New Bedford Standard Times.

New York Clipper.

*New York Commercial
    Advertiser.*

New York Dramatic Mirror.

New York Herald.

New York Picayune.

New York Illustrated News.

New York Saturday Press.

New York Sun.

New York Sunday Herald.

New York Sunday Times.

New York Times.

New York Tribune.

New York Weekly Herald.

Philadelphia Bulletin.

Philadelphia Inquirer.

Philadelphia Press.

Philadelphia Public Ledger.

Philadelphia Weekly Times.

Porter's Spirit of the Times.

Spirit of the Times.

Times (London).

Washington Evening Star.

Washington Star.

*Washington National
    Intelligencer.*

Wilkes Spirit of the Times.

Unpublished Sources

Dissertations

Johnson, Rue Corbett. "The Theatrical Career of William E. Burton." Ph.D. Diss. Indiana University, 1966.

Noid, Benjamin Maunard. "History of the Theatre in Stockton, California 1850-1892." Ph.D. Diss. University of Utah, 1968.

Taylor, Dorothy Jean. "Laura Keene in America, 1852-1873." Ph.D. Diss., Tulane University, 1966.

Playbills

Ford Collection, Manuscript Division, Library of Congress.

Harvard Theatre Collection, Harvard University.

Simon Gratz Collection, Pennsylvania Historical Society, Philadelphia.

Performing Arts Research Center, New York Public Library.

Richmond Surrey Library, London.

University of Tulsa.

Victoria and Albert Museum, London.

Letters

Folger Shakespeare Library, Washington D. C.: Ten from Laura Keene, one from Joseph Crosby.

Harvard Theatre Collection: Forty-one from Laura Keene, three from John T. Ford, two from Dion Boucicault, and one from Charles Reade.

Laura Keene folder, Manuscript Division, Library of Congress, Washington D. C. Seven to Laura Keene, two from William D. Booth and one each from Jamie Bullock, Thomas William Clarke, Evelyn M. Foster, J. T. Lanord, William Wheatley.

John T. Ford Collection, Ibid.: one from Laura Keene.

Performing Arts Research Center, New York Public Library: one each from Laura Keene and Edwin Booth.

The Players Club, New York City: two from Laura Keene.

Civil Documents

Census. Parish of St. George, Hanover Square, Westminster, Great Britain. 1851. (H.O.107/1475).

Moss, Thomas, Baptismal Records, St. James Parish, Westminster, Middlesex County, Great Britain.

Taylor, Clara, Birth Certificate, Number 448, 1848, sub-district of Hanover Square, Middlesex County, Great Britain.

Taylor, Emma, Birth Certificate, Number 157, 1845, sub-district of Chelsea, Middlesex County, Great Britain.

Taylor, Henry, Baptismal Records, St. James Parish, Westminster, 4 vols., 1813-1833, Number 336 for the year 1818.

Moss, Mary Frances and Henry Wellington Taylor, Marriage Certificate Number 60, 1844, in the registration district of St. Martin-in-the-Fields, Middlesex County, Great Britain.

Taylor, Emma and Albert Rawson, 29 September 1872, Marriage License Bureau, Department of Records, Manhattan, New York City.

Keene, Laura. Passport application number 20169, vol. 193, 8 June 1860, Archives of the Department of State, National Archives, Washington, D C.

Rawson, Albert Leighton. Passport application number 3754, volume 433, 24 March 1874, idem.

Passenger Manifests, National Archives, Washington D. C. *Arctic* for September 1852; *City of Glasgow* for June 1853; *Ohio* and *John L. Stephens* for March and April 1854; *City of Washington* for May 1860. *Java* for August 1867.

Passenger Manifest, Archive Authority, New South Wales, (Ref A. O. 891) *M. A. Jones* for October 1854.

Keene, Jane. Death certificate, December 11, 1872, 15th Ward, Manhattan, New York.

Keene, Laura. Grave purchase receipt made out to Clara Taylor, November 7, 1873, by the pastor of the Church of the Immaculate Conception, Montclair, New Jersey.

Keene, Laura. Order to open grave in Greenwood Cemetery, New York, to accept the remains of Frances Lutz (Laura Keene) 19 April 1876.

Lutz, John S. Interment record, Oak Hill Cemetery, Georgetown, D. C., 20 April 1869. Lot 565.

Lutz, Malvina S. Interment record, Oak Hill Cemetery, June 24, 1855. Lot 84. Reinterred 29 May, 1865, Lot 565, Oak Hill.

Lutz, John, Will Book, 5/203/Georgetown, 15 March 1841.

Rawson, Emma. Will Book, 304/345/New York City, 19 June 1882.

Court Documents

Deed, 31 May 1851. Recorded in J.A.S. 25, folio 446, Georgetown. John Lutz to Adelaide M. Lutz.

Docket volume entry and case file in Equity, Case No. 28 of the United States Circuit Court for the Eastern District of Pennsylvania, October Session, 1858, in the matter of Laura Keene vs. William Wheatley and George S. Clarke, National Archives Record Group 21.
A. Handwritten copy of the Bill in Equity.
B. Printed copy of the original Bill.
C. Interrogatories.

D. Commission on part of plaintiff to London, England.

E. Deposition of Tom Taylor.

F. Court's final decree.

G. Depositions, pleadings, exhibits, 84 pages.

Foreign Service Post records of the consular offices of London, Liverpool, Sydney, Melbourne for 1850 through 1860, R. G. 59, National Archives.

Records of the Provost marshal General, R. G. 101, National Archives.

Turner-Baker Files, Records of the Judge Advocate General, R. G. 94, National Archives.

Collections

Daly Theatre Contracts, September 1863 to September 1873. Bound Volume, Harvard Theatre Collection.

Dion Boucicault Scrapbook, Performing Arts Research Center, New York Public Library.

Ireland, Joseph N. *Records of the New York Stage from 1750 to 1860,* extended and extra-illustrated for Augustin Daly by Augustus Toteberg. Harvard Theatre Collection.

May, Alonzo J., "Dramatic Encyclopedia, 1750-1904." MSS in the library of the Maryland Historical Society, Baltimore.

"Notable Players of the Past and Present." Scrapbook of Articles printed in *New York Clipper.* The Players Club, New York City.

Laura Keene Folder, MMC870, Manuscript Division, Library of Congress.
Letters mention *sup.*
Property Mortgage Laura Keene to Jane Keene, 25 October 1871.
Rules and Contract, Laura Keene Varieties.
Copyright Title Pages.
Our American Cousin.
Seven Sisters.
Workmen of New York, etc.
Bogus.
C. Young's statement, 11 March 1862.

Rawdon Pullam Documents.

Laura Keene Folder, Library of Congress, Continuation.

Trust for the benefit of Laura Keene.

Mortgage on Bond St. home.

Undated clipping from *Philadelphia Weekly Times*.

Trust from the benefit of Laura Keene, 10 May 1870.

Mortgage of personal wardrobe, 25 October 1870.

Agreement between Daniel Berrien and Thomas A. Dow for Laura Keene's benefit.

Berrien's report on rental payments and Sothern royalty.

Patent application, 25 May 1872.

Partnership dissolution, 22 June 1872.

Rawson lecture envelope.

Assignment of *Our American Cousin,* 1 September 1872.

Transfer of Riverside Lawn, 9 July 1873.

Accounting for sale of Riverside Lawn.

Index

CERTIFIED COPY OF AN ENTRY OF BIRTH

REGISTRATION DISTRICT _St. L_

BIRTH in the Sub-district of _South Che_

1845.

No.	Columns:— 1 When and where born	2 Name, if any	3 Sex	4 Name and surname of father	5 Name, surname and maiden surname of mother
187	Twenty third of January 1845 at No2 Cooks Ground	Emma Eliza	Girl	Henry Wellington Taylor	Mary Fran Taylor former Hop

CERTIFIED to be a true copy of an entry in the certified copy of a Register of B
Given at the GENERAL REGISTER OFFICE, SOMERSET HOUSE, LONDON, under the Se

This certificate is issued in pursuance of the Births and Death
sealed or stamped with the seal of the General Register Office
proof of the entry, and no certified copy purporting to have b

BX 941386

CAUTION:—Any person who (1) falsifies any of the particula

Form A502M (S.336335) Dd.001406 99999 9/72 Hw.